HOW TO CYCLE CANADA

THE WRONG WAY

By Cycling In A Skirt

Independently published by Cyclinginaskirt
First edition
Text copyright © 2019 Lorraine Lambert.
The author has asserted her moral right under the Copyright, Designs and Patent Act of 1988, to be identified as the author of this work.
ISBN: 9781702234610

All rights reserved. No part of this publication may be reproduced in any form, stored in any retrieval system, or transmitted in any form or by any means without prior written permission of the publisher.
For permission requests, contact the publisher/author at
www.cyclinginaskirt.co.uk

This is a personal work of non-fiction. All events and conversations are portrayed to the best of the author's memory at the time of writing. All content is offered solely as the author's personal opinion. Every effort has been made to check factual information however some errors may occur.
Whilst the narrative of the book is based on a true journey, some names and identifying features have been changed in order to protect the privacy of the people involved, even though they were all very lovely.
Dedication quote by Erada Sveltana
Maps and gradient profiling reproduced from Strava.com
Front cover by Gareth Adams.

For my sister, always.

If it's both terrifying and amazing
then you should definitely pursue it.

Erada Svetlana

A Brief Explanation

For as long as I can remember there have been two passions in my life, my little sister and my love of adventure.

The former started when, at nearly 8 years old I trooped down to our small village hospital one cold winter's day and watched my one and only sister emerging in to the world. It was an eye opening (and watering) experience for a young girl but, being the first human to hold her during those amazing moments as she breathed in the new world, gave us an immensely close bond that has never faltered. She is my best friend as well as my little sister, the person I am closest to and who means the most to me.

We are also incredibly alike in many ways and yet wildly different in others. She is a content person, thriving on the pleasure she gets from her home and her family. As long as I've known her she has known she will be both a wife and a mother and this makes her happy. Turning that dream in to a reality and embarking on raising a child has and will be her great adventure.

I, on the other hand, am a restless soul who still has no idea of what I want from life despite being nearly half way through it. What I do possess however are two things; a perpetual dread of standing still and a craving for the challenge brought by new experiences. Anything that is different, or testing, or will push me beyond my current limits; anything that has the potential to scare me half out of my mind and all the highs and lows that accompany that, bring it on.

This is a true story about one year in both our lives, not so long ago, when our biggest adventures converged. Primarily it's about a bit of a long cycle ride across Canada but within that, it's about the parallels from both our experiences as we go through them and the love and support across thousands of miles which makes both of these adventures possible.

It's also about the life changes we make and the things that drive us to make them. It's about feeling lost and uncertain whatever age you are; it's about the pursuit of life altering challenges be it cycling solo for thousands of miles or bringing a new life in to the world and, underpinning it all, it's about the incredible bonds of family and friendship which help us to achieve the things that matter most.

The Birth Of Something

I'm reluctant to call the whole experience a mid-life crisis, mostly because that would mean I've already reached middle age and, whilst my body may be succumbing, my head stubbornly insists I've yet to hit puberty. Equally, right now, I don't have the energy or enthusiasm to muster a proper full-blown crisis. It's more just a feeling of quietly grinding to a halt and wondering how you got there so early?

Like many people, I suspect that adulthood came as something of a dawning realisation. When you're galloping through your teens and twenties, there's still significantly far more lifetime ahead of you than behind your perky young buttocks.
That boundless sense of opportunity, stretching out to the horizon in all directions, bags of time for exciting things to happen and to make your mark upon the world. All through those heady early years of adulthood I obviously still had plenty of time to win that Nobel prize (for something, don't mind what), become the next best-selling author, broker world peace, record a number one single.
Do they still have singles even?

And then somehow, somewhere along the line you realise that twenties have slipped into thirties and are progressing rapidly to the next decade. Sure there's a whole bucket list of things you'd like to do, still plenty of time too, but first I'll just pay off the car loan, buy a sofa, buy a house, get that promotion, work a few more hours until, on a Tuesday morning you're sat in your brand new, high spec, huge-engined car, doing 5 mph in the usual traffic jam on the way to work and you suddenly think. Is this really it?
That somehow, somewhere, without noticing, you've wandered off of that care-free path of youth and are wading thigh-deep into the smelly bog of mid-life, having lost both the map and the plot.

I don't recall the exact point when I looked down and realised I was so stuck. It definitely wasn't inside a high performance super car either, having never owned anything sportier than a second-hand Nissan Micra. There was no lightning strike moment, just a gradual realisation that as my thirties trailed away insignificantly I was squelching through the mire of every day and it wasn't where I'd expected to be.

Where had all those bright, shiny hopes from my twenties gone, the thought that the world held endless possibilities? Instead I was working every day in a job that was less and less satisfying, commuting, paying the bills, get home from the office, eat, sleep, repeat ad nauseam.

Somewhere along the line life had just lost momentum, I'd started to function and not to live. And, even allowing for my increasingly fluid definition of middle age, there were still a lot of years now stretching ahead of me in this state.

AARRRGGGHHHHH
The sounds of agonised screaming really began to penetrate, dragging me back from my self-obsessed musings into the present. I couldn't believe my thoughts had drifted off so, but then, with over 36 hours of no sleep all reality was slightly fuzzy and wavering around the edges. The howling next to me was quickly building in intensity and volume, rising in an almost perfect scale of pain as, squatting on one of those oversized yoga balls, my younger sister battled through the final stages of labour with her first child - definitely very much in the present.

I was probably a strange choice to be alongside her and her husband at such a personal moment, especially with zero experience (or tolerance) of anything child-related. Despite this, and a near 8 year age difference, my sister Emma and I are incredibly close and I was torn between being honoured and horrified that she'd asked me to be alongside them at the birth.

"*Take the drugs*" – was my contribution from the start – but for her own reasons she'd been hanging back. Now, after 36 hours of increasing pain she finally let herself be persuaded. Lulled for a while by the blessed relief of the pethidine entering her system she leaned back on the yoga ball, no mean feat when you're partially dressed, sweaty and in the throes of child birth and drawing a huge breath she began dictating......an order for pizza, extra cheese no anchovies, chicken wings and garlic bread. Looks like the drugs were working overtime hitting exactly the right spot, even producing the munchies.

This bizarre respite was welcome but all too brief and when the medication wore off the final stages of labour began in earnest. I remember looking at the clock, in my new mid-wifely role, calculating that 1cm dilation = 1 hour in time and thinking what a long night there was ahead. Weirdly, when I next looked nearly four hours had passed and the baby's head, heralded by little tufts of dark hair, was about to crown.

At this point, my respect for women who have borne children went stellar. In everything I've read, childbirth is usually described very fancifully as a wondrous, beatific process blah blah blah. It isn't, it's brutal. It's like watching a particularly vicious boxing match between the baby and the body, full of blood and gore and pain, sitting in the ringside seats and being expected to cheer the fight on.
Being so close to my sister I was, at points, trying to hold back the tears. To see someone you care about in agony and to be able to do nothing was very nearly overwhelming. But, whatever I felt, she had the hardest job by far starting in the wee small hours of the previous night as she spent her early labour in her bathtub; me crouched on the floor beside her whilst her husband snatched a final few moments rest.
It was during this surreal time that we'd developed an odd but effective system of pain relief, counting down the pain.
Starting at 30 and counting backwards through the contractions, it was a surprise method that seemed to work. Since then we'd stuck to it religiously, even if the counting was now decidedly dodgy in the depths of fatigue 29, 27, 21...But by now the baby was on its own countdown and after just a few seconds pause, a small, slimy body

broke through into the light of the delivery room and my new niece was born.

It was incredibly emotional just then to stand back and watch the new little family basking in the wonder and magnitude of each other. Physically exhausted but elated, they formed a tight, protective little knot oblivious to the entire world. It was strange seeing my baby sister holding her own baby.
Stranger still after I'd done the same thing nearly 30 years ago when, at barely 8 years old, I'd been present at her own birth and the first person to hold and comfort the new arrival. Maybe that explains the start of our incredible bond and also my pathological dislike of child bearing!

Despite our closeness and many similarities, we'd always differed in one area. For my sister, children and a life partner had always formed the kernel of her life's wants and desires. In some ways I'd always envied her that certainty, knowing what she wanted was to make a life and a home in which to raise children was always on her horizon. And now she'd done it. Watching her and her little family, I was host to a rolling sea of emotions, waves of all kinds of feelings building and breaking inside me. Here she was starting her new adventure, maybe it was time to start mine?

Three Months Before...

The best ideas almost always start life on a drunken night out with friends. Being quite a lightweight drinker, in my case anything over two small glasses of wine and I'm slouched in a corner snoring and dribbling.

On this night, somewhere in between that brief window of merry and coma, a plan of such breath-taking audacity and daring was hatched that generations to come would speak of it in hushed and reverent awe. A plan that would solve all my non-mid-life crisis fears in one fell swoop; one that would be life affirming, life changing, world changing even. A plan that would lay open to me as never before the mysteries of the universe and how to solve them.

I.

Would.

Quit my job......run off and have an adventure.

Life solved. Cheers!

Two Months Before…

With no better plan appearing for world enlightenment I'd clung doggedly to that pub conversation. There was no reason to, it was just one of those silly, *"what would you do if...."* discussions that you have when drinking cheap wine and wanting to fantasise your way out of real life. But, on I clung. I will have an adventure if it kills me!

So, following on from that evening at the pub, revved up on adrenalin and a slight hangover, I walked into work and handed in my notice.
A month later here I was quitting my job as a locum social worker and stepping out into the unknown and definitely unplanned, a cardboard box with the contents of my desk, good luck cards and chocolates tucked under my arm. The disbelieving and slightly awe-struck good wishes of my colleagues ringing in my ears.

Soon, I would not only be jobless but homeless too, having rented out my house for the next year, the idea being I couldn't run home again if things went pear-shaped. Now I had just days to pack up the last of my belongings and distribute them around long-suffering friends and family for the duration.

In a very Frankenstein-esque way I seemed to have created a monster and the embryonic idea of having adventures, hatched a few short weeks ago, had now bizarrely begun to take shape of its own accord. To kick things off, a good friend, also at a loose end work-wise, had invited me to join her on a month long cycle trip across France. I'd never done anything even remotely similar before but I could cycle, I could borrow a bike, I didn't even have to do any planning as that was all in hand, all I had to do was turn up. Why not?

The French weather in April as it turns out, was why not, at least for the first week or so. As we froze our way South from St Malo I was eternally grateful that at least we weren't camping.

After a week of cold pedalling and a couple of cheeky train journeys we'd finally put most of the bleak frozen North behind us and rocking up in Bordeaux the journey recommenced on pleasant, sun warmed canal paths dappled with tree shade. The pace too was even more relaxed, my friend having discovered she was in the early stages of pregnancy just before departure, the miles were few and the lunches were long. Not exactly slumming it, we stayed in pretty chambre d'hôtes and efficient budget hotels, glorying in French pastries, cheese and wine.

But there was, for me, something missing. My legs grew fidgety at the reserved pace, I was cycling faster and stronger than my poor friend, causing both of us mounting dissatisfaction. It didn't help matters that the miles we did cover were few and flat. I constantly found myself wanting to go further every day, deliberately seeking out more undulating, interesting terrain. I was quickly growing bored of the never-ending tree-line canal routes, pretty though they were.

There was frustration too at the daily long lunch stops. Pregnancy queasiness meant a protracted full-on midday lunch for her whereas for me, a quick sandwich, if that, was more than enough before I'd want to be back pedalling again.

It was a definite lesson in retaining a friendship, which we managed surprisingly well despite the frustrations. It was also a learning curve in discovering how I liked to travel on a bike and of assimilating our varying preferences so that we finished each day on good terms.
In truth, I don't know how long we would have both continued to cycle in harmony before our riding styles and friendships diverged. The world however had other things in store.

Just after Toulouse my long-suffering friend phoned home to find her father was being admitted to hospital following the sudden onset of illness. Although serious but not life threatening it was still enough to know she wanted to be with him and her family. Making the immediate decision to fly home we hurriedly worked out logistics and the abandoning of her bike and gear with the kind owners of our little chamber d'hôte. I however was now faced with 2 choices. Fly home with my friend or continue alone. The latter was frankly terrifying, but somehow the former was even more so. For different reasons, stopping seemed scarier than continuing, even without the GPS and maps and experience and the ability to speak more than 3 words of French.

There was a huge lump in my throat as I waved her off the next day but it was counteracted by a small kernel of stubbornness. I would not quit. Not so long ago I'd wanted experiences and here was my first, going solo. OK, I may be a clueless traveller in an unfamiliar country but I was also now free to choose my own path and the path I chose was mountains, more specifically the Pyrenees.

It was a long, stressful first day on my own, mostly spent getting lost and speaking truly appalling French until I eventually wound up in the beautiful medieval walled city of Carcassonne. Staying for the night in a quirky hostel tucked inside the ancient city walls I both relished and dreaded my lone star status.
The great thing about hostels though is there's always company if you want it. This time in the shape of 2 retired motorcyclists from South Africa who were taking a year out to tour Europe by bike. The grey gap year-ers (as they called themselves) put my day long solo ride to shame. As I listened to them talk of far off places my spirits lifted, I couldn't wait to be back on the bike tomorrow.

The next few days were spent in a flurry of highs and lows, physically, emotionally and literally. Of ascending precipitous mountain roads through a network of hair-raising passes and gorges. Of being absolutely exhausted by the elements, the burning sun and freezing altitude, of being lost, scared, crazily happy and exhilarated beyond belief by the scenery, the achievements and some spectacular downhills.

All too soon I was dropping my bike off near Perpignan, to be housed by some very generous strangers until my friend returned later in the season by boat to collect it.

I was due to fly back from Girona and had run out of time to cycle there, but it had been worth it. On the bus ride between France and Spain I curled up in my seat and rolled around in my head the delicious memory pearls that had been formed in just a few short weeks, riding in company and going solo.

Unwittingly and pretty much unplanned, this trip and the experience of cycle touring, had started to fulfil that drunken pub-brief. To have adventures. So, what next?

One Month Before...

Returning home from France I had a speedy 2 day turn around. Enough time to do my laundry and hunt through tons of packing boxes in various locations to unearth clothes for my next adventure, a trip to Toronto.
I'd arranged, through a volunteering abroad scheme, to help out in a Community Living house in the heart of this iconic Canadian city. The volunteer work itself was to be eclectic, everything from contributing to a vegetarian food website, writing recipes and articles to helping out with the daily chores and numerous projects in the house itself, all in exchange for bed and board.

Over the next few weeks, spending time cycling, walking and running around the city, swimming in the lake, going to concerts in the parks, watching the cherry blossoms dissolve and spending lazy hours in the plentiful coffee shops, somewhere along the line I fell in love. In love with the city, its people, the culture and the country and, like any new obsession, I passionately wanted more time to indulge this love. Time to find out more, to explore, to linger, but time wasn't with me and only a month later I found myself on a greyhound bus from Toronto to New York, from there flying home to await the birth of my new niece. No further plans, 9 months remaining....

Now
Today, with the birth of my baby niece a simple equation has been taking shape in my sleep-deprived brain.
I love cycle touring + I love Toronto + I want to see more of the country = Lets cycle across Canada.
Before I fully know what I'm doing I book a one way, non-refundable ticket to Toronto. Oh Crap, what have I done!

Preparation

It turns out that booking the flight was the easy part as I now realise that I have just 14 measly days, in which to beg, steal or borrow all the kit I will need to cycle across Canada.

Experience-wise I'm also equally ill prepared, my sum total of cycle touring to date being three, happy, responsibility-free weeks for which I did no planning or owned any equipment. Three weeks of idling across France on un-taxing canal paths staying in hotels mostly with a friend and just a few short, off-piste solo days tagged on the end.

When I examine my plan in the cold light of day, there appear to be several large, significant holes. For example I have no idea what route I will take, how far I will be travelling or how long it will take me. More fundamentally, I don't even have a bike, or a tent, or a sleeping bag or a
…..
There is something to be said about preparing for such a big trip in an incredible hurry. I hardly had time to worry, or obsess over kit. I just needed stuff and quickly. As ever, eBay turned out to be my best friend. On a miniscule budget, I quickly discounted the beautiful, top of the range lightweight tents retailing for my entire trip fund. A lucky buy however found me a 2-person (one normal person that is or 2 midget-sized) tent, lightweight at 1kg and the brightest of blues. Not great for stealth camping but I couldn't complain at the price.

Worryingly, a bike was proving trickier to find. Having already spent hours scouring second hand sites and local shops it seemed that nothing remotely suitable was being sold that summer or at least not for my very limited budget of around 50 pence! With time ticking away, it wasn't with much hope that I embarked on a 40 mile round trip to the city to check out an auction bike I'd seen online. The old, aluminium framed Claud Butler was in surprisingly reasonable condition for its age although certainly in need of a little love and attention it was a solid 16 kilograms, dependable looking with basic model 21 gears and v-brakes.

A quick test ride, gamely trying to ignore the lack of steering from a creaky headset and I was convinced enough to make a bid, that and an absence of suitable alternatives. When the sellers found out my plans even they were rooting for me.

Back to the buying frenzy, with one week to go I had a tent and an auction bid on a bike…..

Much scouring led to a stove, lightweight pan and plate set. Actually, the word lightweight can just prefix all my gear, sleeping mat, jacket, multi tool, my friend's dad even donated a front bar bag to the cause.

I was quite proud of myself for buying mostly second hand and it certainly helped keep costs down, but there were a couple of essentials I wanted to get right and I knew would be worth spending some time and money on.

Waterproof panniers for a start. I'm not one for spending long hours delighting in product reviews or the technical ins and outs of each make and model. To be frank that bores me rigid, I'm more of a grab and go shopper. This approach has had mixed success over the years, split evenly between bargains and spectacular failures. But my brief experience in France had at least taught me the value of waterproof luggage, especially when housing your entire wardrobe for months on end.

My final buying session added 2 black Ortlieb rear panniers to the haul (black strangely being the cheapest colour) and a good quality, arctic expedition type sleeping bag, a gift from my parents who weren't all that taken with the idea of me freezing to death on a mountain somewhere.

With the pile of gear growing in my sister's spare room I turned my attention back to the bike. I was due to leave in 2 days and I still didn't have a bicycle – a somewhat fundamental part of a cycle trip. As the auction ran down through its last minutes I had all my surrounding family poised as secondary bidders should, for any reason, my technology fail me. It was the most tense I'd been so far as the final few seconds ticked away. If I didn't have a bike I didn't have a trip but, as the screen flashed up 'Auction complete' I started at it first in disbelief, then in sheer joy. Bouncing across the furniture, arms flying and whooping in delight, I realised I'd won. This was it, bike bought and I was ready to go. I'd also woken the baby. Sorry!

Taking stock, with two days to go I now had all my gear and finally, most importantly, this included a bike.

On collecting my new steed, it became painfully obvious that a bit of tender loving care was needed to get it fully functional and trip ready, the most pressing problem being that lack of steering ability for the front wheel. Unfortunately I'd also run out of time.

A panic call to a local mobile mechanic took care of the worst of the problems, greased bearings and a kindly donated second hand front wheel meant that at least I could now turn the handlebars. Anything else would just have to wait.

With hours to go until departure the other very helpful piece of advice came from my brother in law. As he surveyed the over flowing mountain of gear now invading his home, he casually suggested I may want to try actually pitching my new (second hand) tent, *"just in case, you know, there are bits missing"*…. In the buying frenzy of the last 2 weeks I hadn't even taken it out the bag. What a good idea.

The bag boasted it was a 3 minute easy pitch so, with him timing me and chuckling from the side-lines, I upended the tent bag. Of course there were no instructions but I was a girl, I could do this and low and behold, half an hour later I had indeed assembled a tent-like structure on their back lawn, with only minimal spare parts left over. OK, it wasn't pretty to watch but my tent did indeed seem intact. Phew.

With the minutes to departure ticking away I said my tearful goodbyes to my sister, brother in law and the new baby. With no return flight

booked, who knows how old she would next be when I saw her.
Emma, tired in that way only new parents can be, looked very small and vulnerable, any resolve to be strong dissolved instantly when I looked at her and we both burst into floods of tears. Why on earth was I doing this and leaving just when my niece had arrived, when Emma needed me. But, watching that lovely little family I knew they would support each other and she would be a brilliant mum. Parenthood was the beginning of her big adventure and this, was mine.

My final night was spent at my parents' house. At 11pm my dad and I, neither of us mechanically minded are swearing and growling at each other trying to wrestle the bike, now imaginatively named Claud, into an oversize plastic bag for the plane journey. Having finally worked out how to turn round the handlebars and pedals, the whole bike was cable tied and bubble wrapped to within an inch of its metal framed life. Next to it in the hall sat my luggage, 2 bulging panniers and a dry sack containing tent, sleeping bag, cooker, clothes and five pairs of shoes, including high heels, all squashed into a huge garden rubbish sack and bound with numerous rolls of tape. The plan being to discard the bag at the other end, reassemble Claud, load up and ride away into the sunset. Or something like that.

Right now it was all so heavy I couldn't lift it more than a few inches. There was also the distinct possibility of the duct tape bandaging failing catastrophically, the full contents bursting out all over the place if I so much as looked at it the wrong way.
Enough was enough though and at midnight, dog-tired and having to be up again in 4 hours I fell into bed. I'm so full of nerves however I don't really sleep, I just lie there drifting in that strange state of awake-dozing. When the 4:00am alarm sounds I have to peel my gritty eyelids open in protest.
Oh god, today's the day! What have I done?!
The airport is heaving with humanity as I man (woman) handle both Claud and the dangerously bulging garden waste sack onto a tiny

trolley. Balancing the precarious load it takes 2 people to steer and contain the mound of stuff, my poor, long suffering dad having drawn the short straw of airport departure duty.

Throughout the years I've continued to baffle my very conventional parents with my penchant for full-on sports and weird travel adventures so alien to two people whose idea of a good time is a nice walk and a pub lunch. Ever since I was small however they have gamely accompanied me through various hobbies, from show jumping to triathlon, bemusedly holding on to anything from skittish ponies to race bikes. That or getting up at the crack of dawn for airport runs, to meet returning flights from South America or Uganda in the wee small hours. And whilst they may sometimes question where this strange child of theirs came from, being so unlike them, they're always there, helping make the next off-the-wall scheme happen.

Back to the unruly baggage trolley and I'm acutely and terrifyingly aware that I'll soon be responsible for this entire collection myself with no idea how I'll manoeuvre it single handed. Regrouping at the departure line my wonderful, very practical dad, heads off to get the garden sack shrink-wrapped in plastic in an attempt to stop the contents spontaneously disgorging before he's had the chance to run away. I meanwhile attempt to relocate the bike to the outsize baggage x-ray area, which helpfully turns out to be a million miles away.
Half carrying, half dragging Claud, whose wheels and pedals are cable tied together, across the airport I arrive at outsize baggage point sweaty, swearing and already knackered.

A mini-drama then unfolds as the baggage guys tell me the bike is too big for their machine and I'll have to unwrap him. No Way!
After much persuading and repositioning we finally get Claud into and through the scanner. Surprisingly I feel a sudden pang as he slides through the baggage flaps, both wanting and dreading to be responsible for him again at the other end.

In comparison, check-in with the now shrink wrapped elephantine sack was easy. Finally relieved of my enormous luggage collection I say a choked up good bye to my dad. Trying, and failing to be tough and brave, I feel 5 years old. I want to cling to him, I'm terrified, but I also don't want him to worry – which he assures me he'll do anyway – so, with stiff upper lip, body trembling like a jelly, I march towards the departure line, blurry-eyed and feeling very alone in a big world.

Some serious self-talking to and a large piece of cake go some way to alleviating the wobbles. Seems like I'm already calorie loading for this trip, it may have to be a long one! I have however made it this far and after 2 weeks of planning I'm finally on my way. Oh my god, I'm on my way! From an idea not even conceived a fortnight ago, suddenly I am on a one-way flight to Canada with a bike and enough camping gear to set up home; planning to cycle across a country I know nothing about, other than it's pretty big.

Taking no notice of the copious health advice about alcohol and flying I consume as much free wine as possible, even though it's only 10am and immediately fall into an exhausted sleep, thankfully staying that way for most of the flight.

I'm amazed when, on landing I have no trouble with clearing passport control despite the one way ticket. Either they don't believe me about the cycling or they don't care. I'm still in a daze and slightly hungover as I collect Claud and the elephant sack from the baggage carousel. There's no avoiding it though, as I steer the fully laden trolley towards the exit, unable to see over the top of all the stuff, this adventure is becoming more real as each minute passes.

Mercifully, having been to Toronto earlier in the year I at least have a vague plan for the next bit. I haul my gear and Claud to the nearest bus stop and with the assistance of an amazing driver, pack it all on board disembarking at Kipling, the main metro station terminus (at which there are no exceedingly good cakes – British advertising joke).

Taking over a station bench I proceeded to unearth Claud from his carrier bag. It must have been quite a sight as, bubble wrap and cables ties flying, I attempt to straighten the handlebars, turn the pedals and get to grips with my mini pump to laboriously inflate the tyres to something resembling squishy. I feel I should mention at this point that this is the most hands-on I have ever been with a bike, ever. Any form of mechanic-ing scares the crap out of me, I wouldn't even be fully confident changing an inner tube. With hands shaking like a 90 year old with palsy and adrenalin surging through me it feels like it takes many hours to make Claud resemble a bike again.

Finally liberating my panniers it also becomes clear that I have way too much stuff with nowhere to put it. A practice pack of Claud, which would have been helpful beforehand, having never made the top of the list in the hectic preparation schedule before departure. At last, roughly two hours after disembarking the bus I was as ready to go as I'd ever be. Claud weighed a ton. Wobbling him to the kerb I wasn't convinced he wouldn't collapse under all the weight. With buses and traffic streaming around me I also wasn't convinced I could ride him with all that gear.

Having cycled to somewhere near this point on my last trip I was at least reasonably confident I could find my way into the city from here. Mounting very cautiously, I half scooted, half rode out over the main highway. And was immediately lost.

It turned out my previous foray hadn't taken me quite this far and it was another half an hour of sweating, swearing, wobbling and direction-asking before I finally find myself on a route I knew. Fear and adrenalin pumping through my system in equal, and large, measures, I was shaking and exhausted from stress and lack of sleep, but at least we were underway. More confident now as familiar streets and parks sailed by into the city, I finally began to relax and, if not enjoy myself exactly, at least feel a modicum less terrified especially when, an hour later and I was rolling into my friend's backyard and the place where I'd been spending the next week or so preparing. Claud and I had arrived!

The Countdown Begins

From: Emma **To:** Cyclinginaskirt
Subject: Your new niece
Sending you a photo. Hard to believe this peacefully sleeping beautiful girl could be the same one that kept us up half the night! Good job she's cute!
Xxx

From: Cyclinginaskirt **To:** Emma
Subject: Your new niece
Hang in there, sounds like a Sunday snoozing in shifts on the sofa is the order of the day. She knows she's cute and the cute ones are always trouble ;-)
Off to look for maps later, visited 2 bike shops yesterday.........people all raised eyebrows when I told them what I planned but were very sweet. Looks like a couple of possible places to stay along the way too with friends of friends, so a good start.
Wishing you much love and sleep xxxx

From: Emma **To:** Cyclinginaskirt
Subject: Frasier hour
Hey you,
Its Frasier hour which made me think of you so thought I'd send a short email. How's the planning going? Is it good being back in Toronto? We've got a busy day planned today (I say planned as not sure how much we're get through!) got health visitor this morning, then boob club, then popping to see friend and then another is coming over this evening, Phew, how did I ever fit in working!
Lots of love, Xxx

From: Cyclinginaskirt **To:** Emma
Subject: Frasier hour

Aww, miss spending Frasier hour with you, watching sitcoms and talking but I love the thought that you have 'boob club' in your day :-) I picture it as a room full of half-naked ladies drinking coffee and comparing breasts.......

So how's it going being on your own with the milk monster? Thought of you yesterday, was looking at the photos, can't believe how much she's grown already. I am a very proud auntie.

Are you managing any sleep? I guess the combination of hot weather and baby isn't helping much?!!

It's very hot and humid here so everyone is finding it difficult to sleep at night, there's no air conditioning in my place, just a knackered fan which grumpily shifts hot air around. Didn't help yesterday evening either with my first introduction to skunk smell.....OH MY GOD it's bad. Had to sleep with the window closed as I'm on the ground floor......someone lent me some essential oils too but to be honest they were nearly as bad as the skunk.

Have been very productive getting maps and advice for the trip, will spend some of today plotting my route based on an organised cycle tour I found that rode west to east and helpfully posted their directions. So far I have bought a road map, torn out the east coast (as I'm not going there) and procured a pack of teeny tiny highlighters to mark my route. What could go wrong…..?!

Don't want to work too hard though so will also fit in a swim in the lake I think and maybe an ice cream. Can't believe it was less than a week ago that you made us goodbye pancakes!

Well, have a fun day, enjoy boobs!

Biggest ever hugs my beautiful sis and give the Bean-the milk monster a cuddle from me.

Xxxxxxxxxxxxxxxx

From: Emma **To:** Cyclinginaskirt
Subject: Frasier hour

Hey, how's the skunk?! Bean and I are doing ok on our own, made it out to see mum and dad on Friday (only to drive home and my car to conk out!). Had a busy day Tuesday with boob club! Was really pleased I made it as met a few other mums who gave me loads of good tips though the boob expert lady said it looks like baby Bean's still having problems latching so suggested Chiropractor. I can't help thinking though that if she's putting on this much weight when she's not latching properly what's she gonna be like when she is! I have visions of a giant baby sat next to me as a bag of bones where she's sucked me dry!

Dad said you're getting some warmer clothes sent over for when you're up in the mountains? Is the trip coming together now? Have people given you any more bear advice!?
Lots of love Xxxxxxx

From: Cyclinginaskirt **To:** Emma
Subject: Frasier hour

Hello beautiful sis,
Glad you're getting out and about, blooming well done, I'm proud of you as I know how much you weren't looking forward to it. Really bad luck about the car, Mum and dad Skyped and said that managed to get it fixed pretty cheaply. Mum was also very chuffed about having got to babysit Bean...twice J though she did make sure to tell me that she couldn't look after her for too long as she wasn't able to breastfeed....no comment!
Sounds like you could do with a wet nurse though to give you a bit of a break. I do now have visions of Bean swallowing you whole. Are you sleeping any more now or is the milk monster still keeping you awake at all hours?
It's not the same of course but I can empathise, haven't been

sleeping much as it's so hot and humid here. It was 40+ degrees yesterday including at night, it's like living inside a sauna, I don't believe I've ever sweated so much or had so many showers.

On the plus side, the local outdoor pool is open until midnight in this weather and it's free. Went for a lovely swim at 11pm yesterday which was bliss.

Was being a bit lethargic with all the heat but have leapt - sort of - into action today, spent the day at the library using their free air con, Wi-Fi and chilled water. Have made a list of final things to do before my trip (always handy) and also marked off a good chunk of my route on the map in the tiny yellow highlighting pen - yay.

My aim is to leave by this time next week, with the latest departure date being 29th.

Am a little bit nervous now, it would be so easy to procrastinate indefinitely, but the autumn will come along fast (have been told that August can be cold in the mountains) so that's a good incentive to get going. I'm also excited the more I plan. I bought some of my last few bits today, including a better mini-pump and a packet of dried egg to which you add water....it looks disgusting but better than trying to carry the real things I think?!

Glad you are all doing well, miss you lots, but your photos make me smile. Keep them coming.

Lots and lots of love and cuddles to you all xx

From: Emma **To:** Cyclinginaskirt
Subject: Frasier hour

Hey you,

40+ degrees is crazy and makes me feel a little better about the sweltering heat here! Keep panicking about keeping the baby cool and then I remind myself that there are babies managing in far hotter places then here!

Glad your plans are coming together and that you're making full use of the Toronto facilities whilst you can - love the swimming pool that's open till midnight :) Gross about the dried eggs, bet the idea of a pot noodle isn't sounding so bad now!

Drop me an email whenever's a good time for you – we're up at all hours! Xxxxx

From: Cyclinginaskirt **To:** Emma
Subject: Frasier hour

Oh crap. I've reached the end of the to-do list, I've even cleaned the bike and packed all my stuff. There's now no reason not to go.

Got a flat tyre yesterday, I think the inner tubes had perished they were so old. It took me 2 hours to change it and even then I ended up taking it to a bike shop because I got it wrong. How am I going to manage out there?! I think if I don't go soon I will chicken out completely so, tomorrow it is…..!

Loads of love xxxx

Last Minute Nerves

When I ask Google Maps to plan me a route from Toronto to Vancouver, by bicycle the response was 'none available'. Imagined brackets "*Are you stupid?!*"
The short answer is probably yes.

The route data for a car tells me the distance is approximately 4512km (2804 miles) and would take 2 days, 4 hours and 10 minutes of non-stop driving, staying within the Canadian boundary. Ironically the quickest way to actually cross Canada involves dipping in and out of the United States.
Obviously the above doesn't factor in stops for say food, fuel, calls of nature, sleep or…..just cycling.

So, as I prepare to start, I have no idea what distance I will travel or how long it will take.
Assuming the distance remains something close to the above, I am estimating between two and three months, with two being very speedy and unrealistic and with three sedate.
This is based on nothing scientific whatsoever and of course makes no allowance for such distractions as sightseeing, inclement weather, wind direction, hills, mountains, mechanical hitches, bears, cougars or just getting plain lost.

That aside, I am so excited. Coming from the UK, Canada is an unfathomably large land mass into which many United Kingdoms would nestle comfortably side by side. Weighing in as the world's second largest country, I've heard countless stories from other travellers of its beauty, vast empty swathes of prairies, giant lakes and dizzying mountain passes.
All I know about Canada, after having spent a few sunny weeks in Toronto, is that it's a country full of changing scenery and topography

over which I have yet to cycle and it's populated with some of the friendliest people I've ever met.
Oh, and bears.

As I lie in bed the night before the trip I try and categorise my fears in an attempt to stop my brain exploding.
So far, specific concerns before starting are:

1. I won't get to Vancouver
2. I won't get out of Toronto
3. My stuff won't fit on the bike
4. Punctures
5. Mechanical problems
6. Getting lost
7. Getting tired
8. Getting lonely
9. Finding places to camp
10. Putting up the tent
11. Escaped lunatics or drunk people when I'm lone camping
12. Bears
13. **Everything**

Toronto to Tobermory

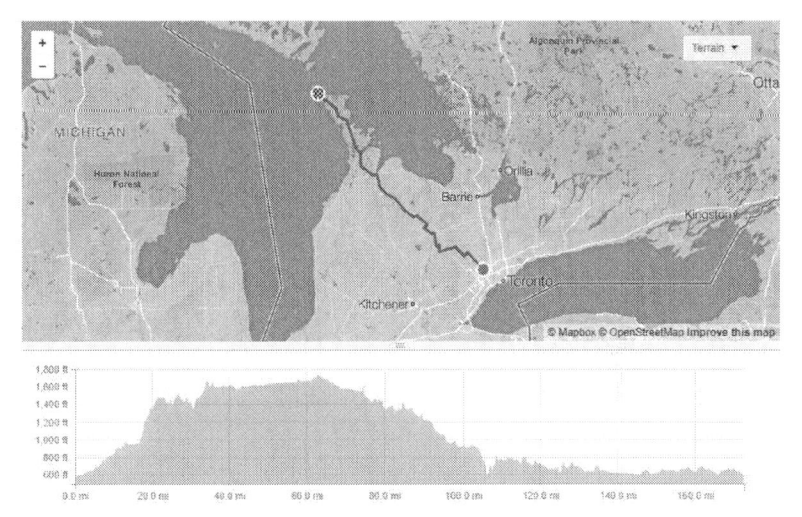

Courtesy of Strava mapping.

Day One: Toronto to East Caledon: 41 miles

Why the bloody hell am I doing this?

I'm used to travelling solo but it's a long time since I have felt so small and insignificant. Vancouver is nearly 3000 miles away but at the moment the end of the street feels like an impossibly enormous challenge.

Having been too nervous to sleep, forcing down any breakfast now seems like an equal impossibility. After literally having to prise open my jaw to swallow a few mouthfuls of porridge I give it up as a bad job. I'm full up anyway as my stomach appears to be harbouring several large house bricks.

Right from the beginning the day doesn't go as planned. Not that there was a great deal of planning but, lying awake in the wee small hours I had gone over again and again in the meticulous detail of the insomniac, the packing and departure bit the following day.

The early start I'd planned however was slipping away from me.

For starters it was taking a ridiculous amount of time to actually load up my bike. Ignoring the added disadvantage of shaking hands and legs, however I loaded it, my gear just wouldn't seem to all fit on the bike. Although I'd bought a few bits for the trip since arriving, map, highlighting pens, dried egg, I seemed to have more stuff than ever.

Having quickly exhausted the space in the panniers and dry sack which filled the entire luggage rack, I'd now resorted to hanging the left over items from any available space. Consequently my cooking utensils, stove, shoes etc. were now artfully tied with string and bungee cords to the luggage mountain. It reminded me strongly of that childhood game called Buckaroo, where players take it in turns to carefully balance items on a spring-loaded mule. At some point the weight becomes too much and the spring releases, the mule kicks and the items go flying.

Gingerly tucking in a jumper I waited for the whole thing to cave in....

amazingly it all held although the bike rattled very musically when it moved.

With my friends trooping out to wave me off, pride meant that I wasn't going to stop, or burst into tears….at least until I'd turned the first corner and they couldn't see me. As I wobbled off along the road hauling over 25 kilos of bulging, teetering, precariously stacked bags, my shaking legs are less from the enormous load and almost entirely from fear. I feel small, I feel 4 years old and very, very alone.

Suddenly I wish I hadn't been quite so gung-ho in telling all my family and friends about my plans. Of course, whether I get there or not doesn't matter to them, they would understand totally if I changed my mind, but could I live with my own mental flak if I bottled it now?

The thing that gets me through those first few minutes is not determination, not guts or courage, but embarrassment. Not wanting to look like a complete prat by giving up is the ultimate driving force in many adult situations.

As these thoughts scrolled through my mind I'd still somehow been turning the pedals and, coming out of my reverie I found myself heading north, joining a quiet path alongside the Hudson River, flowing with it out of the city. I was on my way.

The bike trail also gave me some much needed time to adjust to my cycling cleats. For the happily uninitiated these are metal clips which screw into the bottom of specially made shoes, similar to trail shoes. These small clips then lock into the pedals, welding your foot to them. The idea is that this gives the cyclist extra efficiency by using both the up and down bit of the pedal stroke. The downside of being stuck to the pedals of course is that it makes you fall over sideways when you have to stop suddenly and can't release yourself. After practice it becomes nearly second nature, until then however it adds an extra nerve-stretching element to an already tense time.

Progress is painfully slow and halting and it soon becomes clear the cartoon-style map I found in the local shopping mall, whilst wonderful for highlighting fast food outlets and tourist discounts, has surprisingly failed to accurately illustrate the actual route. Fortunately passers-by are amazingly happy to help and every contact gives me a little tiny drop of confidence and encouragement and the awful weighted feeling in my stomach loosens slightly allowing me to keeping inching forward.

As the day opens up the sun too is throwing out heat in earnest, dappling the peaceful, near deserted river trail. The sound of the water through reeds accompanies the gentle scrunch of gravel under wheels and I'm thinking
"*This is OK, I can do this.*"

"*Oh fuck*". The thundering 3 lane highway came as something of a shock after such a sedate start. Cars roar past the none-too-wide shoulder with which I am now faced if I want to continue. One final, pleading look at the map confirms this is indeed the way forward so, with no obvious alternative I take a deep shuddering breath and plunge on, head down to block out the mayhem just inches to my left.
Bits of broken glass and metal litter the shoulder forcing me to ride over them, whilst drifts of loose gravel grab at Claud's wheels, slewing out the back end in a crazy fishtail, making my already inelegant riding even more farcical.

All this is accompanied by a niggling and growing fear that there is probably a law in Canada prohibiting cycling on something that feels similar to a UK motorway. Getting pulled over by the police, now that would be a great start!
It is around this point that I adopt a policy which is to serve me well for the whole trip. That of; 'If I'm not meant to cycle along here someone will stop/remove/arrest me. Until that time….hum a happy tune and cycle on!'

Ten miles later, the sun is out in blistering force and my nerves are as fried as the shimmering surface of the road. My whole body is aching with that tension borne of extreme, single-minded concentration. Nearly 4 hours after setting out I feel exhausted beyond belief. Woozy, hungry and dehydrated I pull into to a retail park hoping for a café or convenience store or at least some shade.

Checking the trip meter I'm now convinced I'm hallucinating. Surely I must at the very least have covered a substantial distance to warrant feeling this bad.

I stare at the cycle computer in disbelief as it cheerfully displays my total so far as not even 20 miles. Now I could cry, or rage, or both. Stupid piece of junk must be broken as, by my estimation, i.e. the way I feel, I surely must have cycled at least two or three times that.

It's a lesson in managing expectations and one which will take many weeks to master after continually watching that bloody computer inch up, agonizingly, by fractions of a mile. For now though, I'm marooned in the wastelands of outer Toronto, in a tarmac parking lot whose surface is turning liquid in the heat, any fragile new found confidence from this morning melting into the road. One thing is certain, to go any further at all, I need food, drink and a sit down.

The only place that I can see, or have seen for the last nearly 20 miles is a small, cubbyhole of a place nestled against a furniture retail outlet. It's serving hot and spicy Jamaican chicken and goat. This has got to be about the least appealing thing ever in mid-summer temperatures and to someone whose diet is primarily vegetarian. But, not having eaten since early morning, and even then barley at all, I bite the bullet and order chicken, rice, salad and a cold drink.

They're wonderful.

My body is entirely grateful for the food, in fact there's so much I wrap some up to take away. The chatty, cheery lady who serves me is that welcome mix of friendly and curious but sensitive to the fact that I have little, useful conversation in me and, after a quick consultation/confirmation about my progress along on the highway of fear, she delivers my food and leaves me slumped in the corner to recover and eat my meal.

It turns out that food is an amazing restorative but getting back on the bike however was not a welcome prospect to my body, which was now thoroughly at home with the fact that today's cycle ride was complete. Pride though dictated that 20 miles was just not good enough for my first day and, when combined with the distinct lack of camping options out there on the highway, I knew I had no real choice but to move on. Sweating profusely from both the heat and the jerk-chicken, Claud and I groaned forward.

Luck was back with me again though and just a few miles later a welcome exit off the highway gave way to quieter, more manageable roads that in turn segued into peaceful, shady country lanes.

Labouring thankfully along a gravelled cycle path around 4 o'clock that afternoon my thoughts began to crystallise around where I would be spending the night.

With no accommodation booked, a rookie error on the first night, my loose (non) plan had been to find a quiet spot and camp in it. Simple. The further I rode however the more obvious it became that a distinct lack of quiet spots were available.

In fact the whole area was pretty firmly populated, an urban sprawl of homes and cultivated land. Even the cycle path I was on offered little help being bordered by impenetrable dense undergrowth and murky boggy ground beyond.

As this latest predicament began to sink in I discovered that the adrenalin, which had kept me going until this point, had now all but worn off. I was exhausted, mentally and physically after dealing with each fresh challenge of the day. I would have given my net worth at that point for a responsible adult to step in and take over. I was fed up of dealing with things and frankly getting quite desperate.

Now, I wouldn't describe myself as someone of a particular faith, tending to avoid organised practices of any kind, however I hate to think that I live in a world of wholly cold, hard scientific fact where there is no room for the mysterious or unexplained. Therefore, I certainly have an openness or a belief in the possible, be it karma, fate or merely that there are just some things which can't be explained. What happened next was the beginning of a recurring string of bizarre, amazing and downright strange coincidences. Which, for want of a better explanation I am attributing to the universe.

Back to the cycle path and the diminishing prospects of accommodation for my first night seeing the return of my inner 4-year old child. It's then however, that the universe intervenes in the shape of a woman on a bicycle, towing behind her a tag-along trailer and bounded by 2 energetic boys.
In desperation I cycle up alongside her, startling her completely. Not a good start.

Asking hopefully about campsites or small, discreet tent-sized patches of grass nearby quickly drew a blank.
I was, in truth, on the verge of tears by this point, my adventure already appeared to be crumbling about me. I was dog-tired, 40 miles from Toronto and thousands of miles from home. If I could have stuck my thumb in my mouth and cuddled my blankie, I would have.
But, to my utter amazement this saviour then uttered the magical words, *"Why don't you come and stay with us"*?
Disbelief fought with overwhelming gratitude....would it be wholly inappropriate to envelop her in a bear hug and shout wahoo?
I judged yes, but utterly grateful I trundled after the little cycle posse and meet my adopted family for the night.

Tina

Tina, my saviour and new best friend, apparently didn't make a habit of bringing random strangers home. I got the impression it had been a spur of the moment decision on her part and one I was keen she wouldn't suddenly start to regret. I hoped that I was presenting as small and unthreatening a picture as possible as we cycled the last few miles to her home, a beautiful, airy house in the leafy suburbs. It's amazing how much less intimidating places can feel once you're a part of them. No longer a vagrant cyclist with no place to go the neighbourhood looked much more benign than just a few minutes ago.

The family couldn't have been more welcoming, especially since I'd just dropped out of nowhere and into their lives. I spent the evening marvelling in turns at their ability to accept an anonymous stranger in to their midst so completely and also marvelling at how much wine they were plying me with; my good intentions about a healthy, nutritionally-balanced approach already beginning their steep and rapid decline.

The warm shower and a wonderful meal have almost magical reviving properties. During dinner Tina and I compared notes and found that we came from similar work-related backgrounds with much in common. We chatted easily about life, family, work and travel, whilst she and her husband reminisced about trips they'd taken and how much they wanted to take the boys on more adventures, including cycling ones. I loved hearing about different parts of the country too, especially ones I'd yet to encounter.

Throughout this most comfortable of evenings there was a little part of me that remained removed. Almost as if acting as an observer I found myself mentally stepping outside every now and then to watch the scene unfold and to marvel at my good fortune in finding these strangers who welcomed me into their home and their lives, sharing food and laughter in abundance.

Curling up that night I took stock. At the close of my first day I had covered 42 miles of cycle trail and main highway, disgorged hundreds of litres of sweat, consumed a mixture of porridge, nuclear-spicy chicken, spaghetti and wine, been welcomed into a family with whom I was destined to remain friends and covered nearly every range of human emotion on the spectrum. Most importantly my journey had started! Funny how this much needed warm, fuzzy sense of well-being was so, so different to the pangs of hopelessness experienced just hours earlier.

Exhausted and grateful, the anticipation of sleep was a sweet thing.

Day Two: East Caledon to Berkeley 75 miles

75 miles is officially the furthest I've ridden on any bike, ever. I'm almost sure that I feel a great sense of achievement about that, it's just that it's lurking somewhere under all the other feelings of being very knackered.

Leaving Tina's that the morning was almost like leaving my Toronto friends the day before, I'd managed to find somewhere safe, friendly, nurturing and now I was turning my back on it all again.
Packing up I felt that sad, small feeling return. I could go back to Toronto of course I could, it was only a mere day's ride away and no one would think any less of me but, after all the effort, heart ache and huge amounts of 'brave' it took to actually leave, I knew that if I didn't go forward now, I would never have the guts to start this trip again.
Packing, ironically helped focus me on the task in hand especially as my luggage seemed to have multiplied mysteriously overnight. Trying to wrestle it back into bags and under bungee clips I looked more like a travelling camping shop rather than a suave cycle tourist, with pans and shoes again dangling off every available part of the bike.

It wasn't helped by the fact that the bike was so back-heavy it refused to remain upright on its kickstand, crashing sideways the moment I let go. Loading up meant holding it steady with one arm or a foot whilst trying to coax over stuffed panniers in to place working all the fiddly clips and buckles with trembling fingers.
Tina was amazing, having gotten up early to make sure I had a huge breakfast, although I was mostly too nervous to eat. She also sent me

on my way with a food package including a big bar of chocolate – something for which I would be very grateful soon enough.

Saying goodbye to my new friends was tough but I resolutely wobbled down the driveway and back to the road. Heading away from East Caledon my mood lifted briefly as the sun came out and the tarmac opened up ahead of me, definitely calmer and more traffic free than yesterday. Ah, the open road, this is what it's all about, oh, wow, that's a big hill…*

*Looking back now that was nowhere near a big hill, it was a mere bump in the road, a blip, compared to what was to come. Looking back, I'm so glad I didn't know that at the time or I would have turned around and fled.

Mountain View Road, thinking about it, the clue was in the name, turned out to be incredibly hilly. I struggled up each undulation barely moving forward, terrified of grinding to a halt as my feet were glued to the pedals by the cleats.

Every pedal stroke was a mammoth effort, every hill steeper, culminating in a particularly spectacular moment when the gradient and the weight on the back of the bike actually caused the front wheel to lift off of the ground.

Cresting yet another big hill, heart hammering through exertion and adrenalin, it began to rain. Not just drizzle, but big, sploshy gobbets that drenched everything in minutes.

There followed one of what would be many moments to come as a wash of defeat, despair and loneliness engulfed me. How did I think I could do this? I've covered just a fraction of the mileage and it's already taken so much mental and physical effort.

Despondently I pull into a golf club in the middle of nowhere for coffee, cookies and to feel sorry for myself in the dry.

Sipping the hot liquid and feeling marginally less morose I give myself a bit of a talking to (or a kick up the bum). My internal teacher voice sets in accompanied by a strong mental image very similar to a favourite primary school teacher of mine, a stern but kind woman with little half-moon spectacles, sensible hair and comfortable shoes. She (me) proceeds to deliver a straight talking but kindly inner monologue, exactly the kind of no-nonsense pep talk I need, the stiff upper lip kind with a bit of love thrown in.

Coffee break and 'talking to' complete, Claud and I are up and pedalling again. I get into the rhythm of the hills and the road starts to look like a friendlier place, even the sun comes out. Another food stop helps and my spirits lift considerably *"Go on go, you can do it, you're rocking it girl"* I cheer myself on as I negotiate a thankfully flatter network of sleepy lanes.

The quiet Dufferin County Road I'm navigating winds through small towns and hamlets before depositing me on to the busier Highway 10 heading north.

Already the scenery is changing too, with the Toronto suburbs now firmly behind me long stretches of farmland and greenery border the tarmac; windmills now appearing on the horizon instead of industrial units, the road opens up before me, I'm on my way.

Coming up I had a kind invitation to stay with the family of a Toronto friend in their holiday cottage, an offer which, having no idea of my potential daily mileage, thankfully spanned a few days.

In Caledon I'd estimated the distance at approximately 65 miles and had planned in my head to take 2 days to cover this. Then the devil in me kicked in. Maybe I could do this in one day, it would be a challenge…. Never mind that 65 miles would be the furthest I'd ever ridden, never mind that I was hauling near my own body weight in gear. Challenge identified and accepted.

As it happens, this will also be a common, recurring theme. One in which competitiveness and stupidity manage to override common sense and good decision making pretty much every time.

Looking back now, with the benefit of experience, I have learned than when you estimate the mileage to somewhere on a bike (a) it is always at least 10 miles out, in the wrong direction, and (b) they are never, ever flat miles. They are hilly extra miles at the end of a long day when your body is exhausted and screaming in protest. Right now though, I was oblivious. Welcome to the start of a steep learning curve.

On a high and bolstered by both my new found cheer and the prospect of a challenge I pushed on. Fifty miles came and went on my odometer and then 60, 62, 64. Rolling along the road looking at the vague directions I'd scribbled down I was becoming aware that the two did not seem to tally, worryingly neither did the names of the towns I was passing through.
Finally, frustratingly conceding the need to stop for guidance I was met with disconcertingly blank looks from the locals I approached. "*Nope, never heard of that one*" was the general response, their best, and only advice, "*head for the next town, just 5 miles away!*" Just! Just…..!
Pushing down a slight sense of rising panic, I forced down some of Tina's chocolate bar to try and persuade my groaning body to churn out a few more miles. The next town brought more hope but still not the family abode I was aiming for. The day's mileage now topping 70 as I pedalled wearily on.
Just as sheer despair was starting to set in I finally spotted a small sign for the turn off I'd been searching for all afternoon. Four miles of bumpy gravel track later and there, in the middle of a beautiful forest stood a lovely old cottage, surrounded by flowers and my home for the night.
To be honest it could have looked like a garden shed, I was just so glad to get there 75 miles after I set out and the end of day two. Toronto already felt like a lifetime ago.

Magically, once again, the restorative power of a warm shower and chocolate chip cookies did much to erase the worst of the day, as did a night in soft, clean sheets and the chance to log on to Wi-Fi to catch up with the world. Especially with an email from Emma:
From: Emma **To:** Cyclinginaskirt
Subject: Busy Night

Wow this 'roughing it' business doesn't sound too bad so far! I would almost be tempted if it wasn't for all the cycling in between! How's the scenery? Met any other cyclists on route yet?

I definitely feel we're getting there with the baby, I feel so much more confident about going out but we have yet to have a poo explosion or crying meltdown so that might change things! Getting a lot more confident breastfeeding in public, have found that generally people don't realise what you're doing and when they do it's quite funny seeing the panicky embarrassed look on their faces.
It can be tough though and definitely puts a strain on my relationship with M. Evenings are still difficult too, last night between 6 and 11:30 she cried every time I stopped feeding, it's exhausting! Actually resulted in us using a dummy in the end (which I feel very guilty about) but it gave us a few mins of peace each time before she spat it out!! I know it'll get easier and it's all worth it when I wake up in the morning and she's grinning at me! Sorry bit of an off load but I know we agreed to share the good and the bad stuff :) Looking forward to your next instalment :)
Lots of love and Bean smiles xxxx

Day 3: Berkeley to Sauble Beach: 43ish miles

Waking early the next morning I decided to have another attempt at tackling the packing conundrum, not being able to face spending another day listening to the banging and clattering of objects tethered to the back of Claud.

Another sort out of clothes and military repacking ensued until I'd managed to cajole and ram pretty much everything into the 2 rear panniers with my luminous orange dry bag lashed on top of the pile. At least the cars will see me coming!

Waving goodbye to my hosts I felt less emotional and scared than the previous day, wow was I already becoming a hard-bitten cycle tourist? Great.

After an initial protest my legs lost the worst of their stiffness, giving up to the inevitable, that I was going to make them pedal the bike again. My good mood lasted as I coasted along in the sunshine.

By now, the city and the suburbs had most certainly disappeared. The smaller country side-roads I was following were bordered by arable land rather than dormitory towns, disrupted only infrequently by eerie forests of wind turbines and signs to small, appealing places such as Balmy Beach or Blue Mountains lying off the road somewhere to either side.

The blossoming arable land also revealed an increase in the Amish population who farmed a large portion of the land north of the city. The distinctive loaf-shaped barns marked out the farms as did the horse drawn buggies which would suddenly appear, melting over the crest of a hill detaching themselves from the landscape, moving sedately, politely, reminiscent of an era prior to the noisy intrusion of the brash motorcars which sped past, ignoring us both.

I had a sense that we both mourned the loss of a daily life and a road without motorised traffic, thinking wistfully of a forgotten, more sedate era of travel.

Many of the Amish families often appeared in local towns selling their produce from the back of their buggies which skilfully converted into a mobile fruit and vegetable stalls; sometimes complete with a little brazier to facilitate selling hot potatoes or freshly cooked cobs of corn.

It was always incongruous to pull up in a parking area to find one of the unassuming Amish carts sharing the space next to a mobile burger van, oozing greasy cooking vapours from deep fat fryers, accompanied by the racket of a noisy generator.

A shadow from the past reflected in an omnipotent present.

Stopping in Chatsworth for lunch and to mail my excess belongings, it took nearly an extra 30 minutes to leave under the friendly but intensely curious questioning of post office staff. Not about my suspicious looking lumpy package of clothes, but about my trip and why on earth I would want to do it. Covering the parcel in stamps I bid farewell to the staff and the package; mailing the bag of dirty laundry back to my sister I hoped she'd see the funny side.

Heading back out into the afternoon my inner doubts took the opportunity to resurface. Tonight I had no planned campsite or comfy host accommodation. I was going to have to make my own way and rise to the challenge I'd set myself of wild camping.

Wild camping, also known as 'free' or 'stealth-camping' involves pulling off the road along a conveniently located grassy track, through woodland or in a nook of a field and subtly pitching the tent for the night. My gung-ho plan was to 'wild-camp' as much as possible, it being a convenient, easy way to sleep and with the amount of time I'd be away, something that was very good for the budget.

On setting forth my one, unassailable piece of legalese, gained from a friend of a friend, was that wild-camping is allowed on Crown-land in Canada.

With 80% of said land belonging to the Crown I foresaw no problems in finding an abundance of suitable sites in such a huge country.

Things I had not bargained on however:
- That the 20% of private land is the stuff bordering almost all the roads and highways.
- That fields are generally surrounded by thick, impenetrable hedges and ditches, often in close proximity to farm buildings.
- The sheer logistics of manoeuvring a 100lb pannier-laden bike over/through/out of sight of the above are a non-starter.
- The inability to properly camouflage a bright blue tent, especially on open stretches of land and beach.

Wild camping also sounded a fine plan of course in the comfort and security of home, where it was easy to be full of bravado with a lock on the front door, but now I was out in the open I felt amazingly conspicuous and vulnerable.

Starting to scout locations in earnest as I headed onto the Bruce Peninsula it quickly transpired that there was a distinct lack of opportunity to my untrained eye. Not a square inch of ground that wasn't well tended gardens or holiday homes. As the afternoon drew to a close and fatigue set in, the best or only options appeared to be some muddy, scrubby dunes, by the looks of it used by local kids for all night parties. Pushing Claud through the deceivingly boggy scrub I just couldn't settle. I felt vulnerable, exposed and scared. Could I imagine sleeping here? Not a chance.

An internal battle commenced, between my braver, adventurous self who said *"of course I can camp here, I'm a strong, confident woman"* and the small, but insistent voice of fear. The battle inside me ceased raging when I finally acknowledged I wasn't going to feel happy spending the night here so, dragging Claud and my tired body back to the highway, I cycled on. As the sun began to fade on the third day, very un-tough girl tears were humiliatingly close. Exhausted now, I cycled nearly 15 extra miles scouting potential campsites in the annoyingly well populated beaches along the Bruce Peninsula.

The 2 campsites I did try wanted to charge a ridiculous $60 for my bike and my tent, which took up a postage stamp size of ground compared to the enormous, house-sized RVs parked there.

Beyond tired, hungry and sorely despondent, I think I may have started to weave down the road in a sort of misery-trance when a local walker pointed me in the direction of the Provincial Park – a national forestry network almost always sporting a campsite. Here the last shreds of resolve deserted me and I forked out an eye-watering $37 for a camping pitch, denting both my pride and my budget.
With my tiny tent pitched alone in a sea of monolithic RVs I crawled into my sleeping bag. Too tired to cook I opened a tiny bottle of wine I'd picked up at lunch time, curled up and let the tears roll freely down my cheeks.

If the day had ended then I think I may have seriously considered whether to pack it all in. Tired, despondent, alone, with confidence sorely depleted, the whole trip felt like a completely stupid idea. Just then a pair of feet stopped outside the tent.

"Hello in there. Hello. I saw your bike, thought I'd come and say hi. I'm Guy (or Gee if you speak French)."
I don't.
Oh great, just what I bloody want.
I had nothing left in me to be sociable but the prevailing Canadian friendliness had struck again and, despite being the grumpiest person on the planet at that point, my innate Britishness responded with that need to be polite.

I briefly explained my trip to a very interested and animated Guy/Gee, himself a bit of a traveller. It transpired his whole family was having a reunion in the park that weekend and his wife Sharon had seen me arriving and duly dispatched Guy/Gee over to invite me to join them for some food (and the promise of not having to talk if I didn't want to). I already loved this woman.
My evening began again. The family were warm, welcoming and

wonderful as I was plied with mounds of hot food, beer and much advice. They felt like instant friends, and in a day of such solitude that was somehow more comforting than anything.

I was sent back to my tent an hour later with a food parcel and a promise to join them for breakfast.

Not for the first time and nowhere near the last, was my constant astonishment that a day could go from abysmal to amazing at a gift of food or a few kind words and how generous this country was in providing both in abundance.

Day 4   Sauble Beach to Lions Head: 31 Miles

Waking refreshed in spirit, if not in body, by the previous evening I wandered over to meet up with Sharon for an early morning walk to a nearby waterfall. Persuading her in for a paddle we talked about our respective lives finding that despite a difference in age and geography our outlook on life was very similar. She also talked candidly about herself and family and I was struck by her strength and ability to nurture. I also thanked whatever universal gods helped me to land in Sauble Beach last night, despite my earlier cursings of the day.

Whilst my spirit may have been soothed, my legs and body however were not convinced as I selected my next destination from the map, Lion's Head, this time a mere stone's throw - just 30 miles away.
The peninsula itself was beautiful, the sun was shining and suddenly I didn't want to hurry. Cycling out through Pike Bay, the water beside me, I began to feel restored.
I would like to say I had chosen Lions Head for artistic or cultural reasons but it was purely based on the fact that it was close, was reputed to have an amazing bakery and that I am a sucker for cake.

Thirty miles later and Rachel's Café certainly delivered. Decked out in old fashioned 50's diner style, prints of Marilyn and Elvis smiled benevolently on me as I greedily scoffed down crumbly apple tart, buttery sponge cake and coffee by the gallon. It was also the chance

for some life-sustaining correspondence through the miracle that is Wi-Fi. How I'd already grown to love and seek those four happy little letters as an umbilical cord to home, friends and family.
Receiving their emails was better than any sugar rush, words and encouragement were much more sustaining.

Email and sugar fix sated and apparently I'm making good progress according to Toronto friends, which is heartening.
I even briefly considered getting back on the bike but, stopping at the local store for provisions, I firmly and resolutely turned my back on the road, instead setting up my tent in a small site near the harbour. I didn't have the energy today for any raging internal debates on wild camping or miles of scouting for hidey holes to pitch in.

It was a good call as the beautiful, glass-clear expanse of Isthmus Bay made for an exhilarating swim. Drying out on the sandy ground near the tent afterwards, full of cake and cold-water buzz, life and cycling felt do-able again. This sense of well-being was further helped by the numerous glasses of red wine pressed on me by the amused RV dwellers I was again camping alongside.
It seems that bicycles and cycle tourists are quite a novelty hereabouts.

Settling into my tent that night, Sauble beach and the previous day seemed so far removed they were nearly dream-like. Lulled by the gentle lapping of the lake and the warm breeze drying my clothes I prepared to drift into a much anticipated wine and cake induced slumber.

Day 5   Lion's Head to Tobermory: 32 miles

It must have been around midnight that I was awoken by the sound of thousands of large stones being hurled vertically at the tent. A hail storm as it turned out, followed by thunder, lightning and a monsoon of such volume that I lay awake until morning rueing both the lack of rest and the decision to launder half of my clothing and leave it out to dry the night before.

Giving up on sleep, I was packed up and back on the doorstep at Rachel's for breakfast orders. Scoffing down eggs and toast I reviewed my more modest goal for the day, to reach the Tobermory peninsula in readiness to catch the Manotoulin Ferry first thing tomorrow morning.

The map showed either a possible twisty scenic route winding through country lanes or a more direct main road alternative. My conscience put up a brief and feeble fight for sight-seeing before tired legs and body beat that idea to a pulp. The highway it was.

Even the word highway though was an optimistic one for a road barely 2 car widths in places. A headwind accompanied what was otherwise a pleasant 32 miles meandering through pretty countryside, fields of wild-flowers and windmills rolling with me as I easily coasted in to Tobermory in time for lunch.

A quick scout of the town provided little inspiration for food, the main streets boasting what appeared to be mostly over-priced tourist fare. Not in the mood to go searching around I eventually just propped Claud up outside the nearest bar and headed inside.

Trying to tuck yourself inconspicuously in a corner is not easy when you're wearing Lycra, a skirt and cleated footwear that makes little clacking noises with every step you take.

I thought I'd managed it however when, tucked into a dark nook, a family appeared out of nowhere and plonked themselves down beside me.

"*Saw you outside*" – the now familiar refrain went – "*where you headed?*"

I groaned inwardly, cursing my propensity to attract attention and my inability to be impolite.

Fortunately Barb, Bob and Bob Jr turned out to be good lunchtime company and, after insisting I join them in a few glasses of wine, I was feeling decidedly light headed when I heaved Claud back onto the path.

Note to self, must learn to refuse wine when offered (sometimes).

Having no plan and nearly 15 hours to kill until tomorrow's ferry I headed for the waterside. The fresh air thankfully cleared my fuzzy head a little and as I headed out of the main town I spotted a small track with a discrete handwritten sign saying 'Beach'.

Half a mile later the track opened out to reveal a stunning little pebbled cove with the clearest, bluest water.
Leaving Claud in the shade I hurried down for a swim. Floating in the soothing crystalline bay, gently rocked by the swell and staring at the cloudless sky I felt a sense of peace that had been absent so far on the journey, a moment of calm amidst the turbulent emotions and physical exertions of the trip. It may only be a few days since I left Toronto but it felt like I'd travelled a lifetime to get here.

Climbing out to drip dry on a rock I chatted idly with the only other people there, a holidaying family. After they left, the beach remained deserted and with the sun now sinking behind the rocks an idea was forming….could this be my first wild camp site? Could I do this?

After cooking a simple dinner of rehydrated noodles, tinned tuna and dried nori, that thought had crystallised into a firm resolve and I tentatively began pitching my tent on the wooded slope above the beach.
In hindsight, after much more camping experience, it was quite an exposed location, clinging to the top of the shingle, but at least the beach was quiet. The site alone was worth it for an exquisite sunset, only briefly populated by a couple of photographers, after which, I climbed into my sleeping bag, zipped up the tent and waited.

Camping, especially alone, you are almost unnaturally aware of every tiny noise just outside the paper thin canvas. It could be anything from the falling of a leaf to the eerie noise of night insects but each small sound becomes, even in the least fertile of imaginations, a potential threat of danger.

I can't say I slept at all that night and I swear at one point someone, a human, walked past my tent. Willing them away, I was less thinking of any danger, just about not wanting to be moved on for forbidden camping. Thankfully whoever it was left me undisturbed but sleep remained elusive.

Toronto to Tobermory in pictures

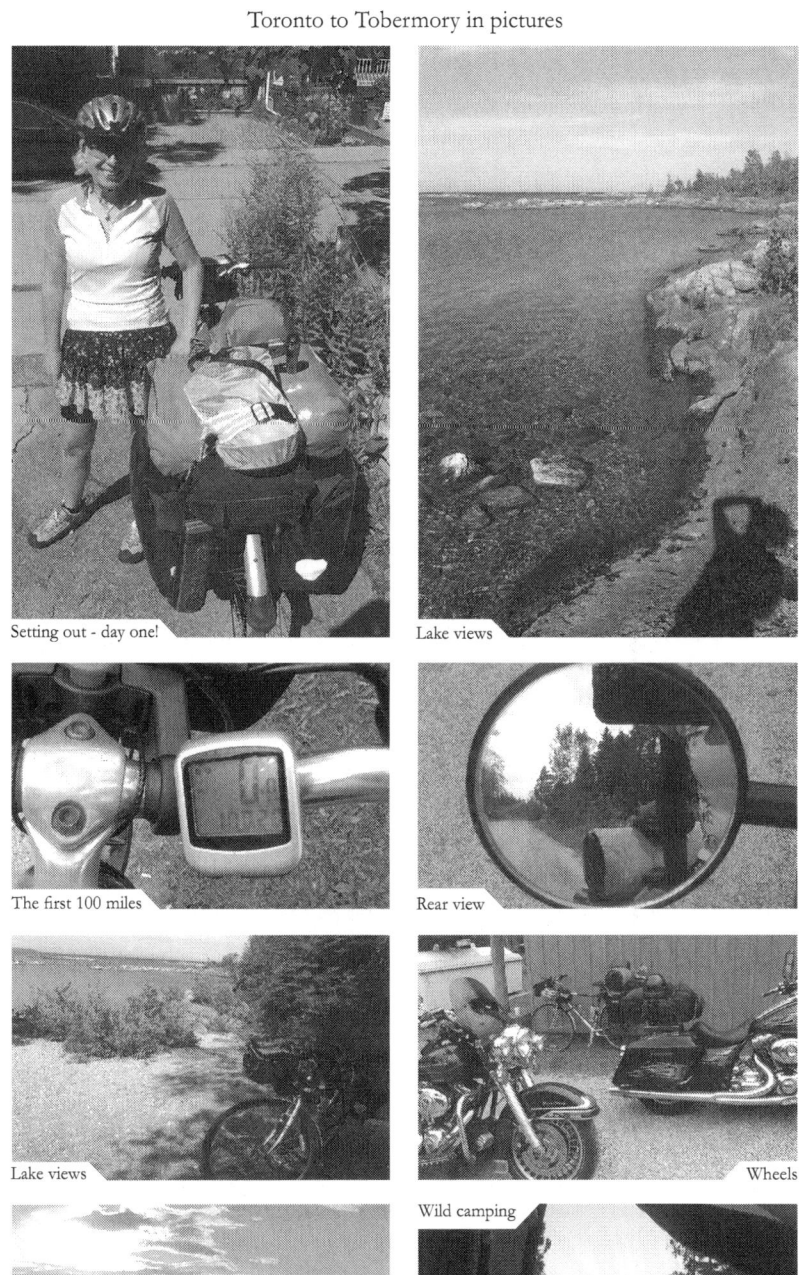

Setting out - day one!

Lake views

The first 100 miles

Rear view

Lake views

Wheels

Wild camping

Evening

South Baymouth to Thunderbay

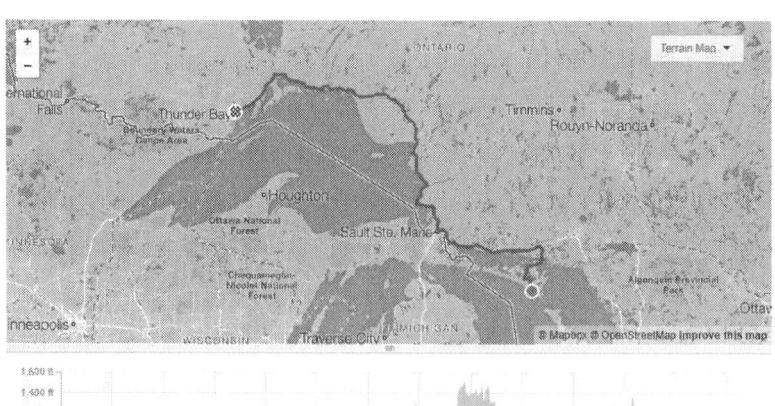

Courtesy of Strava mapping.

Day 6   Tobermory to Honora: 54 miles

I'd done it! I'd spent a night out in the open, on my own, off grid. OK, it's not quite the jungle but I was extraordinarily pleased with myself. After greeting the 5am dawn I finally quit my warm sleeping bag for an icy morning bath in the lake sporting just goosebumps and flip-flops. It was a glorious experience to watch a blood-red sun rise over my little campsite, bathing my progress in a rosy glow as I packed Claud's bags. Cycling away up the track I glanced in my rear-view mirror for a final view of the new-day fire emerging out of the sea.

This exhilaration led me all the way down to the town ferry terminal where another strange experience awaited.

It was a surreal and rather proud moment pedalling off at the head of the long procession of waiting vehicles leading them on board the little Manatoulin ferry. It seemed I hadn't gone unnoticed either and had become a bit of a talking point on board (possibly not much news that day), the skirt and bike helmet making me unavoidably recognisable. One couple approached asking tentatively, "*are you 'the' cyclist*", nonplussed I responded that I was definitely 'a cyclist'?

Chatting about my intended route we were joined by a tough, grizzled looking biker who'd ridden in behind me on a Harley.

He listened and shook his head before telling me what a crazy son-of-a-gun (paraphrasing there) the wind would be in the direction I had chosen.

"*You'll be fighting that bitch all the way*".

He then went into great detail about how often he rode that route and the amount of fuel he consumed being 3 times more the way I'm heading than on the reverse journey, because of the wind.

My fragile spirits were wobbling again and leading the disembarkation I was feeling pretty disheartened as biker-guy shot past me with a cheery wave. On I pedalled.

A stop for home-made ice-cream in Sandfield did amazing things for my spirits; it's still astonishing how much of a pick-me-up food can be. I also consider the fact that maybe I am possibly not eating enough to power my adventure? It's already becoming a noticeably recurring pattern that my state of mind, as well as my physical ability are very much linked to how much food I remember to take on board.

Back to the sunshine in Sandfield and I'd nearly forgotten that for once there was actually a sort of plan for today having prudently arranged some accommodation through my newly acquired membership of the wonderful Couch-surfing organisation. Not being the world's best with technology I was still getting to grips with using the site, so popular because it offers the weary traveller a bed or couch for the night anywhere in the world - gratis. More than that however, it's a friendly face to aim for.

Despite this technological ineptitude I seemed to have arranged to stay with a chap called James who lived on the North of the island. Even better, he'd recommended a bike shop on route run by his friend Jez and, as Claud's gears were in dire need of a bit of love and attention, I decided to stop off.

The Mindemoya cycle shop was a large shed just off the main road, but more than visible with the profusion of bikes surrounding it.

On rolling up outside I was greeted with such enthusiasm I was taken aback, this only increased when I explained where I was staying and who had sent me over.

Jez and his assistant Cath (so good to see a female mechanic) immediately stripped Claud's panniers and got to work on him clamped in the bike stand. As he worked Jez explained the basics of what he was doing – a lesson to me whose mechanical ability just about stretched to changing a flat tyre.

Even better, we also tackled the problem of Claud's twitchy front end. After discovering the propensity for the front wheel to take off on steep hills I'd decided to splash out some of the trip budget on front panniers to balance things out.

Unfortunately the bike shop had the mounts but no bags and wouldn't be able to get them for days. Not having the time to wait I resigned myself to the rearing bike for another few hundred miles, however Jez again amazingly came to the rescue by gallantly donating his own panniers. People are astounding. I did insist on giving him some money but their generosity was amazing and humbling. Riding away from the bike shop Claud felt like a different bike. Instead of the clunky front wheel I'd anticipated with forward luggage, surprisingly the bike was now much better balanced. Instead of expending valuable energy controlling the front end it now stayed put. More than that, I actually felt protected by the wider, stockier front. As Cath had predicted, I felt like a tank, invincible.

Hills still sucked unfortunately and the sudden downpours of rain still drenched me but my fickle spirits were again lifted and a few hours later I rolled into James's driveway.

James

My lack of technological know-how meant I'd failed to properly read James's profile in which he candidly describes his paraplegia caused by a sporting accident in his twenties.
Many people on my journey were to leave a huge impression on me and James did even more than most. His twin passions were permaculture and sustainable living which he studied and practised on a farm that he had created. On the go all the time, I'd no sooner parked Claud when I found myself somehow co-opted in to feeding the chickens. After that he drove us to town, all the time explaining his many projects and schemes. It was dizzying trying to keep up and I was also feeling grateful to sit down after my long cycle, given my companion though you couldn't fail to be acutely aware of being lucky to have that ache in your legs.
Meeting other people and learning a little of their lives always helps put your own in perspective and James was someone who firmly lived life on his terms. Shopping in town took twice the length of time

anticipated, not because of any disability but because, being involved in local politics and running for office, James spoke to everyone.

On the way home he told me how he was planning to hand-bike to Texas soon to visit his girlfriend and how he and Jez were working on converting his mum's bike to an electric one. Endless projects and energy.

Guiltily pleading exhaustion I headed to my room for the night to unpack and dry my belongings. What a room! A cosy little shed close to the house, used for drying plants, it smelled divinely of hay with a jumble of old bikes in one corner. It also came complete with a surprisingly comfortable bed and saggy old sofa over which I laid my sleeping bag and tent to dry out. I found out later the shed had actually been Jez's home and bike shop for a summer before the operation moved to Mindemoya and he was still a regular visitor and part of the family.

James's mum Karen with whom he shared the property cooked up wonderful dinner that evening. An accomplished traveller herself we talked adventures over a glass of wine before Jez appeared with some friends who all piled in for the meal. I very much got the impression that it was always an open house, people dropping in and out, more of a community or an extended family. James even told me that the last cyclist who came for the night ended up staying for 6 weeks. I could see why.

I would have dearly loved to have stayed in the warm, comfortable atmosphere of wine and conversation that evening but fatigue had taken a firm grip on me. Saying goodnight however, Jez extracted a promise to go swimming in the lake the next morning before I left.

Staying a little longer in this wonderful place was so very tempting and the thought played on a loop in my mind as I curled up in my shed, breathing the sweet smelling air. The unaccustomed mileage, the fear and anxiety, the lack of sleep were each starting to take their toll, maybe I could stay for a while......?

Day 7   Honora to Massey: 62 miles

I wake early with the thought of remaining still uppermost in my mind. The feeling of bliss at my first good night's sleep since starting is indescribable as I snuggle down under the blankets, safe and comfortable in my bed.

It was only an unbearably full bladder which drove me, bleary eyed into the yard around 7am looking for somewhere to pee. I was just contemplating a discreet stand of bushes rather than wake up the house when Jez appeared, keen to make good on my promise of swimming.
The idea of cold water seemed less appealing in the light of day but what the hell – this is what adventurers do right?
Grabbing my towel and bikini we headed out on the bikes, turning off down a rutted track about a mile away; as the undergrowth thickened we abandoned the wheels and set off on foot.
Wandering through the early morning woods, damp springy earth beneath my feet, soft sun light filtering through the canopy I marvelled at how the world changes. A few short months ago I'd been sitting in an office, starting at a computer, fighting the commuting traffic and now here I am, striding through a forest on a tiny island, the sun on my face and the only deadlines the ones I choose.

Breaking out through the trees we reached the shore of Lake Huron and a vast expanse of boulders leading to a plunge straight in to deep dark water.
With an uncharacteristic modesty I was vaguely wondering how I was going to wrestle into my bikini when I turned round to see Jez casually stripped naked and diving into the navy blue waters.
Oh well, when in Rome….. Leaving my clothes in a neat pile I followed suit. The cold water shook off any last vestiges of sleep and swimming nearby to each other we chatted, dived and swam until the cold brought us shivering out onto the sun warmed rocks.
Modesty kicking back in we sheepishly dressed facing discretely in

opposite directions and began the walk back. So many thoughts running through my head, the predominant one being how much I wanted to spend more time in this place, with these people, doing exactly this.

That devil was back on my shoulder again though, whispering that need to keep moving and pushing on. I knew in my heart that if I stopped now, got to know these people further, became a part of their lives even for a while, that I would never finish what I'd started. The reserves of courage and will it had taken to start wouldn't hold a second time and finishing what I'd started mattered to me a great deal.

I think the others were surprised too when, over breakfast later, I said that I'd be moving on and it was with much misgiving that I loaded up Claud, including Jez's new front panniers and said my goodbyes to everyone. Cycling away I still chastised myself for going, but if it was this hard to leave after one day, how difficult would it be after 3 days, 5 or 10?

I pedalled on.
Passing through Little Current on the far north of the island I cycled over the bridge back to the mainland, the skies darkening to reflect my mood. It was now 30 mountainous miles to the town of Espanola, pushing up and over some punishing climbs, sudden torrential rain sapping at my energy, the dark, forbidding mountainous rocks looming in like some evil portent.
The sight of a dead bear at the side of the road only served to increase my shivering, even at a distance, the slumped furry mass looked threatening. It also made real a threat which, until now, I kidded myself was make-believe.
I cycled faster.

Hours later I stopped in the grey-looking town of Espanola to refuel guiltily scoffing my first McDonalds in over a decade, strawberry thick shakes had never tasted so good. I also realised that all I'd only eaten so far that day was a small bowl of porridge around 8am. Another reminder of how lack of nutrients impacts on my mood.

Stomach satisfied, though still tired and damp, it was a weary cyclist that remounted Claud. However my goal for the day had been to reach the Trans-Canada Highway (at this point highway 17) the main artery across the nation and one that I would now be mostly following as I finally stopped heading up the map and made my turn west towards the Ontario provincial boundary and, ultimately, Vancouver.

"Fuck me"
The headwind hit me full force as I turned left (west) to join the highway. It was late afternoon and, as I would grow to learn, the wind at this time was especially brutal.
Head down, teeth gritted I was mostly pedalling just to stay still.
Inching along the highway I hit another massive low.
This was impossible, soul-grindingly awful. After nearly 20 gut-wrenching miles I gave in for the day. I was wrung out and distinctly tearful again, my McDonald's calories having long run into deficit.
Too tired and low to even consider wild camping I rolled into a provincial park, barely even squeaking at the $36 for a square of field. The only lightness of the afternoon being when the ranger, in all seriousness, asked me whether I required an electric hook up? We both turned to look at Claud, me pointedly, him sheepishly, and decided it wasn't necessary.

Cooking was the last thing I felt like doing but knowing I couldn't afford not to I opened a can of tuna and poured hot water on instant noodles. That done I lay miserably in my tent berating myself for leaving the island and dreading how I would survive that headwind day after day for another 2500 miles.

Day 8   Massey to Iron Bridge: 65 miles

The morning brought with it its usual lightening of mood, helped along by some friendly fellow campers, although my desire for an early start to beat the wind was hindered somewhat by their desire to chat. I compromised and talked whilst packing. I learned that these particular people had driven past me on the road much earlier the previous day and were amazed to see me pull in at their campsite the same night. Kudos it seemed.

Back on Highway 17 the headwind was much more bearable though still present and I made good time, however I could feel it begin to build throughout the day and by mid-afternoon it had again reached what felt like hurricane force for a lonely cyclist.
The wind played games with me too, taunting me. Every time I began to despair it slackened slightly so I would start to move forward more easily, I'd hearten and gather my resolve, pedal a few hundred metres or more and then it would return, pushing hard against me and slowing progress back to a crawl. A bit like an invisible hand of the gods, holding me back, letting me go, holding me back.

It was during this time that I invented one of my many coping systems called the 2 mile mark. I would tell myself I'd pedal for just two more miles, that's all, watching the painful clicking up of the odometer or better still daring myself not to look at all and judge when 2 miles had passed, singing to myself or reciting the alphabet backwards, anything to make the miles pass. And they did pass, two painful miles at a time the little towns ticked by. Spanish, Algoma Mills, Blind River and a long overdue lunch stop; again where I realised I'd eaten only a scone and some nuts and raisins since breakfast. When it comes to food I'm not the world's faster learner it seems.

By mid-afternoon there was little left in the tank but I'd set my sights on reaching Iron Bridge where I'd arranged to stay with the cycle-tourist equivalent of Couching Surfing called Warm Showers, more wonderful people who would donate just that, a warm shower plus a bed for the night.
This thought alone spurred me on.
Wobbling off the turn for Iron Bridge, I was my usual exhausted self,

not helped by spending a further 30 minutes trying to find my accommodation, so it was in a state of near collapse when I finally arrived at the wonderful home of Wally and Chloe.

The usual magic followed, a shower, food and wine and the world instantly becomes a happier place. I'm constantly amazed at how quickly such strong feelings ebb and flow, emotions all over the place dipping and soaring with the road, the weather, people I meet and food I eat.

Stern note to self. Must. Plan. Food. Better.

Day 9   Iron Bridge: 0 glorious miles

My first rest day!!! Total distance covered so far 405 miles in 8 frenetic, non-stop painful, exhausting, wonderful, scary, exhilarating days.

And now, the welcome opportunity to return to semi-human. Washing, drying and re-packing my gear, it was also a chance to find all the bits and pieces I'd lost to the depths of the panniers (socks, food, sun cream) and to winkle out some fossilising, smelly pieces of bread and cake.

Wally and Chloe

Were the most wonderful hosts, the kind of people who are interested in everything about the world around them and the people in it. I didn't know then that this would be a recurring theme with my Warm Showers stops or that I'd come to look forward quite so much to these little oases in the craziness.

Passionate about the land around their home and about its preservation, they both worked to teach and inspire others, Chloe as a school teacher, Wally as a traditional craftsman, often working with the First Nation groups to revive native building skills and boat crafting.

Cycling across Manatoulin, I'd started to really become aware of the native Indian or First Nation population within Canada. Somewhat naively I had previously only associated native Indians with the USA, a mistake I'd soon realised as the number of First Nation sites grew the further west I travelled. The relationship of the First Nation populations with other groups appeared to be an uneasy one, noticeable in things such as the political graffiti and angry slogans adorning buildings and bridges as well as a perceptible tension in the air.

Chloe, as a teacher, saw this more than most, describing a disaffection and malaise in the students but one that wasn't just confined to First Nation groups but across a far larger number of young people. Noticeable around the Great Lakes were the signs of towns in rapid decline. Where high levels of unemployment saw an exodus of the young to find work in the cities, leading to shrinking, ageing populations and, correspondingly, a lack of tangible opportunities, facilities and services. Government reports had recently shown that the levels of unemployment for those living on-reservations were also significantly higher, along with the predictable correlations of worsening health, housing and life expectancy.
The kids, she said, saw little in the way of future prospects so the incentive to work hard at school for instance, just wasn't there. This was compounded, she went on to explain, by an inflexible learning system that took into account little in the way of different learning styles for such diverse populations. Add to this the fact that many of the parents worked away from home, often for months on end, leaving little in the way of support or guidance for the kids, school attendance was often patchy at best.

As with many disaffected populations drugs and alcohol most frequently filled the gaps left by low prospects and absent parenting, only intensifying the issues. Motivation, for students and prospective teachers alike was hard won it seemed. They were both committed however, to shining a light in to that future darkness for as many kids and people they could reach. Wally talked passionately about initiatives, like those he was involved in, that aimed to build ties through mutual activities such as boat building, kayaking and sustainable construction. Projects and activities which seemed to hold real potential for engaging not just singular sections of the community but a whole swathe of disaffected youth.

One particular project worked with a local First Nation group to reintroduce traditional skills alongside useful trade skills such as carpentry and construction, building boats and houses using methods that had all but died out in the current generations.

Wally and Chloe's enthusiasm was infectious as was their desire to share both their knowledge and their beautiful environment. Both keen and very able kayakers, Wally was also a qualified instructor. Excited about showing me around, that afternoon he loaded up their big 4x4 with boats and equipment and we all headed down to Lake Huron so he could initiate me in to the mysterious art of paddling.

I've never been great in boats either big or small. A couple of tandem canoe trips in the past with a previous partner had nearly ended the relationship so it was with some trepidation that I embarked on my inaugural solo jaunt.

First though, before we could head out on the lake, I needed to pass the safety test, the main part of which seemed to be turning the kayak upside down so my head was in the water and then hauling myself out. Now, I love swimming and scuba diving but, for some reason the thought of doing this irrationally terrified me. Every time we came to do 'the roll' I bottled it, heart beating a tattoo, palms sweating, what was it that was wrong with a little dunking?

Fortunately Wally proved a calm and patient teacher and this, combined with the other powerful motivator of not wanting to look like a chicken, was enough to tip both me and the boat over the edge. Coughing up water like a fountain I emerged triumphant from this manoeuvre and was at last told I had earned my water wings. We were ready to paddle.

The lake proved surprisingly bumpy, at least for a rookie like me and whilst Chloe and Wally paddled away smoothly gliding through the waves, I was quickly left floundering and splashing by both lack of technique and experience. They were both incredibly patient however, it must be the 'teacher' gene and once underway I developed something of a rhythm.

The lake itself was stunning, sun glinting off its dark surface and it was wonderful to be travelling via a different method entirely. My legs, grateful for the rest, let my arms take the strain. Meanwhile I watched the world and the wildlife glide past. We circled around a few small islands and rocky outcrops, nosing the craft down skinny channels, beak height with the birds. It was enchanting, the lake stretching away to the horizon on all sides, I'd never seen a stretch of water so vast other than the ocean.

An hour or so later I'm finally getting the hang of it although my arms hate me and it's certainly chilly after my enforced soaking. When a stiff breeze blows up, whipping up little white cap waves we decide to call it a day and head back to shore.

Back on land I'm buzzing. What a wonderfully unexpected way to spend time exploring. Through the generosity of my hosts, through talking and paddling, I'd been fortunate to have just a little glimpse of a world I never would have seen from the highway, even by bike.

Back in my warm bedroom I ponder what I've learned whilst reverently savouring the sheets for one more night. Logging on to the world and its web I indulge my other guilty pleasure, my final fix of messages from friends including the biggest boost of all, sister mail.

From: Cyclinginaskirt **To:** Emma
Subject: Hugs to you
Hellooooo,
Thank you so much for your messages, I've just got internet access again and a chance to sit and write. It's really lovely getting emails and blog comments, it's really been spurring me on and giving me a boost when I'm needing it most.

Had my first rest day today which was certainly welcome and probably a day overdue. The cycling is really enjoyable but I've been covering a lot of miles, 60 -65 a day sometimes and since I've started heading west the wind is now fully against me so progress has been hard won.

However I've been staying with a Warm Showers family who have looked after me really well and I'm feeling rested and ready to head off shortly. I've also been camping a bit (sometimes on campsites, sometimes not). I woke up the other morning to a stunning sunrise on my own private beach. Time for a quick swim before I left too, who needs a swimming costume!

How are things going on the baby sleeping front and with you guys in general? Have been thinking about you lots.

I've found the last few days hard with the headwind and disheartening. I do keep thinking about stopping and/or catching the bus part way. It's silly but it would seem like a cheating, plus so many people have been saying it's such an amazing journey it would feel wrong quitting. To address it I've decided to do one day at a time and re-evaluate at the end of each day. There, that's my little wobble for now. Still enjoying it too though.

Lots and lots of love to you xx

From: Emma **To:** Cyclinginaskirt
Subject: Hugs to you
Hey lady, so sorry I missed your Skype call, I must have been in

Boobie Club at the time :(your pics are fantastic! I hope you're still enjoying you're trip?) Been thinking about you and how tough it must be, especially not knowing where you're going to stay. I know you've set yourself this task and you'll feel deflated if you don't do it all to plan but like you advised me with the whole dummy/expressing thing - do what's right for you :) you gotta make sure you're still enjoying this trip otherwise it's not worth doing, might as well be back in Toronto or here! So, if that means the odd bus day or whatever then let yourself do it. Hope it's ok to say that - I know you'd say the same to me but I also know how stubborn we both are! No hope for Bean - she's already a little madam!

Things are good here and better with M - feel like he's been really supportive, just little things like taking her for half hour in the morning and evening to give me a little extra kip! We've been super busy this last week or so, had last appointment now with Chiropractor which has definitely helped, we also registered her birth. Lots of coffees planned with people, and ice creams. Found this amazing hidden ice cream place to show you, you'd never know it was there unless shown. I had Baileys and a scoop of blackberry sorbet :)

It's great to hear from you, Bean sends a little smile your way and maybe a little poop too – 'cos that's just her :)
Lots of love Xxxxxxx

From: Cyclinginaskirt **To:** Emma
Subject: Hugs to you
Thank you for your words of wisdom and talk of ice cream that made me laugh. Can't believe how much the little milk monster keeps changing, and growing....keep up the good work :-)
Unlikely to have email access for a few days now but will be thinking of you both lots as always. Lots of love xx

From: Emma **To:** Cyclinginaskirt
Subject: Made me think of you

Hey, nice to read your blog, can't believe how much ground you've covered! Well done you! Just a quickie 'cos I thought of you - M is out for the evening, the Bean is asleep in her magic rocking chair and I'm enjoying dinner with a glass of wine! Made me think of when I'd pop over to your place after work and grab a glass of vino or a beer in the garden and when that turned into a bottle and a take away!
Raising a glass to you Sis xxxx

Day 10   Ironbridge to Joseph Island: 48 miles

The day presented an inauspicious start with squally gusts of rain and wind blowing around the bike as I loaded up Claud's panniers. My mood too was as grey as the sky as I pedalled away from my hosts. Again the thought of stopping or at least taking longer off of the bike circled through my mind, but that stubborn, belligerent bit in me was telling me to move on. So that's what I was doing, wind and rain swirling around me.
Turning right, back on to the Trans-Canada Highway, I braced myself for the face full of headwind I'd already learned to expect. Only it wasn't there…. By some miracle of nature I had my first proper tail wind! Wahoooooo.

It was impossible to describe the feeling of delight at such a moment and the perfect boost it gave my damp spirits. And what a difference it made.
Claud and I were flying, clocking up an average speed of nearly 20mph which was something I would have been proud of on any bike. Now this was the kind of bike touring I'd signed up for, the minimal effort variety.

Being a sailor, Wally had explained in detail about the strange weather systems created by the great lakes, the vast expanses of water providing a cooling effect on the air influencing its course of travel. Not being meteorologically minded my understanding was minimal, however I did grasp the basic premise that generally, the worse the weather was, the better for me in terms of wind direction. I could get to like the rain.

Back on the bike and as far as I was concerned this day could go on forever. A short stop in Desbarats for some of the best lemon meringue pie and all too soon I was rolling up to meet my second Warm Showers hosts in as many days.

I could get used to this too I decided as I was shown to my home for the night, my own perfect little lakeside cabin.

My hosts were a wonderful, warm couple, one of whom was no stranger to endurance feats being a multiple Ironman contestant in one of the sport's toughest triathlon distances.

Settling in with another welcome dip in Lake Huron which fronted my little cabin, I emerged to be treated to my first experience of sliders (mini hamburgers), chocolate brownies, ice cream and much wine, all washed down with some great talk of travel and the stupid human pastime of endurance sport!

Given their sporting pedigree I was chuffed that my hosts were impressed with the distance I'd already covered. It was also really heartening to find out that they'd also previously had staying another cyclist who was riding an east-west route, a huge source of relief as I was beginning to think I was the only idiot who'd attempted it.

Finally, as keen walkers and kayakers they sent me off to bed with a raft of recommendations for camping and swimming spots along the lake shore.

Feeling strong, happy and slightly fuzzy with wine I curled up in my cabin that night, drifting off to sleep to the sound of the lake lapping against the shore.

Day 11 St Joseph Island to Sault St Marie: 36 miles

Distance-wise today should be an easy day but my nemesis the headwind returned with a vengeance. Inching my way into the city of Sault Saint Marie it was quite a culture shock being back around so much traffic, so many stores and people. Since leaving the outskirts of Toronto I'd become accustomed to small towns, sleepy roads and minimal traffic but in 'The Soo' (as the locals' called it) it returned in bucket loads.

My campsite that night was a bike shop, legendary amongst cycle tourists. *Velorution* provided a city haven for bikers, offering free camping on a tiny patch of land behind the shop and 24/7 access to a shower, toilet and Wi-Fi, the holy grail to all weary pedal pilgrims.
Bizarrely located in the heart of an ugly, urban industrial park it also offered the opportunity to tackle my growing list of 'things I need to get in town', a new adapter plug being the most pressing. Having annoyingly left my one and only plug converter in an unknown socket, all electronic gadgetry was getting severely depleted.

But the best bit about my new campsite.... Other cycle tourists! Jim and Etta, travelling separately, converged on the shop throughout the day. Etta with a fishing rod strapped to the bike frame and Jim with plastic buckets for panniers. It was a real high to meet other people doing the same daft thing (albeit in the opposite direction). As dusk fell and a curtain of rain moved in we all moved our camping gear into the side porch of the shop and shared travel tales along with cheap beer and instant noodles. Alongside these veterans of the road, 41 and 30 days respectively I felt very wet behind the ears, a mere novice.

I was particularly intrigued to hear Etta's story. She'd started her trip in Vancouver doing the opposite of my ride and heading back to Toronto...with a female friend. It had quickly transpired however that she and her companion, Chris, travelled at very different speeds and somewhere along route the tensions caused by this discrepancy had boiled over and caused the pair to split up. I admired Etta's resourcefulness riding solo and was relieved to find another (my first) lone female rider.

Jim and Etta were also great at passing along a whole host of useful information including road layout and free camping spots and most importantly the promise of huge, face-sized ice creams within a day's ride from here.

Still nervous about wild camping, this gen and Etta's example came as a real boost, as did her advice about the headwind, bizarrely both her and Jim had encountered their share even coming from the other direction. Etta's advice: make friends with it, don't fight it and most importantly, "*Don't let the wind break your spirit*".

Hmmmm.

Taking time out to add to my newly minted blog, I bask in the glow of being fed, showered and slightly drunk on 2 bottles of beer. Curling up in my sleeping bag in the shop porch, my 2 companions snoozing next to me I felt contented, almost like a proper traveller. As I drifted in and out of sleep I wondered how long it would take to feel I'd earned my panniers and the right to be an adventurer of the road and more importantly, when I'd stop feeling like a frightened kid and feel like I really belonged.

Day 12   Sault Saint Marie to Alona: 72 miles

Four am and I'm wide-a-flipping-wake, sleep is not happening much at the moment, right when I desperately need it. I make the most of the time by tramping round Walmart shopping for pannier food items (tuna and noodles) and random impulse purchases such as the pack of muffins which I inhale in the checkout queue.

Etta and Jim are packed up when I return and hit the road not long after. It's lonely. As I sit waiting for my tablet to squeeze the last drops of electrical juice from the new charger, I have that small abandoned feeling again realising how nice it was to have some company for a while and to feel like a part of something.

I've often found it's one of those strange abilities of the itinerant, the hobo, the back-packer, the dispossessed, to be able to set down in a new place and to make it feel like home after a few hours. To lay out your things, strike up quick and easy friendships, bonds that form deeply over a few tales, a few beers, when strangers become close friends for that one night only. Then in the morning, you move on, probably never to see the people or the place again. Keep moving forward, don't look back.

Funny how those pop up friendships still stay with you in your head though, hazy around the edges, but with more clarity than a 24 hour acquaintance would suggest.

Back on the road I give a nod to the International Bridge dividing Lake Superior neatly between Canada and the United States. Crossing here in to the US would make my journey shorter ironically but I was determined to make the crossing completely on Canadian soil. Even if it was hillier and longer!

I'd been hearing some tall tales too about the even taller hills guarding the exit to the Soo. Loins girded and the sugar from 3 breakfast muffins pumping through my body it turned out those hills actually disappeared with relative ease. As always, the best bit about those ups….. were the downs. With complete abandon, Claud careened down over 300 foot of descents, the weight making him an unstoppable force. I'm fairly sure the brakes would have had limited effect given the gradient and load so my finely honed policy was becoming one of just steering around the worst potholes/roadkill/abandoned shoes and riding the adrenalin wave. My downhill speed record to date now is nudging over 33mph.

Drunk on speed I pull in to one of the random trading posts lining the highway.

These groups of shops sold everything the bored/tired/naïve traveller could demand at a rest stop. Everything from a range of beautiful First Nation crafts to the inevitable tacky tourist souvenirs, fridge magnets, baseball caps, dream catchers, animal horns. But most importantly, nestled amongst the huts I discovered the fabled kiosk of ice cream as described by Jim and Etta.

In wonderment, I bought a 'small' ice cream roughly the size of my head for the bargain price of $2, from an enthusiastic, rotund teenager who clearly had a different concept of 'small' from the measly portions depicted on the menu card. I did wonder if his employers would be as entirely supportive of his generosity?

As I tackled my football of ice cream a smiley couple plonked themselves down beside me, with the sole intention it seemed of telling me how horribly, horribly hilly the next part of the route was. They went on to describe in detail its awfulness and the fact it was so steep their truck of a campervan could hardly make it up the climbs. After all of which they cheerily wished me a lovely trip and departed. Thanks!

I think people thought they were being genuinely helpful by warning me of the terrain to come, such as the motor-biker on the Manatoulin ferry but actually all it did was scare the pants off of me and dent my confidence. No longer hungry now and with ice cream remains congealing in splodges all around me, I gave up, collected Claud and headed off.

All day it had been on my mind, squatting like a toad, where will I sleep tonight? Can I, do I, dare find another wild camping spot? Etta's example spurred me on as did her words of wisdom, as the wind began its usual afternoon hurricane impression, my grim mantra became, Etta's *'don't let the wind break your spirit'*.

Reaching Alona Bay I paid my respects to my adversary the wind and bowed out for the day. The sugar highs had worn off and I was tired. When the sole pedestrian I encountered told me the nearest camp ground was another 25 hilly km away this sealed the deal on wild camping. Kindly, she also pointed me towards a track just a few metres away which she thought led to an area that was sometimes used for partying by the local kids.

Bumping Claud down the grassy trail it quickly opened out into a small clearing looking out onto a stunning view of Lake Superior. Evidence of the aforementioned teenagers was prominent in the, litter, bottles and fire remains making me slightly uneasy. As lone female, hidden in this remote spot, I felt vulnerable but, I was tired and also determined that I could do this.

Dinner was the usual uninspired noodle/tuna combination and the last of Tina's chocolate (how it had lasted that long I've no idea) and 2 more muffins, all consumed sat on the shore of the great Lake Superior watching a heartbreakingly beautiful sun melt into the water.
Washing up before bed I just had to sort my final chore of the day. As a responsible camper and following much sage outdoorsy advice I determined to try and hang my food pannier in a tree, far enough away from the tent so that any passing bears would leave me alone in favour of the delicious dried noodles I was carrying.

Discouragingly all the trees around me had very high branches and I can't throw for toffee. After many failed attempts at coaxing my nylon cord into the upper echelons I settled for just out of reach, being only 5 foot 4 tall this wasn't ideal, but the bag was a little way away. It would have to do. The rest of the panniers I tucked snugly in the tent.

Heading inside I gripped another addition to my armoury which I'd found under the trees, a large pointy stick, whether for protection from bears or humans I'm not sure.

Lying tucked up in the tent I read, with a mix of utter pleasure and home sickness, the cache of emails I'd downloaded from home following my earlier blog post. I jealously hoarded the words and memories they conjured as I lay in the dark, wide awake, listening to every pop and snap of the undergrowth, imagining the beasts, murders and lunatics that were marauding outside, whilst with every shift of my body I managed to impale myself on the damn stick.

It was going to be a long night.

Day 13   Alona Bay to Rabbit Blanket: 57 miles

Despite fears for the safety of life and limb I did actually manage to doze off. It must have been sheer exhaustion having not slept well almost every night since leaving Toronto.
The next day, emerging to an ominously gunmetal grey sky I streaked past startled birds to plunge naked and shrieking into the lake. A beautiful but freezing bath provided a quick wake up and a glorious view. Then the clouds opened.
Getting dry and dressed in my tiny tent I watched the stair rods of rain beating the earth knowing it was in for the long haul. Not wanting to linger if the rain was set in for the day I squelched around packing up in the downpour.
Hauling down my food pannier from the tree for breakfast I was surprised to find it full, not of groceries but maps, books, money and my passport?
Weird….then it slowly dawned on me. With both front panniers being identical, in my brain addled weary state I had carefully hung my travel documents 6 foot in the air whilst I slept cuddled around the bear-attracting food pannier in my tent. Oops.

Unnervingly, it was a mistake I would make more than once.

Unwilling to linger over breakfast in the pouring rain I gulped down a banana as I pushed Claud back up the track to the road. I was getting soaked but my spirits were curiously high. I'd wild camped again. I was a woman of the woods. I was beginning to feeling like a proper traveller at last……. A proper traveller who really wanted breakfast! Up until now there had been a surfeit of rest areas, cafes, petrol stations and small towns lining my route making the choice of food stops plentiful. Now, when I needed it, of course there was nothing.
My stomach howled in protest, the banana being long deployed to ungrateful muscles, when finally, around a bend in the empty road I

spotted a campsite.

Huddled on the lake shore sat a small bunch of grey cabins, a run down and desolate looking place nearly obscured by the rain. The whole resort had that out of season holiday camp air and I held little hope of finding anything open.

As luck would have it however a little breakfast cabin provided a decent egg sandwich and coffee as well as company in the form of Edie, a Toronto artist and film maker.

I answered her questions about my trip as best I could through ravenous bites of sandwich. In between she told me about her current film project, recording the memories and recollections of the older generation of Canadians who had grown up on the lake shore. Their reminiscences were of the many changes to their home as the world progressed and these isolated communities had begun to falter, decline and often wither away.

As I'd seen back in Ironbridge, all around the lake it seemed that jobs were disappearing and with it the younger generations who defected to the towns and cities to find work. Caught in a circular spiral of decline these dwindling communities then found it harder to retain vital services; doctors and teachers wouldn't come, schools closed as the population needed to sustain such services fell below critical.

Those that remained, the elderly, the sick, the stubborn, the die-hards, were living a tough, often lonely existence in the decay of these once thriving communities.

The dark, grim weather made for an excellent back drop to the monologue. The greyness of the day was almost oppressive, lightened only by the warmth of my new companion who, as I said goodbye, plied me with offers of hospitality should I return to Toronto. People are so genuinely, openly hospitable here it amazes me.

The wet blanket of mist and rain now hung over me like a suffocating blanket. Stopping for lunch I optimistically unpacked the tent and hung it from a tree during a brief respite from the drizzle to try and dry it off. Ten minutes later it rained again. Giving up the idea of cooking food I grazed some trail mix instead, packed up Claud and pedalled away again.

Riding deeper through Lake Superior Provincial Park the roads were eerily quiet. This natural preservation area was spectacular but I was rapidly becoming a grouchy, hungry cycle tourist in dire need of shops or cafes or….human life. All of which were spookily absent.

It was only now that my small brain cells were dredging up the forgotten advice of my previous Warm Showers hosts – namely that there was a roughly 60 mile stretch of road around the lake with no services or provisions. Bugger!

The sign for Agawa Bay visitor centre loomed out of the misty drizzle and like a shipwreck survivor in sight of a flotsam I pedalled towards this glimmer of respite with hopes of warmth and hot, comforting food.

The small visitor centre, as it turned out, sold jars of jam, books and toys. That was all. I could have cried. A begged-for flask of hot water made an insipid cup of tea but it was at least warming and surprisingly restorative and I drank it taking advantage of the Wi-Fi to check emails and pilfer the dregs of my pannier for something quick and edible. Crisps. More trail mix.

Pleasingly I did have a moment of genius by attempting to dry out/warm up using the hand-drier in the ladies rest room, which, for 20 minutes I commandeered to dry clothing, bedding and tent, much to the amusement/surprise of unsuspecting toilet goers as they encountered me in my bra, holding a t-shirt over the drier nozzle.

Feeling somewhat better I return to Claud to find a random stranger intensely looking him over. Not sure of his intentions – he didn't look desperate enough to steal a damp, muddy touring bike, I hastened over.

Bert actually turned out to be a real enthusiast. A keen cyclist and triathlete he'd been considering trying cycle touring and was fascinated by Claud's creative packing layout. As his wife joined us we chatted about the route, mine to come and theirs following their annual pilgrimage south to Florida.

Before leaving, Bert asked me about my bear strategy and I explained my pointy stick approach as a look of horror slowly crept over his face. Pressing me to wait he sprinted back to his van and returned with a small aerosol device. "*Bear spray*" he explained (to repel, not attract) "*just in case*".

With a warm glow from this encounter I cycled away, straight onto a beastly section of hills. I tried hard to focus on the stunning scenery, trees, the lake, anything instead of the creeping tiredness and crushing headwind.

It will not break my spirit, it will not break my....

At one point the going was so tough I actually got off the bike to check the brakes thinking they were stuck on the wheel. Nope, just headwind. Twenty or so miles short of the destination I had in mind I pulled off the road at the first campsite I'd seen for ages. Exhausted, too tired for the stress of wild camping, I berated myself as I paid the exorbitant $40 fee for a pitch designed for giant motor homes - the only ones on offer.

Eating the now ubiquitous noodle/tuna combination I read the new emails I'd downloaded earlier and that perpetual stab of loneliness flared in my gut making the food even more unappetising. Again I'm wondering what it is that's driving me to do this. No one minds if I don't, it's not like there'll be hordes of people expecting me at the finish. Tired, lonely and for the first time, really cold, I curl up deep in my sleeping bag only to be greeted minutes later by a voice outside.

Climbing out of the tent there are 2 laden bicycles sprawled on the floor and behind them 2 very tired people, equally prostrate.

These late arrivals had been despairing of somewhere to stay it seemed as the campsite was full. When they spotted Claud and my tent they knew they had found a kindred spirit. In turn, I more than happily accepted their offer to share both cost and company. With plenty of room for all 3 of us I was very happy to have camp mates. Thank you universe!

Chris and her bike buddy Jack had met only a couple of days previously it turned out, whilst both cycling a west to east route starting in Vancouver. Things got even more bizarre when it transpired that Chris was Etta's long-lost companion now travelling at a different pace. Small world.
At this point I got the impression that Chris wasn't as comfortable with the split as Etta was and that it had left a big hole in what was previously a close friendship. I hoped for her that, given time and distance, their splitting up and subsequent adventures would become a positive part of her travel tales and that the different opportunities it produced would maybe help to heal the friendship, but that's their story.

There followed the usual catch up on wind (who had experienced the worst), places to stay, free camping and general news of the road. It was here I learned there were 2 French guys cycling ahead of me by a day or so as well as another British guy. I wonder if I'll catch them?
After this unexpected but enjoyable social interlude I retired back to my tent in a weirdly better frame of mind. Again the day had swung unexpectedly from awful to good at the turn of a conversation and some company, simple things which make the world alright again.

Day 14   Rabbit Blanket to White River: 84 miles

Now officially my longest ride ever in both time (10 hours) and mileage and I'm knackered!

Two weeks on the road and I've developed my own little routine already.

- Wake early – dawn lights up the tent in technicolour so no chance of sleeping.
- Put off getting up for as long as possible, usually until I'm desperate for a wee.
- Wash (if there's water) and get dressed in still slightly sweaty cycle gear trying not to think about how damp and tacky it feels.
- Stuff down a quick breakfast of dried muesli or muesli with water if I can be bothered to wash up. Brew fresh coffee if I'm really treating myself. My one luxury, a travel coffee press mug. Sheer heaven.
- Pack tent and load bike, a tedious chore which, no matter how much I try, I can't reduce to below 30 minutes.
- Cycle.

The details of the day then seem to take on a life of their own but the greater picture always seems to entail riding an awful lot of tough miles; pushing to and beyond limits before rolling half crazed with fatigue into a campsite/spot. Pitch tent, cook noodles, sleep if lucky. Get up again the next day and repeat.

Why? It's a question I will ask myself again and again throughout the trip, especially at the low points of hunger and tiredness. Originally the idea was to have an adventure, to do something outside of work, to do something, although somehow the journey seems to have taken me over, shaping my days for me whilst I dumbly comply.

But at least the miles are falling away, I've crossed several pages of the map now and each new page turned brings a new goal to aim for as the thin ribbon of luminous highlighter pen marks the road ahead.

The end, in Vancouver is still an inconceivable amount of miles away, too far to imagine, but at least I can now see the miles racking up on my odometer. I think less about turning back now, partly because I know how bloody far I've come and I don't want to retrace those hills. I fought for those miles and I am inching forward, slowly. It's also kind of addictive.

Bidding farewell to Jack and Chris, I tackle the next steep, hilly 20 miles to Wawa, really glad I hadn't attempted them yesterday in my beleaguered state.

Wawa is an odd little town that it seems is most famous for its gigantic statue of a goose!
As I travel through these small communities it's definitely becoming apparent that there something of a competition going on here; with every little town wanting to stand out from its neighbours it seems that there's been some sort of programme of covert one-upmanship involving giant statuary. No restrictions appeared evident on what the statue should be of, just that it was BIG. Consequently towns boasted giant models of strange, random objects such as hay bales and animals including polar bears, camels and geese. Obviously, the bigger the better.
Within this weird world, Wawa's goose was, erm legendary.
Pausing to photograph the bird and be mildly confused as to its presence, my mind quickly wandered on to other things, namely food!
My other great discovery to date has been the Canadian institute of Tim Hortons a ubiquitous chain of bakery/restaurants spanning the entire country and frankly, cycle tourist heaven.
After paying brief homage to the town's concrete feathered legend, the lure of air conditioning, Wi-Fi, toilets and cheap baked goods put the giant goose firmly in second place. Parking Claud up outside Tim Hortons I proceeded to order and demolish half a cheese sandwich, a doughnut, a cinnamon bun, a cheese scone and large coffee all in an indecently short space of time.

Stuffed and happy I headed back on the road waving at the goose as I pass. The day was warm and sunny and, as the temperature climbed, an inviting lake made the perfect mid-afternoon stop and the chance for a swim to cool off. Only slightly perturbed by the very red-looking water I spent a heavenly half an hour splashing about before draping my bikini to dry over Claud's rear end and pedalling off again thinking *"This is why I do it"*. And it is, for moments like these and of course, to be able to raid Tim Hortons with impunity.

Further on I see 2 cycle tourists approaching on the other side of the road. I've found that etiquette dictates that one party always pulls across the carriageway for a chat and to pass on news of the road.

I like these meetings, it makes me think of pre-automobile times when gossip, stories and information were swapped by travellers on their journeys from town to town, an old fashioned bush telegraph.

Pulling to a stop I meet John and Jean, cyclists from Montreal. We spend a pleasant few minutes talking of our journeys, road conditions, campsites and places of interest. I pass on the details of my ice cream extravaganza the previous day and they of a cyclist less than a day ahead of me going my way, the other Brit spotted by Jack and Chris it turns out whose name is Tom.

Maybe he too was heading for the fabled free camp ground at White River? Galvanized by this thought, I set out to catch him up.

Four hilly hours later and there's no sign of any more cyclists as I finally reach the small town of White River in my usual utterly wearied state. This was the furthest I'd ever ridden on a bike and boy did I know it, so much so I'm weaving down the road with tiredness.

The town is primarily known it seems as the home of Winnie the Pooh complete with the obligatory giant statue erected in his honour of course. Cycle touring legend has it that cyclists can camp for free under his benevolent gaze in the grounds of the Tourist Information centre.

You'd think that locating a 20 foot high statue of a yellow bear would be pretty easy. Wrong. Cycling round in circles I kept asking groups of people where the giant bear lived. They smirked and pointed towards a patch of open scrubby grassland next to a wooden hut (the closed up Tourist Information Centre it turned out).

For the life of me I couldn't see it but, with the light and my final drops of energy fading fast, I pitched camp on the lawn defying anyone to move me on.

Hanging my damp bikini out to dry I walked across the grass to a depressing burger joint at what appeared to be a truck stop. The only place open other than an even less appealing bar. After a lack-lustre refuel and struggling to keep my eyes open I decided to call it a night. Sprinting back across the field to my tent pursued by clouds of mosquitoes, I dived, Indiana Jones style, through the flysheet and curled up in bed. It had been a long day!

An hour later and I'm lying in my sleeping bag, listening to the groups of drunken locals stagger past me on their way home, feeling intensely vulnerable, alone and conspicuous. This wasn't helped either by realising my bikini was still hanging from a branch outside. Nothing says 'lone female' like a bra top in a tree. Wary, but too tired to move, I lay waiting for my usual fitful sleep to arrive. Despite everything I was also really proud of myself, for the day's crazy mileage, for toughing out the lone camping, hell, for just being there.

Tent mail:

From: Cyclinginaskirt **To:** Emma
Subject: Airport ride

Hey, thank you for the lovely emails. Just got Wi-Fi so thought I'd say hi.

Loved the photos of Bean that girl has attitude :-) All is well with me, I did a 'Heathrow day' today 84 miles - 135km (the distance from my house to the airport in case you were puzzled), at least 60 of which miles were into a bit of a headwind. However, it was still a stunning ride though. I stopped for a lake swim and to stuff myself with an obscene number of donuts. The highway goes through some truly stunning bits of country, mirror lakes, grassland, rock cliffs and beaches and, before yesterday, Lake Superior dominating the vista at every turn.

Bloody knackered now but I made it to the free campground at White River, home of Winnie the Pooh. I'd been told the campsite was behind a big statue of the bear himself.....at the end of such a long day the last thing I need is to be searching for giant fictitious animals.

Still can't see the damned thing but tent pitched on grass behind tourist office, Marathon tomorrow – the place not the distance - if legs still work in the morning.....

Take care, love you loads

From: Emma **To:** Cyclinginaskirt
Subject: Express –oh!

Hey you,

Loved reading your email - pictures look magical and bring back fond memories of west Canada, and the 'bear warnings'!

You sound a lot chirpier in your email - even for someone who has done 84 miles! We had a productive weekend, went out for yummy afternoon tea and a friend's 40th birthday party - Bean was very good, slept right through the noise of the DJ!

Had first go at expressing today - nothing less sexy than an electric breast pump! We were hoping to try her on it before we put her to bed, annoyingly however, she's actually fallen asleep ridiculously early and we're sat here in bed waiting for her to wake up!
I think we'll pop into town tomorrow for a bit - it's a hard life :)
Lots of love and squishy hugs xxxx

Day 15   White River to Marathon: 67 miles

I found Pooh Bear! Turns out he was directly behind my tent. The 20 foot high giant red and yellow concrete icon grinned smugly at me as I plodded sleepily over to the diner for breakfast. I must have passed it yesterday without noticing?!

On the road again and there are just two words for today. Fucking headwind.
Every inch is a battle against the invisible arm which descends out of the sky and holds my bike still.
Occasionally the wind will tease me and let me roll a few metres but then it's back. Imagine if you will, a cat, playing with a live mouse it's just caught. Letting it go, watching it, catching it again, toying with it. In my mind the wind has become that cat, tormenting me.

Places to stop, rest and eat are few and far between as I'm still on the edges of the Lake Superior park. So I do what I usually do and push on. It's raining too, great big squally gusts which accompany the wind, all but obscuring the road ahead.

I've the tentative offer of a Warm Showers place in Marathon for the night, but at the turn off I hesitate. The town is a further 3 miles down a long, long steep hill. Not so much a problem tonight providing my host is home but a bitch to climb back up in the morning with heavy panniers, especially for a 'tentative' offer. I weigh this against the

shakier knowledge of a possible wild camping spot around here behind a shop, maybe a mile or so along the road?
I procrastinate and eat some nuts.
My inner adventurer says I should push on, find the shop and wild camp. My outer knackered body says head downhill to the slightly greater chance of a comfy bed and hot food.
Body won.

NB: As it turns out, when I next re-joined that road, I never did spot the wild camping place.

The glorious downhill, free of headwind revived me a bit. Rolling through the deserted streets however, I remembered my other reason for hesitating at the top, I had no address to head for.
Finding a solitary diner still open I try emailing and have a coffee. No response, it's getting dark now. My cell phone which I can only use for internet access still stubbornly refuses to work in this country so I try the pay phone in the lobby but to no avail.
Seeing my desperation the waitress takes pity on me and lets me use the diner's phone to call my host who is thankfully still happy to take me in and lives just a few minutes away. Relieved, I head out through the gathering dusk to meet Jilly.

Jilly

Walking up the driveway I was assaulted at close range by a small ninja with a water pistol who drenched me thoroughly before running away laughing to hide in the bushes.

As it turned out I hadn't wandered into a bizarre Canadian Kung Fu ambush but the tail end of a 5 year old's birthday party.
From the outset Jilly is one of those truly lovely people you can't help but warm to. Here she was, not only single-handedly holding her son's 5th birthday party – ninja theme, all home-made costumes, games and

food - she was also playing Warm Showers host for the first time to two separate, unknown cycle tourists,!

The other inaugural guest was Arthur, a young French cyclist heading from east to west. After brief introductions and dodging ninja fire, Arthur and I were shown to a small caravan on the driveway way where we'd be staying that night. Balancing armfuls of panniers with plates of party food we swapped stories about headwind whilst we unpacked, both hanging out damp clothes to dry in the even damper air of then van. I'd like to say that it felt odd sharing a small caravan and sleeping space with a young guy I'd met minutes before. But it just didn't! One of the (many) things I'd discovered is that, when you're tired, hungry and soggy, inhibitions play no part if you've been offered food and shelter.

Heading over to the house I was keen to learn more about with Jilly. Chatting away as we both cleared up children's party debris she talked a little about herself. At 24 years old she had 2 lovely children, one a small baby and had just separated from her husband. But as she marvelled at my cycling adventures I felt in awe of her ability and courage to raise 2 small beings by herself so efficiently. Even more so on finding her daughter was just 3 months old, nearly identical to my new niece.

The more we talked, the more my admiration grew. Far from being overwhelmed by life Jilly had decided she wanted to meet more people and broaden her horizons. Marathon was such a small, isolated town and she wanted to know more about the world and find out about the people in it. And if she wasn't able to travel at the moment, then she would invite the world to come to her by signing up as a Warm Showers host. Quite understandably her friends were sceptical and slightly alarmed that she'd be inviting strangers to stay in her home, but, as I'd already learned, she was a determined lady. I hoped now I could make her first experience a happy one.

With the kids in bed and the party clutter tamed we sat and talked a little more, with Jilly playing the guitar and singing for a while, something, she casually mentioned, which she did on stage from time to time! Listening to the sweet, soft music I had a lump in my throat. Thinking about Jilly's courage and care for her little family reminded me strongly of my family back home. How I wished they could be here right now, to be a part of this.

Later, as I lay in my creaky caravan listening to Arthur sleeping, I marvelled again at how far the day had travelled, not just in miles but in a mountain range of emotions. How little I knew when I woke up in White River under the elusive Pooh Bear how the day would play out. Wind-fighting crushing lows and some sweet, nostalgic highs.

What next I wonder?

Day 16   Marathon: DAY OFF

Actually, a glorious day off was what next! Jilly had been more than happy for me to linger another night and as we sat with kids eating blueberry pancakes and watching the rain lash the windows I think Arthur was rather regretting his decision to cycle on.
Waving goodbye to him I felt both sorry and smug in equal measures but only for his drenching, not for my day off.
My body was rebelling again with a sore throat, achy joints and an equally sore bum. A rest day was exactly what was needed sitting in a warm house catching up on emails and writing my blog. Only venturing out to replenish pannier supplies and buy beer and food as a thank you for Jilly.
The rest worked wonders and after cooking the family dinner I curled up on the sofa to sleep very contented; the temperature having plummeted that night I was really glad to be both indoors and not on the highway in a tent. Poor Arthur!

Day 17   Marathon to Schreiber: 65 miles

The dreary cold morning reflected my feelings and it was with real sadness that I said farewell to Jilly and the kids as they stood waving on the front driveway. I liked Jilly a lot and her little family reminded me so much of my own back home, my sister and little niece.
It was becoming a pattern now it seemed, such close connections forged with people over only a day or 2 meant that leaving again felt like another parting from a friend and one whom, realistically, I would probably never see again.

The 3 mile long haul uphill and back up the highway helped to divert both mind and body. Despite dreading it the previous day, it actually rolled past under my wheels with less effort than expected. Back on the trans-Canada the wind was giving me a break for once, the bike however was not.

Grinding up yet another steep section of hill Claud's pedals suddenly stopped dead. It wasn't just the gradient making them stop either. Looking down I saw with dismay that the chain had fallen off the inside of the front cogs and gotten wedged solid between the pedal crank and the frame.
Even worse there was precious little stopping room on what was a fairly busy part of the highway, just a strip of dirty gravel a couple of foot wide with great trucks thundering past.

My heart plummeted, as I mentioned, I have little or no mechanical ability other than changing a puncture and even that can be debatable. Fishing out my meagre set of tools, bottom lip wobbling and stomach churning I set to work.

It was soon clear that trying to pull and prise the chain loose with my fingers was not going to work, especially as the bike threatened to topple into the road with every tug. Nothing for it but to unload all the panniers, fingers black with oil and grease everything else soon became covered.

Turning Claud upside down I cajoled and rattled the chain around but still it wouldn't budge. It was about then I lost the plot a little, part panic, part frustration, I was in the middle of no-where and, for the first time, with no kindly offers of help forthcoming I resorted to unashamed violence. Selecting the largest (only) spanner I had and a nearby sturdy rock I spent the next few minutes bashing and swearing at the errant chain which, all of a sudden, slipped liked butter into my hand.
Hallelujah!
Chain now reintroduced to cogs, I righted Claud and spent 10 minutes reloading the panniers, everything now a filthy oily-black. Gingerly setting off again up the hill, I prayed to the universal gods that the chain would stay put. I was also in the world's foulest mood.

Ironically, just a kilometre up the road around the next bend was a little restaurant with a handy rest area. If only I'd known!
Ordering their biggest burger and fries on the menu I cleaned myself up as best I could and consoled myself with the fact that I'd survived my first mechanical crisis, by myself.

The errant chain played on my mind though as I cycled on that day, especially on hitting a stretch of roadworks which meant leaving the nice tarmac surface and moving to unpaved, rutted gravel.
It constantly amazed me how a busy highway such as the Trans-Canada could be quickly reduced to a single file flow over a dirt track.
Now I'd ridden through construction works before but it turned out these were mere blips compared to my current position. Twelve kilometres of heavy road improvement, all road surface gone, exposing a muddy, gravelly soup which grabbed the wheels, or threw them skidding. I now rode grimly, using everything to focus as I cycled up slippery stony hills whilst huge logging trucks bore down, tailgating me and cars threw sharp stones against my body.

I was reaching that too-familiar near sobbing point, it had been a stressful day already and adrenalin had given way to tiredness yet again. All the calm reclaimed from my rest day had seeped away I was tired, lonely and afraid.

As I've mentioned, I'm not a religious person, but I do have an open mindedness that there are maybe forces in the universe greater than us unwashed masses. A guiding hand, a guardian cloud sprite or whatever floats your boat. What happened next though was one of those uncanny moments when the world seemed to step in, with exquisite timing, just when I needed it most.

Waiting at a red STOP/GO boards operated by luminous vested men with walkie- talkies and tans I was near breaking point, miserable, homesick, done in. I'd had enough, all I wanted was to go home.
It was then that I noticed the construction worker operating the 'STOP/GO' board seemed to be gesticulating at me, oh great I think, I'm about to get yelled at for something. Beckoning me to the front of the queue, he sets about pulling some paper from his pocket. Instead of a reprimand however, silently, he hands me a printed card, a cartoon of a great bird swallowing down a small frog.
I'm mystified but looking closely at the cartoon I suddenly notice that the canny frog has his little hands around the bird's throat, holding on for dear life and safe for now. A caption printed at the bottom simply read. "DON'T EVER GIVE UP!".

Whether you believe in coincidence, signs or none of the above, at that particular moment in time it gave me the most amazing boost at the exact point that I needed it. Maybe it was just that someone had cared, someone had reached out to me, had understood, but the effect was instant.

As the board swung to GO board we began to move off, now however the rest of the roadworks began to flatten out and mercifully, shortly after, Claud and I were reintroduced to wonder of multi-lane tarmacadam. Pedalling too seemed easier after the off-road slog. Lost in a sea of emotion, I was startled when a short while later another cycle tourist made a bee-line across the road to me.

John, in his 70's had grown up near my home town in England, though he now lived and toured in Canada, he also told me that Tom the British cyclist was approximately 2 days ahead of me (after my Marathon stopover), heading for Thunder Bay. As well as quite a lot of details about Tom's family history I also learned that the 2 French Canadian tourers were somewhere not far up ahead too. Loneliness banished, I waved goodbye to John and re-joined the road.

Feeling so much happier I decided to blow the budget a little and treat myself to a motel that night. As I pulled into Schreiber it felt like as good a place as any.
The Sunset Motel gave the impression of somewhere you may go to end your days, a transit lounge for the afterlife, an image not helped by the creaky 91 year old proprietor or the furnishings that even my grandmother would have considered dated.

That aside the room was spacious, clean and comfortable and in possession of a wonderful bath tub.
After soaking off the grease I felt much more human. A lightening quick recce of the town showed no obvious (or open) shops or diners although I did catch the briefest glimpse of what looked like another cycle tourist. Nah, must have imagined it. Heading back to the motel I wanted only to collapse on my indescribably comfortable bed, eat dinner (instant noodles) and drink the last of my wine whilst wrapped in clean sheets.
The Ritz or any other flashy hotel tonight could not have competed with that experience. Sleep was quick and merciful not long after.

Day 18   Schreiber to Nipigon: 62 miles

The sore throat that's been dogging me for the last week woke me up like a persistent alarm clock. If I were cleverer or more self-aware I might think my body is trying to tell me something, but stubbornness makes me push it to the back of my mind in the same way that I now ignore the insidious tiredness in my muscles and bones.

Taking advantage of the heavy old fashioned motel furniture I upend an arm chair to use the legs as an impromptu bike stand. I have no idea what I'm doing really but being keen not to repeat the chain fiasco of yesterday I try to unearth the advice that Jez from the Manatoulin bike shop gave me.

After confidently twiddling a few cables and turning some screws, the pedals now completely refuse to turn. It's also patently clear that I have no mechanical aptitude. Twenty more minutes of panic fiddling and I manage to undo the worst of the damage before deciding to accept both my bike repair limitations and the dodgy chain.

Straightening up the room ready to depart my tablet starts making curious noises which turn out to be a Skype call, from my mother. At this point I don't know which of us is more shocked. As a confirmed technophobe who is still baffled by the TV remote this is a huge leap for her and I'm touched that she's tried. We haven't always had the easiest of relationships so this small, but large, gesture means a lot me. I've noticed that absence really highlights the things that are important in your life. For me, it's not my house and my possessions I miss but friends and family and it's this contact with them via the electronic world that's keeping me going.

Call over and I set out with a lighter heart.

Not having managed to go shopping the previous day, breakfast had consisted of pannier dregs – slightly iffy tasting nuts and raisins - so I'd planned to stop off as soon as possible for food. The pretty, chocolate boxy town of Rossport seemed ideal, unfortunately it was also completely shut. No shops, no people, just imaginary tumbleweed blowing through the deserted streets.

After trying the locked door of the only café I could find I was about to go on my hungry way when the lovely owner saw me and took pity, opening up especially so I could buy a coffee and muffin which went a long way to restoring much needed energy.

By the time I leave Rossport the temperature had climbed again and so has the road. Hills dipped and, more often than not, soared. It was a work out for both my legs and Claud's gears but luckily the chain stayed put this time.

By afternoon a highway café lured me off the road with the promise of hearty plate of fish, chips and salad, just the job for a ravenous cyclist.

This meal when it came though could have passed for an offence under the trade descriptions act, my food fantasies vanished staring down at a piece of limp lettuce, 1 tomato slice, a handful of chips and a measly fish-finger sized goujon. I'd have walked out if I wasn't so hungry.

The culinary part of the day may not have been going well but it was easy to set aside when, going back to Claud, I stumbled across 2 more cycle tourers. A lovely retired couple form Montreal who were cycling home from Vancouver (sensibly riding from west to east). Whilst attempting a chat in our pidgin French/English, a third cycle tourer suddenly pulled alongside us. Bizarrely it was the apparition from Schreiber the previous evening and even more amazingly he was going the same way as me!

Matthew, cycle tourer number 3, was 'commuting' to work at a school in Winnipeg from his home in Toronto. Whilst most of his gear was being driven up by friends, he had a road bike, tent and panniers and a big smile. He was also the apparition who'd passed through Schreiber last night on route to a campsite further on!

We chatted for a little while before heading in our own directions, me to the road and Matthew to lunch, having been advised against the fish and chips! Riding lighter and faster than me there was a good chance I would be seeing him again before long. I would keep an eye on my mirror.

That afternoon the hills unbelievably got even tougher and whilst the glimpses of the lake I got were still stunning, my eyes seemed to spend a lot of time firmly on the tarmac beneath my front wheel.
I'd begun to notice that each hill climb plays out like a lot like a miniature relationship between cyclist and road. Bear with me on this.

Firstly there are the quick flings, hills that are crushingly steep but short. They're incredibly hard work, they make your muscles burn and your lungs scream, but they are at least over relatively quickly, leaving you breathless, a bit wobbly and reeling but cycling away pretty much unscathed.

Then there are the rollers, ones that, from a distance look like they are going to be trouble but actually turn out to be fun. When you reach them they're not as arduous as anticipated and you can coast up them with minimal effort knowing you won't be tied down for long. On these, a fair sized bump in the road can often disappear under my wheels without noticing as my mind follows an (inappropriately long) train of thought about bananas.

Finally, there are the hills that call for a serious commitment. You can optimistically skirt the slopes in the mid-cogs but very quickly you're trickling down through the gears....when you can't go any lower, you know you're in it for the long haul.
'Granny gear' is the lowest of my 21 gear options. It requires the least effort to turn the wheels but in turn provides the least forward motion. It's reminiscent of those cartoon characters who run off a cliff, feet pedalling madly in mid-air, going nowhere. That's me going uphill, Wile. E. Coyote on a bike.
But you do get there, slowly inching forward, counting off road

markers, bushes, clumps of grass, anything to aim for and mark forward progress. And when the wind bends that grass clump further away, the world feels like it's truly conspiring against you.

However when you stop fighting it, find a rhythm and you realise that, inch by inch the bike is moving forward, the effort is bearable, you also realise you will make it, albeit slowly, it will just take a while.

One of the hard-learned lessons of journeying anywhere is that you must deviate from those time schedules in your head and adapt to the environment, stop battling against it, trust that you'll get there, eventually.

Summiting these last climbs is the most exhilarating, bringing a real sense of achievement, made even sweeter by the expenditure of all that physical, mental and emotional energy, alongside, in some cases blood, sweat, oil and tears.

Going through all that you can't fail to leave a small piece of you indelibly bound up with the place where such an intense relationship has been formed and played out.

Matthew eventually caught me up later in the afternoon, his lighter bike indeed making better time than Claud and I. After a rest and a chat we made a vague plan to maybe meet up in Nipigon at the end of the day at the omnipotent Tim Hortons.

After waving goodbye to him the afternoon dragged on, the sun blazed relentlessly down with the heat haze making the tarmac ripple like water.

I also seemed to have developed the rather disconcerting habit of weaving across the road a little. I was dimly aware that my thinking seemed to get more sluggish in such intense heat and with it my bike handling abilities. I also no longer noticed the hunger from so many miles ridden on just a muffin and one fish finger and I had no desire to drink, which was fortunate as I'd run out of water an hour beforehand.

Nearing Nipigon I had the curious sensation of floating, as my vision began to constrict and the blood pounded in my head I pulled off the road and loitered on the narrow verge, drifting in and out of reality.

Karla

Faint and dizzy I somehow wobbled the last few hundred yards into Nipigon centre. A friendly dog walker was just directing me to a campsite (which I sincerely hoped wasn't far) when a car pulled up alongside. Assuming the diver, a kind-looking middle aged lady, wanted to speak to the pedestrian I concentrated on the dog-walker's directions.

But for the second time in as many days it seemed the Universe was stepping again. Karla had actually seen me wobbling by her house moments earlier and jumped in the car to come and find me. She had a daughter my age, she explained, and would hate to think of her alone and in need of help.
It also turned out that Karla owned a beautiful B&B in which she offered me hospitality as her personal guest.
Overwhelmed doesn't come close to describing how I felt as this lovely woman scooped me up and took me home. And what a home, a beautiful organic vegetable garden under shady green trees led to a peaceful, white weatherboard house.
Inside, a shower, a gallon of water to drink, both followed by some home-cooked food and I marvelled at how restored I felt compared to just a brief time ago.

That evening, whilst Karla went out to visit a friend I took her little dogs for a walk around the town; which now appeared much smaller and friendlier when not in a fatigued, dehydrated state.
Of course who should I run in to again but Matthew who was staying at the campsite there.

Back at the B&B Karla had returned and, settling in with cups of tea and blankets, we sat up talking into the night. What I discovered was a fascinating, cultured and well-travelled 72 year old woman with a passion for education and travel. Talking about everything from her pilgrimage on the Camino de Santiago to a burgeoning passion for China, it was one of those surprising jewels of a conversation where you're privileged to get to know so much in a short space of time and leave feeling like old friends. As the evening slipped away we also shared stories about family, love, adventures as well as hopes and plans for the future.

Karla, Tina, Guy, Sharon, Jilly, Wally, Chloe and others, so many people I'd met these last few weeks who'd let me into their lives with their warm welcomes and generosity. These people alone had more than offset every hill and hardship and already made the journey worthwhile.
Again, the motel this morning seemed like centuries ago. But my body is stepping up its protests, my asthma has been growing steadily more insistent and the utter fatigue experienced today was not helped by the lack of food and water.
Very strong note to self, more organisation needed and a few more rest days!

Day 19   Nipigon to Thunder Bay: 71 miles

Any day that starts with pancakes and strong coffee is set to be a good one. And it was. The six and a half hour ride to Thunder Bay fairly rolled past in a blur.

Saying a fond and heartfelt farewell to Karla, my rescuer, I had to try hard to resist the urge to tarry, but the addiction of the road was a strong as ever.
After Nipigon the pretty, sleepy towns faded out to give way to a wider, busier highway. There was the usual good deal of climbing thrown in although mercifully less so than the previous day.
I was aware too that, after today, I would also be saying goodbye to Lake Superior whose perimeter I'd been doggedly navigating since

Sault Saint Marie.

Riding round just a small portion of Superior is one of the best ways to drive home the knowledge that it is truly the largest (by surface area) freshwater body of landlocked water in the world. It's essentially a sea, but with a shoreline all the way around. Whilst appearing placid in the lazy summer heat, the calm waters can turn ferocious; its vast depths mean the lake has the power to affect weather systems and can produce storms which terrify experienced sailors and sink shipping.

Coming from the UK it's easy to become complacent about being surrounded by ocean. There is a trivia titbit I like which says that when in Britain you are never more than 70 miles from the sea. In Canada however, those in the interior can be thousands of miles away from the coast, for them to see the ocean is a pilgrimage in itself, not the short car ride away it is at home for me.

Meanwhile, I'm agog at this vast body of water which looks to me like an ersatz ocean. I can't put my finger on it but something feels different, not quite right. Maybe it's the missing ebb and flow of a large tide, maybe it's the lack of huge waves and rolling surf hitting the shore or perhaps it's the more subtle absence of that salt tang in the air. It confuses my ocean-knowing senses making me slightly uneasy. In balance however I have enjoyed some of my most beautiful campsites nestled in to quiet spots on its remote beaches and had some of my coldest morning baths in the lake's waters.

A further shock has been the discovery of the scale of the water contamination here. Growing up, Canada always seemed to me to be a country of pristine forests and crystalline rivers, one great big advert for the healthy outdoors. A huge misnomer it seems as in reality high levels of ground water pollution from oil extractions, from farming and from construction have left much of the surface water in rivers and streams undrinkable.

The great lakes too have not escaped unscathed. In Toronto, locals had looked at me askance for swimming in Lake Ontario which, like it's big sibling Lake Superior, experiences high levels of E-Coli amongst other pollutants, with strong advisories against drinking and/or bathing in some areas.

Nowhere does Canada show her beauty and her seedy underbelly more closely than these stunning bodies of water rendered hazardous no-go zones by human activity.

Back on the road and powered by those early breakfast pancakes and chocolate milk from a handy grocery store, I'm flying along, contemplating the scenery and getting to Thunder Bay, a small landmark on my road map and a hopeful opportunity for another rest day.

I'm incredibly weary but also weirdly energised, I'm on the lookout too for a memorial to a man I'd not heard of until a few days ago but whose story it seems has not just captured one hapless cyclist but a whole country. Terry Fox.

In 1980 Terry, an accomplished athlete, amputee and cancer sufferer began his 'Marathon of Hope' running a full marathon everyday across Canada. He wanted not only to raise awareness of this disease but to raise awareness of the power of sporting achievement despite it. To seize the opportunity to do something more, every day, despite all that life throws at you.

In the course of doing this he inspired a nation.

Because of him there is now an annual Terry Fox 'Marathon of Hope' festival giving people the opportunity to tackle a whole range of sporting activities, big and small.

Terry's declining health brought his epic run to a close after 3000 miles, just outside of Thunder Bay where there is a memorial marking his achievement. But his legacy continues to motivate an entire country, encouraging people to set goals and push boundaries.

For them, for Terry, for the ordinary and extra-ordinary folks, for the differently-abled, the runners, the walkers, the one step at a time-ers and, in a small way, for me, it's that motivation that means so much.

The joy, pain and exhilaration of identifying a challenge and then meeting that challenge head on, whatever your circumstances.
It's the opportunity to expand our idea of what is possible and the sense of achievement, pride and confidence that completing that challenge brings.
So here's to challenges, whatever they may be, and here's to hills. Bring them on!

Seventy one miles later, after passing the Terry Fox memorial on the outskirts of the city, I pedalled into Thunder Bay to the home of my next Warm Showers stay with host Dan.

Dan

From the attic of Dan's 2-storey wooden house I could look down over the long, beautiful garden which contained a lovingly tended vegetable bed, a huge workshop for various carpentry projects and an inviting hammock strung between two old fruit trees.
Dan himself was similar in age to me and the veteran of quite a few cycle tours. He'd also just started a whole new career as a fireman after leaving a long standing job as a park ranger for reasons which would become clear later.

Now though, it was time to focus on practical matters. It was becoming increasingly obvious over the last few days, not least after the chain incident, that Claud was in need of some overdue care and attention. So, after briefly settling in we piled him and ourselves into Dan's little car and headed to the nearest bike shop. Leaving Claud in the hands of the mechanic for the night, at Dan's suggestion we headed out to a local river and beauty spot for some swimming.
Floating around in fast flowing water as evening drew in, the long day being washed away in the current, life felt pretty good.
Back at Dan's we chatted over beer and dinner. He was good company and was very open about his life which encouraged me to be the same, covering everything from family and relationships to the difficulties of

mid-life career changes. At some point he also decided to share with me the reason for his own job-switch. One day whist on ranger duty he and a colleague had fallen victim to a horrific bear attack. Fortunately, miraculously, he'd managed to survive and also save the life of his colleague, but the experience was understandably traumatising. No wonder life had changed.

The rawness Dan experienced from telling his story combined with my feeling of being stripped bare by the endless miles of cycling meant that we had both shed tears by the end of the evening. We headed off to our rooms that night both slightly drunk, tired and emotional and more than drained from laying feelings open in front of a stranger. Despite the exhaustion though, sleep would not come.

Day 20   Thunder Bay: 0 Miles

I briefly considered pedalling off today but Dan had offered for me to stay an extra night and both Claud and I were in dire need of a break. I was exhausted.

Thunder Bay was also the largest town I'd seen in a while and I needed to make the most of my time here so, with Dan off helping friends for the day, I set about wading through my list of things to do.

- Laundry - ✓
- Collect Claud – ✓ although his gears still felt niggly after their service, I was too lazy to return to the shop by the time I noticed.
- Food shopping – ✓
- Find more asthma inhalers – having imprudently run out of my daily medication there followed a swift induction to the Canadian Healthcare system. Fortuitously I secured an appointment at a walk-in clinic, with the two hour wait giving me a chance to rest in air conditioned comfort and a sympathetic doctor being so helpful I was near to tears. Big ✓

The only other happening of note was my first puncture. On leaving the clinic I returned to find a flat front tyre. In the scheme of things it could have been a lot worse. At least the bike was mercifully pannier free as I upended him in a sheltered spot, wrestling the tyre off the wheel to affect my first, relatively smooth, tube change.

With Claud restored to the road I headed back to Dan's to take full, gratuitous advantage of the garden hammock.

South Baymouth to Thunder Bay in pictures

Bear hunting

Traffic

Refuelling

On the lookout

The Wawa Goose

Lake views

Manatoulin Island

Thank you!

South Baymouth to Thunder Bay in pictures

Local barns

Trans-Canada

Sharing the road

Claud's new front luggage

Thunder Bay to Regina

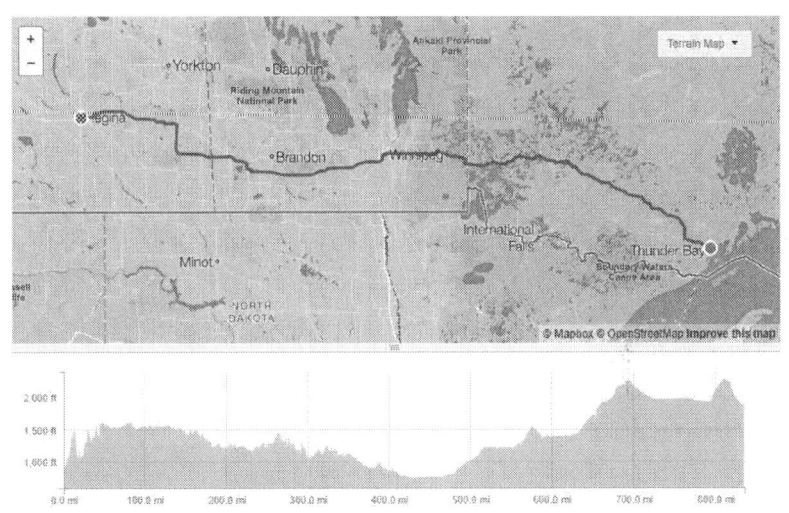

Courtesy of Strava mapping.

Day 21   Thunder Bay to Savanne River: 75 miles

One of the best night's sleep ever, perhaps unsurprisingly, I was dead to the world until 9am. Dan's brilliantly prepared breakfast of homemade porridge full of fruit, nuts and maple syrup also combined to produce a lazy, indulgent start.

In a very gentlemanly manner Dan also biked with me to the edge of town, describing various landmarks including the Sleeping Giant, a formation of mesas and sills which resembles a giant lying on his back, a prominent local feature it seems.

Another day and another goodbye but, by 11am, Claud and I are heading westward once more and meeting up with our old friend the headwind.
Ugh, feeling sluggish and less than motivated, we cruise past huge advertising hoardings for the country's largest sex shop. I'm tempted to take a detour but laziness and the thought of the extra mileage puts me off the idea.

Turning a corner Highway 17 heads north and the wind finally lessens and we're on our way again. My motivation and oomph is helped along somewhat by a delicious lunch of beef stew and chocolate milk and randomly an email from Matthew, the cyclist I'd met in Nipigon, saying that he too was leaving Thunder Bay today and giving details of his proposed camping spot. A plan and company, both of which had been lacking until now, drove me forwards.
With renewed purpose I headed back into the wind.

After hearing dire warnings from other cyclists about using the Highway 17 instead of the more usual option of the 11 road to Fort Frances I passed through with no problem, hitting my pedal stroke with ease. Apart from the sex-shop signs the road remained busy but anonymous. No more of the lovely lake views from around Superior but thankfully slightly fewer hills. It was also evidence I was heading towards the much flatter prairies, I was making progress at least. Well, sometimes I was convinced of that!

In the late afternoon I was thrilled to cross over my first ever time zone on foot (or wheel).
Living on a small island and point zero for the GMT measurement, to move to another time zone means a plane or a boat ride to cross this mysterious, invisible line occurring somewhere out in the murky depths of the English channel. But now I have finally gotten to travel through time myself, going from Eastern Standard to Central time. Stupidly excited I circled the marker board by bike, childishly relishing the ability to pop backwards and forwards in time at will, gaining and losing an hour at each pedal stroke.

Feeling 'high' on Central Time, I rolled along the final few miles of road, easily spotting Matthew's campsite, a beautiful shady patch of green by a small cluster of cabins, nestled in the bend of a river.
It was a really wonderful experience to see a friendly face, someone to chat to and compare the journey with, to moan about the wind and tired legs and have a laugh and joke. Even better I persuaded Matthew to join me for a swim in the river.
With the river meandering right past the tent door I was amazed at why anyone wouldn't just jump straight in! Matthew was hesitant at first but, seeing me splashing around he couldn't resist for long before plunging in. What better way to end a long, hard day than soaking tired muscles, watching the sun dip behind the treeline.

The incessant and vicious mosquitoes put paid to lingering outside over dinner, so early bed and through-canvas chatting commenced before curling up in the warm softness of my sleeping bag, glad to be back in the tent, glad to be right here, right now.

Day 22:   Savanne River to Ignace: 85 miles

Breakfast is fast becoming the feature meal of the day. Deciding to forgo the usual pannier fodder I risked the (very often) shaky intelligence that a 'great breakfast place' existed just up the road. Happily for once the information was spot on although I could dispute the 'just up the road' part. Ten inaugural morning miles on an empty stomach and my body was complaining by the time I pulled Claud into the diner's parking lot.

Two English muffins (or muffins where I come from) topped with eggs and sausage followed swiftly by blueberry pie and ice cream made a pretty good start to the day however, as did chatting with three lady motorists, all bizarrely called Shirley.
As the Shirley's gave advice on what (and what not) was a must-see on route I demolished my mammoth meal. Matthew finally showed up just as I was licking the last blobs of ice cream from the bowl. We'd already decided, because of our different cycling speeds, to go at our own pace rather than risk the frustrations of cycling together and, being far more organised than me, Matthew had pre-booked his campsites for the whole trip. However he had invited me to join him there, daily plans/mileage permitting.
Challenge accepted and something to aim for, I left Matthew and the diner and headed off. The first 50 miles seemed to fly by and with little wind, the countryside rolled under my wheels.

The Trans-Canada Highway:
Since passing through the town of Spanish, just after I left Manatoulin Island, the Trans-Canada Highway remains with me, or I with it. It's comforting and has begun to feel like I am journeying with a friend.

This massive highway, completed in 1971, is one if the longest in the world, going through all 10 Canadian provinces to connect the Atlantic and Pacific oceans. During the journey so far it has ranged from a roaring, fast flowing multi-lane torrent, to a single lane trickle, unmade in parts due to construction. It carries along in its flow all manner of traffic from cycle tourists to gargantuan multi-sectioned trucks which pass inches from you in a never ending thundering wall of steel. Alongside these are the huge RVs towing cars, cars towing trailers, families, travellers, Harley Davidson's and, as mentioned, the odd, wobbly cyclist (I've counted around 42 bike-tourers to date).

It's a fascinating road, not least because of the pace at which I travel. The visual aspect isn't done justice by my photographs but one of the many reasons that I love cycling is that it's a form of travel that excites all the senses.

The smell of pine wood from the forests and wafted from the back of the massive logging trucks thundering past or the indescribable stench of a flattened skunk that can be stifling from a good half a mile in either direction. All underscored by the ever present smell of hot asphalt.

The silky feel on your body of lake water, wading out in to warm sandy bays and the welcome chance of a cooling lunchtime swim washing off some of the dust, bike grease and insect life that is drawn to the skin like a magnet.

The noises of the road also form a strange soundtrack to trains of thought. Insects and the numberless bird calls, as well as the ever present wind, roaring or whispering in the grasses and in quiet moments the sound of water lapping; the growl and ground-shaking of the monstrous trucks, the friendly (I think) hooting of cars and the soporific swish of bike tyres meeting road.

There's much time too to watch the stunning scenery slip past but, equally fascinating to me, is the morass of debris discarded on the side of the road; a deciduous layer of the lost and abandoned remnants of a thousand daily journeys.

Having had much time over the weeks to ponder this I've compiled a list of my top 3 things to see at the side of the road. Presented in reverse order these are:

Three: Wildlife, especially insects. In parts there is literally a carpet of crickets covering the road and making a rather sickly crunch underwheel. There's also a plethora of other bugs often hitching a free bike ride and appearing in my line of sight, on handlebars or bare legs when least expected causing much shouting and furious waving of hands.
The amount of road kill too is both prolific and morbidly fascinating. Numerous deceased and flattened birds and mammals reduced to surrealist 2-D versions of their former selves. Oh look, flat-pack skunk.

Two: Abandoned shoes, so many of them and always the left ones. Some are worn-out specimens probably best forgotten but some are new and expensive looking, sitting forlornly waiting for the unlikely return of their mates. How can someone lose one shoe? Surely it would be noticeable.

One: By far and away the winner though are the copious number of plastic drinks bottles all filled with a strange amber liquid…..No, not apple juice as I first naively thought, but the mobile toileting solution of the male, vehicle driving population (sorry chaps, but I have yet to meet a woman who can aim accurately into a bottleneck).

One of my many roadside games has become the fleeting analysis of the colour of these yellow offerings, linking it to the hydration state of the owner. Ooh, I think, that one was a little dehydrated, or, gosh, that really looks problematic.
My favourite to date is a mineral water bottle, refilled by a driver, whose label proudly proclaimed "A Canadian product, naturally filtered and bottled at source". Still technically as advertised I guess!

Back on the road, Matthew passed me at some stage and then I him after a lunch stop. This leapfrog pattern repeating a few more times until he finally took the lead later in the day. As usual the wind began its torment in the early afternoon, the joyful morning riding was gone and the head down grinding returned.

The scenery remained a mix of small towns and long hilly stretches where road signs teasingly advertised restaurants and motels as only a 20 minute drive away. My rough equation estimated that 1 driving minute = 1 cycling mile, a hard slog right now.

The dry wind also meant I was rattling through my water very quickly. Looking back, the 2 x 0.75 litre bottles didn't hold anywhere near enough for my needs. Not too much of an issue when shops and houses were plentiful but, in their absence and with dire warnings about the ground water pollution, I hit a problem. Seventy miles in and for the first time on the trip I had run out of liquid with nowhere to refill.

I had no choice but to cycle on into the parched, brutal headwind. By the time I reached Ignace my tongue felt like wood in my mouth and I would have seriously sold my granny for a glass of water. Finally reaching the outskirts of town I found a precious lone vending machine outside a hardware store.

Raiding it for as much fizzy cola as I could buy I sat on the shoulder of the busy highway, drinking the stuff of life whilst huge trucks thundered by.

The campsite was a welcome relief after those last miles, as was Matthew who'd been there relaxing for far longer than was decent. How great it was to again compare days on the road, to laugh at the peculiarities and peccadilloes. Even better was a swim in the campsite lake and a disgustingly large submarine sandwich for dinner.

Lying out on the wooden lake dock that night and chatting to Matthew I again felt a deep sense of calm and contentment. I liked the company and as a companion he was easy on the eye too, although of a far too religious persuasion for either of us to be anything other than buddies.

Not cycling together in the day was perfect, but I did like meeting someone at the end of the route and sharing the experience, especially after such a hard day. Sadly however he'd soon be reaching his end destination of Winnipeg which was just a few days ahead. No matter, I was a hardened female adventurer going it alone, wasn't I?

Day 23   Ignace to Vermillion Bay: 103.5 miles

It's not the first time I've broken my personal distance record on this trip but again today saw my longest ever cycle ride and my first century! I am very proud. I am also very knackered. Now there's something new!

It certainly hadn't been my plan on getting up this morning. Saying goodbye to Matthew after our Subway breakfast, I wished him well, knowing he was planning a long haul ride that day whilst I fully had no intention of doing such a stupid distance myself. I was sad that our little joint portion of the trip was coming to an end, the evening companionship and rugged good looks of my newly acquired cycle buddy were definitely appealing. But, such is the way of road life, people drift in and away. You enjoy the coming together, of the moment, and then you continue on your separate journeys.

The day rolled out well under Claud's wheels, aided immeasurably by a kinder wind and a cooling swim at lunchtime. Chocolate milk and a sandwich helped me power through and after 70 miles I pulled in to sample the delights of a Tim Hortons in Dryden and have a think.
I was feeling good, could I go on?
Of course, after 70 miles and after a run of tough days, it would have been an excellent and very sensible decision to stop right there.
Hmm, but knowing Matthew was aiming for Vermillion Bay was a bit like a red rag to a very competitive bull. It was 30 more miles. Do-able. And, as a fall back, my map showed a truck stop just 20 miles up the

road in which I could stop and pitch my tent if needed. It was a plan.
Twenty miles, 21, 22 came and went but no truck stop, I was tiring by now, the heat fast draining my strength but my cycling century was near, as was Vermillion Bay. I was determined.

A mile or so later and I was surprised when a couple in a passing car pulled over at the side of the road and flagged me down. Even more bizarre was when they greeted me by name?! It disturbed me greatly in fact until it transpired that these were friends of Matthew, driving to meet him. Apparently Matthew had described me in detail and said to look out for me. It seems I was easy to spot in my skirt.

Wonderfully these kind souls gave me a bottle of ice cold water, fine words of encouragement and told me I had 11 miles to go.

More than I'd thought but, head down against the wind I ploughed on.

Pedalling into Vermillion bay at just over 100 miles I was ecstatic but exhausted! I'd done it! My only slight problem was there was no campsite. I had passed one a mile or so before town but surely that wasn't it? By this time most of the few shops were shutting down for the evening and I started to get a little concerned. I'd nothing left in the tank now but camping options seemed thin on the ground. A lovely lady at the souvenir shop informed me that the nearest provincial park camping was 6 miles or so up the road.

In slight desperation I explained I was meeting friends who must be somewhere nearer and she very kindly let me use her phone. As it transpired Matthew's group were in the provincial park 10km away, but by this time I had nothing left in me. I'd really looked forward to celebrating the day's achievements with my new friends, but I also knew it was time to stop. Defeated, with euphoria and adrenalin draining away I turned Claud round and pedalled a weary mile back to the previous campsite. $30 for a piece of soggy, mosquito plagued ground, no Wi-Fi and showers you had to pay for! I was too tired to argue.

Pitching the tent, my spirits were restored somewhat on discovering a can of beer in my rucksack. A clean-up dip in the lake and a stunning sunset later I reflected on the day, proud that I'd made the decision to stop and very proud to have cycled that far. I think at last I might feel like I've earned my cycle touring stripes. No longer a wet-behind-the-ears-weekend-wonder, I was a bona fide cycle tourist, albeit a knackered one being eaten alive by mosquitoes.

Day 24   Vermillion Bay to Kenora: 70 miles

Looking back through my diary, I've often written 'tough day' or 'hardest yet'. Today was ostensibly no different although it does win the top prize so far.

By late morning temperatures had reached over 32 degrees Celsius (37 with humidity), super-heating the head wind to furnace levels. My asthma which had been increasing in frequency also jumped up a gear. At one point, cycling up another, never-ending hill, headwind blasting me, legs screaming and lungs gulping and sucking for air like a drowning thing it all just got too much. I began to sob.
Looking back I don't know why I didn't stop and take a break at this point, I think the sun had made me a little delusional, so I just pedalled on, the world misted by tears, snot, sobs and generally feeling very sorry for myself.

In the middle of this self-induced misery-fest I thought I'd truly begun to hallucinate when, on the road ahead I saw a touring bike appear on the horizon, and then another…!
I seriously thought I was seeing things but, needing to validate my sanity, I kicked up a gear and raced to catch these ghosts up.
I fully expected the mirage to disappear once I got closer but to my surprise instead it formed in to 2 solid shapes. The French cyclists from Montreal I'd heard tell of a few days back.

The boys were really friendly, laid back and in no hurry, a good thing as they were limping along with some broken spokes, but partying in style as they went. It also turned out they'd run into Matthew and company the night before at the same campsite. Small world!

Leaving them to their leisurely pace (and secretly galvanized by catching them and overtaking) I pushed on towards Kenora and my overnight stop with another Couch Surfing host - Jill.

Jill

Meltdown number 2 of the day nearly occurred after collapsing gratefully into Tim Hortons, where we'd arranged to meet, only to find that Kenora boasted 2 such establishments and the one that I wanted was, guess what, on the other side of town.
Pretty much crawling those final few miles I eventually, gratefully made it to Jill's lovely home.

Jill explained that she'd been a Couch Surfing host – and guest - for a number of years, quite often paying return visits to those who'd stayed with her. She'd also used it when travelling vast tracts of the country to visit relatives. Unlike most of the teenagers and twenty somethings who seemed to make up the majority of Couchsurfers, it was refreshing to find someone closer to my own age who was a real advocate of this way of travel.
Jill was also fantastically knowledgeable about her home town and its water systems in particular. A keen kayaker she talked with passion and enthusiasm about the area and some of her expeditions. I loved finding out so much about the lakes and towns I was passing and Jill was happy to oblige. My personal guided tour continued into town that evening, past the flying boats and the newly installed, first ever roundabout (traffic island). Apparently this was so left-field and confusing for residents that a civic film had been produced instructing drivers how to navigate it after a spike in the number of traffic incidents caused by its installation. I wondered wryly how Kenora residents would fare in the UK which is entirely filled with these little circles of doom.

A very welcome pub meal followed with a few local beers. Just as we were preparing to leave we were treated to a burst of some particularly drunken singing and hollering, which, it turned out, came from the French-Canadian cyclists I'd met earlier. Apparently they'd limped in to town on their broken bikes and propped them outside the first pub they'd found before settling in for a long session at the bar.

Well on their way now to complete oblivion they were happily propped up at a table, looking for all the world like they intended to stay the night there.

Maybe not such a bad idea. As Jill and I stepped outside we were ambushed by the worst hail storm I've ever encountered.

Ice pellets the size of golf balls bombarded us as we sprinted for the car. Inside we could hear them ricocheting off the windscreen as the wipers, going full tilt, failed to make an impression on the avalanche of water washing across our path.

The drive back was hair-raising in the extreme with both of our noses pressed against the windscreen playing spot the road!

It was about now that I also questioned the wisdom of having left both my tent and sleeping bag hanging outside to air in what was, until recently, a balmy summer's evening.

Arriving back at the house I sprinted through the rain to gather up my stuff. Not an easy task with half of it blown into tress, all of it as wet as it could possibly get.

Jill's poor house looked like a laundrette/refugee camp an hour later as all my worldly possessions were draped across surfaces to dry.

Later that evening, curled up in a soft bed, listening to the storm outside I was immensely relieved I wasn't camping that night. I've no idea if my poor little tent would have survived the onslaught of ice balls but I was glad I didn't have to find out the hard way.

Day 25   Kenora to Prawda: 66 miles

The first few hours of the day were spent tumble drying my sleeping bag and helping Jill to collect up all her patio furniture and garden pots, artfully redistributed in the hedges following last night's storm.
I enjoyed the slower start as well as a long breakfast, chatting and putting the world to rights. Jill talked about life, love and kayaking, me about aging, adventure and my increasingly weird east-west tan lines, branded in the left side of my skin by the sun and wind.

Another hard day on the road awaited but nowhere near yesterday's all-time low. My companion, the headwind, was ever present but now being so near the Provincial border spurs me on.

To reach Vancouver I need to cross 5 out of the 10 Canadian provinces, currently, after 25 days and 1345 miles I'm still in Ontario, my first one. It's never-ending.
Back at home I would have cycled the full length of mainland Britain by now. But here, I was seriously beginning to feel stuck in some weird geographical twilight zone, one in which every road only heads uphill and where the provincial boundary between Ontario and Manitoba was just the stuff of fiction. Like Narnia, only believed in by a few delusional souls and gullible cycle tourists.

But today, 32 miles in to the morning I finally found my way through the wardrobe, entering the second out of five provinces, Manitoba. A celebratory stop at the near deserted Visitor Centre and a dubious selfie outside the Manitoba sign and I'm cycling away, re-invigorated, re-enthused, flying.

This invigoration lasts approximately another 2 miles until the headwind and a distinct lack of food combines to kick in big time and, in cycling terms, I bonk.
Bonking is the bike equivalent of your car running out of fuel producing a pretty much total shut down. Thankfully the universe was

on my side again in the shape of a mobile chip van in the next lay-by, rarely have small bits of fried potato tasted so good.

They did the job, just, but my body had obviously noticed the lack of care and attention and mulishly refused to do more than grunt along. At least the road was flattening out, significantly.
The famous Canadian shield; the great swathe of Pre-Cambrian igneous rock which covers half of Canada; was visibly diminishing, softening from the jagged rocky hills around the great lakes into a flatter, more rolling landscape, eventually giving way to the vast acres of the promised prairie land to come.
I looked forward with glee to these prairies which everyone assured me were positively pancake flat. For now Manitoba, being just over 300 miles across, at least promises a welcome, short ride through.

As the afternoon heat haze shimmers on I begin my usual scout for camping spots. I find a couple of possibilities down marshy forest tracks but my usual dilemma surfaces. Ideally I would like to stop mid to late afternoon when I'm tired. When wild camping however, so one isn't spotted, the optimum time to pitch your tent is near sunset, currently many, many hours from now.
If I do stop on this lonely stretch of highway it means a long period of time either sitting in the bush or risking putting up my tent – the brightest of blues – and being spotted.
The tent, being so tiny, also wasn't the comfiest place to hang out for long periods unless sleeping and the vampire mosquito inhabitants of Manitoba were currently making it less than pleasant to sit outdoors.
I adopted my usual solution, if undecided, just keep cycling.

Chip van guy had told me of a campsite up ahead near Prawda and it at least provided a vague solution in my mind. Unfortunately for now, Prawda was appearing to be as elusive as Manitoba had been.
Still cycling, the afternoon heat intensifying, I began to develop one of my strange cravings. This had happened a few times before and I found that once an idea entered my head, usually food or drink related,

it just wouldn't leave. In fact it was as if the whole notion expanded like a big soap bubble to fill my entire head.
Today's craving was for ice cold, bubbly beer.

I had no hope. One of the many things I had discovered about Canada was their strict licensing laws. In Ontario for example alcohol was only to be sold at government approved outlets, the expensive LCBO (Liquor Control Board) shops, with strictly regulated hours.
Coming from an island that liberally purveyed alcohol at pretty much any shop at any hour, I found this approach odd at best, annoying at worst. The funny thing is I drink very little usually. I think it was more the idea of being 'restricted' that made me rebel.

With no campground on the horizon, I'm eyeing the farm gateways again, obsessing about beer and entirely grumpy with life. As a gas station comes into view I'm determined to be sensible for once, I'll stop and ask for directions, although fully expecting the campsite to be either miles away or non-existent.

What followed next was another of those odd moments when you feel that the universe has read your thoughts out loud and catered to them perfectly.

The gas station served beer!!! As I'm thanking the universal gods and ordering a cold bottle the cheery proprietor also informs me the campground is just around the next bend in the road, a mere 400 yards or so.
A fellow customer who's also there, paying for fuel, then saunters over. He's seen the bike and wants to talk about my trip. For once, feeling high on good fortune, I'm more than happy to oblige, even more so when he pays for my beer and orders a pack for himself, so we take them outside and sit in the sunshine.
Bob, my beer companion, it turns out, has just sold up his house and packed the entire contents in to his car, including his bike, to go roaming around the country for a while. As fellow knights of the road

we toasted our adventures with another cold bottle.
Half an hour later as I get back on Claud I'm decidedly light-headed as I wobble away, 2 more bottles chinking in my panniers, donated by Bob.

Even better, the campsite was indeed around the corner, quiet, beautifully kept and amazingly sporting a tiny crazy golf course. I spent my final hour of the day stupidly grinning and whacking little golf balls around the course with a fellow camper, sharing my beery treasure and thanking the universe for such a beautiful, well-timed intercession.
Winnipeg tomorrow and some time off!

Day 26   Prawda to Winnipeg: 75 miles

The world is getting stranger still. I awoke to an email from Tom, the British cyclist I've been vaguely chasing down for the last few weeks. Apparently he'd run into Matthew who'd given him my contact details. How very odd. Turns out he'll reach Winnipeg today too, a few hours earlier and is likely to be in the same hostel (there being few, if any options).

I send out a quick response and hit the road. I'm really looking forward to a couple of days off in Winnipeg, the first city since Thunder Bay and a chance to stock up on food and equipment and attend to Claud's ever growing needs. I really want a rest too.

The flat tarmac ahead shimmers in a fierce heat haze rolling away to melt into the horizon. God, I couldn't believe I was already missing the trees and rocky hills of Ontario.
Stopping by a busy stretch of highway for lunch I resolutely turn my back on the traffic to stare out at an endless wavy green field and was overcome by the most bizarre sensation.

Do you ever get those moments in life where you just stand outside of yourself and think wow?! This was one of those times. Sat at the side of the highway with my bike, munching a sandwich, deep in the heart of Canada, I took stock. Just a few short months ago I'd been sat at my desk, a busy social worker in an even busier office, worried about targets, frustrated at a computer system which was often broken and at a social care system which seemed not far behind.

Now, here I am, in the middle of nowhere on a bike. The desk and computer seem in another universe, my worries now being mainly of the practical, body nourishing kind. I'm a whole adventure away from my job a few months ago. However tough this journey, would I opt to go back now if I had the choice?

Not for anything.

Time to get pedalling.

My usual pattern ensued whereby I'd under estimated the distance for today, forgetting that the mileage on road signs usually only indicates the city limits, not the extra tarmac you need to cover in order to actually reach your destination.

Soon the anticipated 60ish miles turned into 75 and the usual exhaustion brought me to the door of the hostel where I raised only a weary half eyebrow at the fact it seemed to be a disused hotel with bunk beds hastily erected in a few Spartan rooms.

Further eyebrow-raising at the $40 per night charge for a bunk bed in a hostel, but fatigue, as ever, won the day.

Tethering Claud in the tiny internal garden I took note of a sturdy framed racing bike with panniers, my fellow road traveller perhaps? But the need for a shower and oblivion drew me irresistibly to my new room.

Hours later I was woken by an insistent knocking at the door. Stuffing a pillow over my head I let one of my new room-mates deal with it, after all I didn't know anyone here…..

Enter Tom.

The mystery British cyclist whose wheels I'd been trailing for weeks.

He was nothing like I'd imagined.
At a little under 6ft with light brown hair and blue eyes, a cyclist's figure combined with a relaxed, cheeky 24 year old's confidence. Apparently we were going for a beer.

It was great to sit and chat about our experiences, many of them shared in terms of places, horrible hills, headwinds, temporary campsites, wonderful people encountered.
Tom actually started a day later than me from Toronto and had generally been doing shorter mileage. However he'd had fewer days off. After nearly catching him near Marathon the lead opened up again when I'd spent that extra day with Jilly.
One beer turned into several, followed by a very decent curry courtesy of the family running the near empty hostel-hotel.

Finally falling into, or trying not to fall out of, my bunk that night it felt really good knowing that I'd found someone a) as stupid as me... what wind direction? and b) someone to share experiences with who understood. The fact that he was easy on the eye didn't hurt either.

I was going to like Winnipeg.

Day 27 – 28   Winnipeg: 0 miles!

Winnipeg Shopping List:

- Fix bike gears – in serious need of tlc ✓
- Clean chain-set ✓ not needed thanks to new cogs. Result!
- Sort out tax return ✓ Hard enough to do at home let alone from the middle of another country. Thank goodness for the power of proxy
- Get a massage for my tired legs ✗
- Buy food + drink ✓ ✓ ✓ Mostly chocolate, biscuits and wine
- Buy bottom-soothing cream ✗ oops
- Contact potential Warm Showers hosts ✓
- Look at map ✗
- Buy small provincial flag stickers to mark progress ✓
- Write blog ✓
- Email the world ✓

Taking Claud to the cycle shop for the aforementioned tlc the mechanic heaved him into the bike stand and, after a considerable amount of silent pedal spinning and prodding, began to suck a lot of air in through his front teeth. Never a good sign. After explaining the various issues he diagnosed the need for the minimum of a new set of rear cogs and a chain. I baulked at the idea of replacing the front cranks as well, even though it's the recommended procedure, try and failing to push aside the dawning realisation that my already second hand bike had just covered an additional 1500 miles.

The sporadically working front gear shifter was at least an easier fix. The mechanic's first suggestion, empathising with my limited budget, was to just for me to lean down at a precarious angle when pedalling and yank the wire gear cable directly on the frame. A solution certainly, but not an attractive one when going full speed downhill. Fortunately, a flash of inspiration ensued (him, not me). Undoing the offending part he discovered the cable end had merely dislodged from its holder inside the shifter. A merciful discovery about which I don't know who was more relieved/pleased.

The final work was to fit a set of new, ergonomic handle bar grips. By now, both hands from mid-to little finger were completely numb from the road vibration and limited positioning, a worrying symptom I didn't want to continue with me to Vancouver. As a veteran of various tours the mechanic swore by these. Only time would tell, but I left Claud in his capable hands until the next day. Now, freed from bike responsibility, I did what any girl would do in a new city. I went shopping.

The Forks Market at Two-Rivers Meet turned out to be produce heaven. I spent a happy few hours there sampling everything from falafel to wine, lots of local produce and being photographed with a (stuffed) bear.

Writing postcards to family, sat in the sunshine listening to a local choir perform jazz and blues numbers, I began to relax. Most happily I also managed to buy some small provincial flag stickers to commemorate the 5 Canadian provinces through which I will be riding. They will be ceremoniously placed on Claud's front mud guard as and when I pass into each new area.

From: Emma **To:** Cyclinginaskirt
Subject: Dawn Chorus

So, it's 5:30 here and Bean's wide awake so we thought we'd send a short email!

Mum and I went to the cinema on Monday – to a parent and baby showing for the under 2's, where once a week they show one of the latest films, but the volume is not so loud and the lights are turned up - brill idea and meant that we got to see the new Johnny Depp movie (getting Bean hooked early!). Only one minor poo explosion.

We've got a house warming/baby warming next weekend, quite a few people coming so I'm a bit nervous. Hope all good your end - mum and dad say you're now in Winnipeg!
Lots of love and baby gurgles – she's starting to chat now.
xxx

From: Cyclinginaskirt **To:** Emma
Subject: Dawn Chorus

Got to Winnipeg yesterday. Haven't found much Wi-Fi until now but will try and catch you on Skype if you let me know when's good? Sounds like 5.30am is the best time :-)
Hope you have a lovely time baby/house warming, thinking of you.
Love ya x

From: Emma **To:** Cyclinginaskirt
Subject: Dawn Chorus

House/baby warming went very well but oh-my-gosh a lot of people turned up! Felt like my wedding day again when you're just trying to say hello to everyone! Also quite funny when M decided to take everyone on a tour of the house just as I was upstairs feeding Bean with my boobs out!

Well, glad that you're getting into the swing of Winnepig! Enjoy the break :)
Love and big hugs Xx

From: Cyclinginaskirt **To:** Emma
Subject: Dawn Chorus
Love that M is showing you off! Photo attached of current (and very much platonic) companion!
Glad your day went well xxx

From: Emma **To:** Cyclinginaskirt
Subject: Dawn Chorus
Seriously - I need to get into cycling, he's fine :) or is that just a really flattering photo?! Xxx

From: Cyclinginaskirt **To:** Emma
Subject: Dawn Chorus
Hard to tell, it's the only pic I have. S'pose he's cute in a young puppy kind of way. He made sure to tell me he likes older women! Oh dear :-)

From: Emma **To:** Cyclinginaskirt
Subject: Dawn Chorus
Sounds like the ideal opportunity for a cycling fling! I would say you go all 'Mrs Robinson' on his arse and enjoy :) Xxx

From: Cyclinginaskirt **To:** Emma
Subject: Dawn Chorus
I have a nightclub stamp and a hangover this morning. Went drinking with the (24 year old) British cycle guy I met up with called Tom. He was hitting on me big time. Eek, it seems I've reached that age where I've become a cougar.
And before you ask, no, I didn't go there!

Last night I'd somewhat sceptically, agreed to go clubbing with Tom – not my thing at all but hey, nor is cycling across Canada. We set out to walk the couple of miles Google maps assured us it was to the club, but somewhere along the way took a wrong turn. Wide, well-lit pavements and the bustle of people somehow quickly deteriorated into smashed street-lights, broken pavements and boarded up, derelict houses. More worryingly, the only people visible were hooded, slouching shapes, merging in and out of the shadows.

I finally stopped a dog walker to ask for directions in my suddenly frightfully British accent. Incidentally, why does that happen abroad? Every time I open my mouth I seem to sound all BBC English and enunciated vowels.

With no preamble the guy told us he'd give us the best advice we'd be likely to get on our trip…. And that it seemed was to:

"get the hell out of here before we had a very bad tourist experience".

Apparently we'd wandered into what the locals affectionately called the 'murder district'. So, get the hell out we did, thanking the guy and flagging down the next taxi we could find.

The nightclub we'd been looking for was called 'The Cavern' a dimly lit, crowded cellar, full that particular night of goth-style music, wall to wall people and over-priced drink. But the atmosphere was happily charged and so was I, helped along by my inaugural and probably last Jaeger-bombs, the current drink of choice for most twenty something lads across Britain. Procured by a gleeful Tom, it tasted overwhelmingly like cough medicine.

Drinking, dancing, laughing, the night was cathartic, after so long on the bike it was great to do something different and spontaneous. I was happily drunk and feeling very benevolent about the world as a whole.

That feeling of bonhomie lasted as we arrived back at the hostel sometime after 2am, when as fellow adventures travelling against the tide, or at least the wind, we cemented our friendship by agreeing to cycle out of town together the next day.

Before stumbling off in that elaborate, tip-toey way that only drunk people think is really quiet, we said goodnight and headed to our respective dorms.

Day29   Winnipeg to Elm Creek: 45 miles

So here we are, Claud and I, one of us with a lovely hangover, standing in the hostel lobby preparing to leave. As I'm pumping up tyres, trying to ignore the throbbing in my head, and doing final checks I vaguely recall agreeing with Tom that we'll cycle out of the city together?

I'm slightly perturbed by this although, given the loneliness of the last few weeks, I figure it could be nice to have some company for a change? But not for too long though. This is my journey, besides, I like being on my own too much.

Between the hangover and a permanent state of weariness my body is very resistant to the idea of getting on a bike again anytime soon. My leg and arm muscles would certainly be more than happy to stop longer, rest and recuperate.
But, weirdly, every time I do stop, there's an underlying restlessness to get going again, itchy feet (or wheels). I don't want to be still. I miss the momentum and it seems I've gotten a taste for the road now.

Tom arrives in the lobby looking not much better than I how I feel which is heartening. I even manage to force down some breakfast which helps a lot. Afterwards, with accompanying headache, tired muscles and new travel buddy, Claud and I head out into a gloriously sunny morning.
I guess it's roll on with the adventure and whatever is next?

Cycling away from Winnipeg it feels great to be on the road again. I'm certainly not sad to be leaving it behind. The murder district thing was an eye opener and the city itself felt like it held a certain tension/edginess to it. A place in decline, like a lonely old man long past the prime of life, quietly giving up and settling into old age on the seedier side of self-neglect.

I've also gotten used to the smaller towns and quieter roads which have marked much of the route so far, much more pleasant than city riding and I find myself looking forward fondly to more of the quirky statues and little bakeries.
As I trundle along it's also clear that the bike shop has done great work on Claud. The gears are running beautifully and not having to operate them by reaching down to yank cables is a big plus.
I'm keen too to start reaping the benefit of my new ergonomic grips, both hands having lost much of their feeling due to the constant road vibration, not an ideal state.

Heading east on The Redcoat Highway 2 the urban sprawl soon fell away to the quiet rural roads I'd been looking forward to. I was kept amused as much as anything by passing through a scattering of small towns with quirky names such as Fannystelle and Starbuck. No coffee there though, in fact not much of anything in any place, whole towns either being shut for the day (no Sunday trading) or just uninhabited.

Being decidedly hot and thirsty by now and stupid enough not to have stocked up in Winnipeg, it was a bit alarming after leaving the city behind, to suddenly find that there was nowhere to buy food or drink.
Luckily Fannystelle took pity on us or at least a cafe owner there did, kindly opening their doors just so we could buy much longed for cold drinks.
Given the lack of groceries available, lunchtime produced the need to apply all my powers of creativity to sustenance, finally eliciting a rather weird sandwich concoction of mushed up banana, spread over bread and sprinkled with chocolate beans. Mmmm, tasty.

Whilst lunch was always a welcome respite from the heat, getting back on the bike after any stop is always a chore and even more so after a few days of rest. My legs had definitely seized up a bit during the Winnipeg break and this far into the day they were stiff, sore and protesting loudly. The usual headwind was back too and the day soon settled into a long, hot grind, not helped along by the sweltering temperatures, topping out at 35 degrees Celsius which combined with the wind to make it feel like riding towards a very powerful hair-dryer.

Tom turned out to be good company however and having someone to chat too definitely took my mind off the worst of the riding.

My usual aim for a day in the saddle had long evolved into doing a minimum of 100km or roughly 60+ miles. Today however, wasn't going to be one of those days.

Pushing relentlessly against the heated headwind, legs crying in frustration, it was Tom who finally persuaded me to call a halt at a paltry (for me) 45 miles. As someone used to covering shorter distances he had no problem calling it a day, especially when we spotted a little diner up ahead. Annoyingly, it made sense.

What a place to stop! Ma's Drive-in, one of the only food places we'd seen all day, was a little shack on the side of the road, but obviously popular especially with the motorbike riding fraternity.

It was here I sampled another Canadian first – Poutine, a national dish of pure comfort food aka calories.

After a tough day the steaming, dripping plate of fries covered in rich gravy and cheese was heavenly.

The shack owner, amused at our delight, also kindly gave permission for us to pitch our tents in a wonderful grassy area behind the diner. Shaded by overhanging willow trees and a little wooden bridge, the site looked out onto green, deserted fields. Even better, she agreed to leave the toilets unlocked for us for our exclusive overnight use. It was perfect.

After putting up the tent and chatting to some of the diners, I sat and shared some red wine with Tom, watching the evening drawing in, the sun setting prettily behind the wavering fields. It felt entirely more civilised than some of my previous campsites. Maybe travelling with someone wasn't so bad after all? Maybe I could get used to this?

Day30   Elm Creek to Glenboro: 61 miles

An 8am early start under a disturbingly-bright blue sky meant that it promised to be another hot day. Even the wind was up early, but at least I was feeling good as we ploughed into the headwind mile after mile.

One of the many quirky things I love about Canada, especially being a Brit, are the place names.
Many are quite obviously linked to the early pioneer settlers from the UK and beyond, naming their little patch of earth after the place they'd left behind in another country somewhere. Whether in homage or irony I was never entirely sure? What this happy quirk meant however, was that I could perform geographical miracles in the space on an afternoon that would take days by bike at home.
For example, over the space of a few hours I cycled from Somerset to Norfolk before landing up for lunch in Holland.
Holland, as well as a miniature windmill, also supplied a very shady foot bridge under which I had a delightful snooze; I'm definitely slowing down with Tom for company. No more forging ahead mile after mile on a handful of nuts and chocolate. Was I changing how I rode already?

Getting back on the bike my body reminded me why I don't like stopping for lunch. This morning's supple muscles had seized and the afternoon now dragged.
To help with the lethargy and sanity, I introduce Tom to the 'Alphabet Game'. A fiendishly simple but engrossing travel strategy used over many a long journey. Simply pick a topic – pop songs for example – and then take it in turns going through the alphabet thinking of song title beginning with each consecutive letter….
The number of topics is exhaustive and strangely addictive and that afternoon we cover everything from music to infectious diseases to cheese. The miles slip by again, the headwind not forgotten but diminished in my mind at least.

The 17 foot high camel guarding the edge of the highway stops us in our tracks. Sara, as she as affectionately known, perches randomly and conspicuously by a rather nice looking pub, presiding proudly over the town of Glenboro.

A helpful sign proclaims that Sara had stood sentry for Glenboro since 1978, an emblem of the Spirit Sands (also known as the Manitoba Desert) in nearby Spruce Woods Provincial Park.
The area itself was mapped much earlier by western expeditions in the 1730's during which the good quality of the soil, wood and water meant that it was settled early, quickly growing into a hub for farming communities.
Happily for wayward cycle tourists this early development also meant that it boasted a pub, bakery and community campground.

As it turned out these community campgrounds would play a huge part in crossing the prairies. Often with minimal charge, or occasionally free, they mostly operated on an honesty box system or were vaguely staffed by someone from a local house. It seemed that nearly every small town offered the chance for the itinerant wanderer to have somewhere to rest on their journey across the plains. Perfect.

Glenboro's campsite was situated on a racecourse with rather welcome showers and toilets and no other people, perfect. Seeking me out that evening, Tom appeared in the women's loos and his jaw dropped in amazement. Apparently, never having sampled public conveniences for the fairer sex, he was struck dumb at the difference. Mostly, I hasten to point out in the levels of hygiene and smell, but also in comfort and decoration. Sometimes being female has its advantages, smug smile.

Tents pitched, we cycled back to visit Sara and the rather promising looking pub. Not disappointed, I wolfed down a hearty plate of roast beef, gravy and potatoes followed by a cocktail or two and a few genial games of pool.
Wobbling back to the campground on Claud I reflected again how nice

today had been, having company to break up the long miles and adding some humour into the day. Even if the company had beaten me 3 games to 2 at pool.

Day 31   Glenboro to A field past Souris: 58 miles

Feeling good on the bike this morning, my legs are working well and Claud's wheels roll easily over the lumps and bumps in the road. Having Tom there spurs me on too. Partly it's the company, partly it's the competition.
There are many reasons, I tell myself, why I shouldn't be trying to compete with a 24 year old boy. Muscle bulk, youth etc. etc. but that doesn't stop me one bit. Competitiveness it's like an in-built button that gets activated as soon as anyone pulls ahead. If I spot a bike on the horizon, there's no choice, head low, I'm charging like a crazed bull, no matter how tired my legs are or how wheezy my asthmatic lungs get. It's always the same, got to win, got to be first.

Today was a particularly smug day for that too when Tom, being thirsty, decided to take a detour off to a small town, hoping for a drinks stop. Wanting to push on I said goodbye agreeing to meet up later in Souris. In theory, Tom's detour should loop back to the main road at some point ahead; with him confidently predicting he'd catch me up or even over-take me there.
Game on.
I cycled away, picking up pace as soon as I was out of sight, hammering up and down some increasingly big hills. It's a myth, by the way, that the prairies are flat.

It was further than I thought to the town which meant I stopped a couple of times to check directions. Souris; in a dual French/English speaking country I'd assumed this was pronounced as in the French for mouse, 'Soor-ee', and put on my best accent when enquiring. Not so, after asking for directions and getting blank looks off of several locals I found out it's 'soor – iss'. Lesson learned and town located I pushed on, finally rolling in to Souris, hot but happy, especially when a quick scout round revealed a definite lack of Tom or his bike.

Settling down in the shade with a slushy and a sandwich I had lovely time dozing and watching the world go by.
Until finally, over an hour later, a sweaty, exhausted cyclist came in to view. I tried to keep the smug to a minimum as Tom explained that not only had there been no shops on his detour there had also been no road. The connecting bridge having been deemed unsafe years ago and shut down, he'd had to retrace his steps, hot and parched.
I'm trying hard not to gloat but may be a tad unsuccessful.

Sitting in the shade by the river as Tom recovered, I'd hoped to go for a swim but the local geese had other ideas as the shallow water was a stinking mess of goose poo. After making do with a bit of splashing downstream we quite reluctantly climbed back on the bikes at 4.30pm, three hours after I'd arrived. As ever my body protested the long break, despite only 40 miles covered so far it didn't see the need to press on.

The usual pattern now emerged where the afternoon dragged again, I'd already learned that the mercury had hit 44 degrees centigrade in Souris, with humidity to match and, out in the middle of the melting tarmac, the sun's haze turned the endless road into a wavering, shimmering heat river.
With no overhanging tree shade I felt like I was slowly cooking, my head boiling in my helmet, roasting to perfection. Even the liberal stops to apply more sun cream brought no relief.
The afternoon wind had worked itself up in earnest too but instead of a cooling breeze it just felt like riding through a blast furnace. In my estimation though, I'd covered nowhere near enough miles, so pushed on.

It was Tom who brought some sanity to bear that afternoon. Getting progressively quieter and slower he was looking pale under the sun burn. Starting to get concerned I suggested pulling off into one of the endless fields for a drink and a rest.

Hunkering down by a hedge, emptying the last of our water bottles that we'd filled just a few miles back I got the feeling Tom wasn't going to be able to go much further. I was still pondering this as we saw a tractor racing towards us across the field.

My immediate assumption was that it was the farmer coming to tell us to get off his land so I wearily stood up, preparing to haul Claud out of the grass and maybe beg for a few more minute's respite. Things, as it turned out, couldn't have been different.

It was the farmer alright, but beaming from ear to ear, he'd spotted us and come racing down to see if we'd like an ice cream, or a cold drink….?
It was again that strange experience of the universe having manifested your thoughts right in front of you.

Daniel, the farmer, was like a whirlwind of welcome as were his family. Wobbling up to the farm gate on the bikes we were greeted effusively by his wife Cath who bizarrely pointed us in the direction of an ice cream cart standing on the dirt driveway and simply said the magic words, "*help yourself.*"
Unbelievable! As it turned out the family had been selling these ice creams at various county shows all summer and were now happily using up the remains.

Whilst Tom and I struggled to believe our luck Daniel was busily unloading our bikes for us. "*Right – these can go in the barn – now then, we've only got a bit of space in the house or….much better, if you like there's a quiet field by the river which is all yours. There's a BBQ tonight and a few beers too.*"

Stunned by such amazing hospitality and hardly daring to believe our luck we bundled our bags into the farm 4x4 and Daniel bounced us across a field full of curious horses and cows to an idyllic spot on the banks of a small creek.

Leaving us to pitch camp with a cheery wave and a dinner invite for 7pm Tom and I stood around stunned. In a few minutes we'd gone from heat exhaustion, with the prospect of an angry farmer evicting us, to honoured guests with a private campsite and as much ice cream as we could eat. Wow.

Pitching camp quickly I stripped bare and made a mad dash for the creek. Watched only by a few curious bovine and a surprised Tom I did what I'd been longing to do all day and plunge into cool water.
Emerging half an hour later I felt like a different person, Tom carefully (or not so) averting his eyes. Luckily I have no shame when it comes to skinny dipping, though Tom steadfastly refused to join in, splashing around in his shorts instead.

The evening passed in a blur of full-on Canadian hospitality. I was literally blown away by the kindness of these strangers who had not hesitated to open their home to two weird, unknown people on bicycles found squatting in the corner of their field. Would our country have been as generous to them? I like to think so but I also have niggling doubts. As a nation we are very kind hearted but we're also pretty reserved whereas, almost without exception, the Canadians I had met were just so up front and open.

Talking to our hosts that evening, it turned out that Daniel, Cath and their 4 children were more than used to hosting all kinds of guests including students, volunteers and random travellers. As we sat chatting into the night, drinking beer and putting the world to rights I again marvelled at the whims of a universe that would have you near heat exhaustion one minute and being cosseted by strangers the next.
At the end of the evening Daniel made the mistake of offering us use of the quad bike to drive back to the tent.
Both a little the worse for beer and sunstroke I gamely informed the

crowd that I had plenty of experience in driving these machines (technically true, though a few years ago now) and volunteered for the role.

With Tom seated on the back a tense few minutes ensued as I reacquainted myself with the clutch and gear mechanism, accompanied by a great deal of crunching, grinding, lurching and squealing (the latter being Tom's obvious lack of faith in my driving abilities) but familiarity returned and we shot away at an enthusiastic speed into the darkness of the fields.
The quad's lights made alarmingly little headway in the pitch black as we careened over grass and ruts. I also had a vague recollection that the ground plunged down to the creek at some point on route but luck and the gods were with me and, after an exhilarating few minutes we made it safely back to the tent, accompanied by of all things, the family's 2 pet goats.

Settling into our camp Tom and I sat outside on a blanket, stretching out and looking at the night sky, gazing up at the stars. It was such a perfect clichéd, cheesy moment, Emma would most definitely be laughing at me.
The goats however had other ideas, looming out of the night they playfully charged us, nibbling at clothing and chewing up the blankets, the torch light throwing their little horned heads into devilish caricatures against the side of the tents.

Falling about laughing it was definitely now time for bed, although the tents gave little respite from our new best friends who, curious about the guy ropes and canvas continued their exploratory munching long in to the night. Every now and then the peaceful silence punctuated by cries of *"Gerroofff"* as an inquisitive goat tried to eat its way inside the tent.

I finally fell asleep ruminating about Tom and the possibility, indeed the wisdom of a fling. Not a good idea I decided, too young and too full of himself. Besides I would be going my own way soon, fun though this had been it wasn't my intention to have a companion of any kind on this voyage of discovery…..

"GO AWAY GOAT!"

Day 32:   Souris to Maryfield: 61 miles

I awoke, thankfully to a lack of goats, but a distinct smell of cow shit. In my hurry to get away from the goats it seems that I'd managed to walk through a large dollop the night before, coating my shoes and subsequently everything they'd touched. Now, helped by the morning sun, the delightful odour of hot crap was filling the whole tent.

Falling over myself in the effort to reach fresh air I was in no mood to linger in bed. After a quick breakfast we packed up the smelly, goat chewed tents and Tom claimed his turn on the quad bike back to the farm.
Personally I thought my driving had been much better as I clung on grimly to the back seat, the quad bouncing and skidding over potholes, it was a relief to disembark.
Loading the gear back on to the bikes Tom discovered, much to his annoyance, that his erratic driving had cost him a favourite flip-flop, lost somewhere in the mile-long stretch of deep grass between the campsite and farmhouse.

With him still moaning about it we said goodbye to the lovely Daniel, Cath and family and headed off down the road. Trying to divert Tom's attention from the flip-flop was a non-starter so I left him to sulk. Just as things were getting tedious however, we heard a large car revving and hooting behind us. Bloody drivers I thought, we're well in to the side of the road, why don't they just pass.
Just as I was about to turn round and let fly with some colourful hand gestures and language our motor stalkers revealed themselves to be Daniel and one of his sons.

It turns out that after we left they'd combed the fields and miraculously found the errant flip-flop. Amazed and humbled we thanked them profusely and carried on our way.

The sun was back again with a vengeance as the morning wore on. Stopping in Virden for lunch I could only pick at some fries and a milkshake, wrapping my burger up for later, the heat making my appetite non-existent.

Same mistake, different day and it seems I never learn as come the afternoon the lack of food started to take its toll. Toiling away in the 40 degree heat I felt distinctly light headed. As I swerved across the tarmac it was Tom's turn to play the adult and suggest a rest break. The shade of a small grove of trees helped a little but by now we were both out of water and not a town in sight for miles.

Ploughing on for another 22 miles it was with a relief bordering on hysteria we reached the general stores at Kola, only to find them shut and the town yet again deserted; another mining or farming town fallen on hard times and abandoned by its occupants.

In something of a parched frenzy we were bordering on desperate when out of the heat haze a woman appeared in a truck. Who knows where she came from but, unbelievably she had water which she offered to us and ice pops which we gratefully seized like the parched desert survivors we felt we were. The woman disappeared as she arrived, in a shimmer of dust and heat. Five minutes later I would have sworn it was all imaginary if it hadn't been for the sticky lolly wrapper in my hands and the cold water now re-filling my bottle. It was all a bit surreal.

Kola was just one in a long line of defunct or non-communities which existed only in a map reference or town sign. No matter how far I travelled in the prairies I never got used to these ghost towns. Referring to the map was useless in discerning which were occupied and which left to rot in the elements. This also meant each day was becoming something of a lottery when trying to plan sustenance and rest.

I'd quickly learned that large-looking towns on the map could, in reality, be as dry and empty as disused film sets, whist tiny hamlets with barely a mention could be bustling communities.
Getting it wrong meant long arid stretches without food or water and today especially I seemed to be getting it wrong, a lot.

For every down though there's always and up and the next one was a huge boost to morale. Entirely unexpectedly, with little fanfare I realised that I'm now in my next Province. Having scooted through Manitoba in barely a bike week I suddenly came upon the understated sign which welcomed me to Saskatchewan, Province number 3 of 5. It also necessitates another time change, minus 1 hour and of course a 3rd provincial flag sticker to be stuck to Claud's mudguard. Simple pleasures.
Ontario now seems a long time ago.

I'd originally thought of stopping in Kola but, given the distinct lack of human habitation I pushed on to a tiny town marked on the map as a mere speck but, infinitely more lively as it turned out.
Another day, another community campground but this time heaving with life. As in other places no one seemed bothered about collecting a fee and we were waved in for free.
Passing through the entrance by a neat little farmhouse, Helen the farmer's wife took an interest in us and came over to chat. It was harvest time, she told us, an all-out work-fest against the coming autumn hence the busy campsite. Her husband who owned much of the surrounding farmland was out on one of many gruelling 16 hour shifts on the combine harvester. Maybe would we be interested in joining him – after dinner of course?

I was again dumbstruck by the open generosity of people. And as I made camp for the night people were literally appearing from nowhere with offers of beer and food. Maybe it was a slow night on the campsite, populated by a handful of farm labourers and crop dusting pilots hanging out for the last of the season but it almost felt like the giddy heights of celebrity.

It was also somewhat overwhelming, especially after a long hot, tiring day on the bike.

Really, all I wanted to do was curl up in my tent and go to sleep, but, not for the first time, that innate British politeness wouldn't allow me to shut out the world and hibernate.

Saying 'yes', even out of politeness, can sometimes lead to good things though and as it turned out this was to be one of those evenings.

It's patently obvious that farming dominates the landscape here on an enormous scale. Surrounded, as I have been, for days by fields of wheat, barley and canola (which smells like over-boiled cabbage) grass land and acres of sunflowers which flow in unbroken seas as far as the eye can see.

Helen and her husband Mick had lived in the tiny community of Maryfield their entire lives, farming this land. Here though the acreage is so vast that the farm actually spans 2 time zones which meant that crossing their property, some fields are an hour ahead of others! Farming across time and space!

I was incredibly lucky to be offered an insight into how these 3000 acres of crops were managed. After a very welcome dinner with Helen she drove Tom and I, along with Mick's dinner, to an endless field a short distance from the campsite. Spotting the monster harvesting machine we headed towards it on foot before climbing skywards to reach the cab.

Mick was very happy to see his food but also explained he was glad for the company, 16 hour shifts getting lonely and tiresome especially by the end of the day. As he drove, we chatted, sitting as high as a house above the crop you could see for ever. There commenced a wonderful hour at sunset riding high in the space-age cab of the 3 tonne, £250,000 machine, marvelling at the size and speed of the grain harvest.

It was an education and an eye opener too. Farming in Manitoba and Saskatchewan is a modern, thriving business but whilst (as I'd experienced) some communities are slowly fading away, others, like Maryfield are diversifying and growing.

Mick mentioned this had been helped by an influx of Chinese citizens over recent years, buying and farming land that would be hard to find at home, and adding to the culture. Bizarrely, it hadn't gone unnoticed that many town high streets consisted almost entirely of fuel, farm machinery shops and Chinese restaurants.

Incongruously, also squatting on the skyline were the hunched, vulture-like shapes of oil pumps, pecking ceaselessly at the soil.

Mick explained that ownership of most farm land in Canada is divided into two; consisting of surface rights and mineral rights.

Canada's land ownership laws are a contentious issue, in particular for First Nation communities and farmers. Since 1763, following the British acquisition of eastern Canada over 80% of land was declared as owned by the Crown and leased out to various agencies, including the farming rights. This means that most farmers therefore have tenure for the surface land but not the mineral rights for the soil beneath which are retained by the government.

Therefore, if oil is found, the government will most likely sanction drilling on current farmland based on their ownership of the mineral rights. The oil companies do pay rental to farmers for the land space but the machinery can be awkwardly sited, with rigs constantly burning off toxic fumes, spewing great plumes of flame and smoke across the crops.

This went some way to explaining why my notion of sourcing water from crystal clear streams across the prairies had been quietly debunked. This toxic combination of crop maintenance, oil extraction and mineral mining taking its toll, rendering ground water undrinkable in many parts.

My head was spinning as Mick wound down the machine for the night, depositing his grain load in one of the huge silos nearby. He was incredibly amused when I described for him the scale we farmed on back home compared to here. At a fraction of the size UK farming must have seemed like a hobby compared to the vast tracts he covered.

Finally back at the campground I fell exhausted into my sleeping bag not even caring that the tent still smells distinctly of cow shit. At least having crossed a time zone I'll have an extra hour of sleep tonight.

Day 33:   Maryfield to Whitewood: 66 miles

The patter of rain woke me, reminding me I'd left my clothes out to air last night. Bum. Scooting out from the tent I begin to scoop up armfuls of soggy cycling gear dragging the whole sopping mass back inside.

It turned out not to matter that much as by the time I'd packed up the rest of my gear I was wet through anyway. Damply stuffing my tent into its bag and the final bits of kit, the clouds then cleared and the sun shone through making a steaming spectacle of me and Claud. Bugger, it was going to be that kind of a day.

This sun/rain combination was also a perfect joy for the mosquitoes, out in force already and happily breakfasting on the final bits of my body not already itchy and swollen.

My breakfast subsequently consisted of a couple of antihistamine tablets donated by Tom and the need to get moving to escape the tiny vampire insects.

Looking at the map my intention was to head to the town of Fairlight for a slap up breakfast. Just 7 miles away it was do-able on an empty stomach and the promise of food meant I pedalled hard.

Not again! Like so many other towns before, it turns out Fairlight exists only as a name on a map. Once a thriving community it was now deserted, devoid of inhabitants, commerce and most importantly breakfast.

F**k it!

Swearing at the empty town didn't help the food situation though and my whole body, so rudely awakened and drenched was near mutiny. Finally, over 12 miles later a greasy spoon diner in Wawota came to the rescue, to be honest I would have eaten mud at this point.

At least the heat had lessened today although not the hills. Whoever said the prairies were flat just blatantly lied. It's the funny thing about maps too, especially ones without contour lines, with the roads all laid out grid-like on paper they look, well flat. In reality though they are anything but.

Despite not being flat the prairies are incredibly vast and the lack of trees to block the view means that one of the current favourite passtime seems to be 'guess the distance of that thing on the horizon'. For example, a building which looks nearby can actually be anything upwards of 5 miles away. Some spectacular storms too can be seen from huge distances and lightening is a regular, arresting feature.

By now, Tom and I slipped into easy conversation, discussing life, the universe, and everything in between. Even the alphabet games were still in full swing with diverse topics ranging from rare and disgusting diseases to chocolate. And it does help to pass the miles. Chatting away hour after hour, sharing the difficulties and frustrations of the journey time truncated, creating that bizarre phenomenon that makes you feel like you've known someone for years not just mere hours or days, fermented by those shared intense experiences.

The distances slip by with the scenery. Near endless fields of produce or my favourite, the sunflowers; thousands of them nodding their sleepy sunny heads like some psychedelic landscape from a 1960's album cover.

An incredibly friendly farming co-operative store provided today's welcome lunch stop. Crouching in the building's shade, the amused manager found us setting out our food and invited us inside to use the 'break' room, complete with comfy chairs and good, cold water.

By late afternoon the bikes rolled in to Whitewood campground on the edge of town, even better it was wonderfully and mercifully deserted. We both breathed a huge sigh of relief at not being the local curiosities, for once setting up tents in peace.

A nearby pub provided some satisfyingly large gin and tonics as well as a few more games in the ongoing pool duel, after which, pleasantly hazy we headed back to the campground.

Tom, who had made many disparaging comments on my erratic/non-existent cooking had, in a prim, house-wifely way, decided to cook that evening. Pitching in together we made a very passable vegetable/instant noodle concoction which probably doubled my vitamin intake for the trip so far followed by cake, chocolate and ice cream maybe somewhat lower down the nutritional scale. All chased down by a few glasses of red wine.

We were both feeling pretty relaxed and social by now, so when the vampire mosquitoes started their evening rounds we headed over to Tom's tent for a game of cards.

It was pretty cramped for 2 people but a card game was soon underway whilst quickly deteriorating into the usual competitive banter. Travelling together so closely these last few days, sharing emotional highs and lows, that feeling of familiarity and let's face it tension had definitely thickened the atmosphere until….

There are moments when you weigh the advisability of a decision, consider the pros and cons from every angle and make a reasoned judgement. And then there are moments when you plunge in feet first, eyes shut, ignoring any voice of caution.

For the second time today I thought f**k it and took the plunge, embarking full throttle on my sister's sage advice back in Winnipeg.

Day 34:   Whitewood to Broadfell: 49 miles

Dear God, I am officially a cougar.

The walk of shame was tempered somewhat by being the first one up and awake. I was however immensely glad I'd returned to my own tent. Not sleeping well at the best of times I much preferred insomnia in my own space.
With plenty of time to mentally masticate in the wee small hours of the morning I came to the general consensus that I had no regrets. My thinking from the start had been that Tom and I wouldn't be cycling together for long, if nothing else, it was a fun farewell. I was actually surprised we'd made it this far together as it was anyway.

Tom emerged from his tent as I was cooking a very hearty breakfast of fried eggs sandwiches. Any slight awkwardness was soon dissipated by my refusal to act anything other than normally. I insulted him as usual and then told him I was leaving shortly, if he was coming along he'd better get his ass into gear and pack up.
The unasked/unanswered questions brushed aside we slipped into the usual routine and not long after we were packed up and on the road.

Turing away from the country back roads and back onto my old friend the Trans-Canada Highway, the ability for conversation, even if we'd wanted to, was swallowed by some of the worst headwinds so far. Overcast grey skies whipped up the most brutal headwinds which bullied the bike down into granny gear. Infinitely harder than riding the steepest hills, on which you could at least get a rhythm going, now if you stopped for respite the bike was blown backwards. Just moving forwards was painfully slow, the relentless headwind throwing the bike around all but halting progress.

Perhaps if I had paid more attention in school, instead of looking out of the window, dreaming of adventures, I may well have known that:
- Every country has a prevailing wind direction.

- This is influenced/impacted upon further by a layer of exceptionally strong atmospheric winds known as the jet stream
- Both stretch across the North American continent from west to east

I'm riding from east to west. It is very windy. Sometimes brutally so.

From then on the day turns into the longest grind and my spirits quickly begin to plunge down a slope of despair. I couldn't describe to you any scenery at all, over the course of the next hours as my gaze rested solidly, fixedly on the tarmac under my front wheel.

To top it all an asthma attack kicked in with a vengeance. Set off by prolonged, strenuous exertion the hills and headwind had made for it the perfect storm.

A pre-cursor of my worst asthma attacks are bizarre, uncontrollable tears and these were soon in full flow, followed by wheezing and a chest so constricted I was forced on to the verge of the highway gulping for air like a stranded fish.

Tom, faring better against the wind, had long disappeared and I sat there miserably, wheezing at the passing traffic feeling utterly spent.

At some point the misery must have morphed into anger, the feeling sorry for yourself, it's-just-not-fair type of rage. Abandoning Claud to the grass verge I ran full tilt into one of the vast, horizon-less fields, screaming, shouting and railing at the wind.

It did my asthma no good, nor made one iota of difference to the howling gale, but weirdly I felt a lot better.

"Don't let the wind break your spirit"

With Etta's advice looping around my head I tramped back to the highway, rescued Claud and headed west.

Somewhere down the road Tom was waiting for me, parked up for a quick lunch break at a windy truck stop. My body ached from the aftermath of the asthma attack and that annoying residual tearfulness remained making me grumpy that I felt so pathetic. I hate to cry in front of anyone but, as I'd already found, when your body is at a low ebb, all energy squeezed out and running on reserves, tears are always near the surface. Liquid tired.

My goal for each day was still at least 100km (62ish miles), but after 49 miles I neared the town of Broadfell and knew that my cycling was over for today.
Tom, still with energy in the tank, decided to push on. So after a quick coffee break we said our goodbyes.
Fatigued, sore, wheezy, that small abandoned child feeling returned watching him cycle away. I'd enjoyed much of the company, however this was my solo trip and not one I wanted to share a large part of. Maybe best to say goodbye now, get back into the single rider groove.

I began to give myself a pep talk again as I hunted down the campground, a mosquito-infused patch of woodland staffed by a rather reticent character my addled mind somehow equated with Norman Bates from Psycho. It didn't help any that he emerged from behind a derelict wooden house hefting an axe (allegedly doing some maintenance). As I paid I still wasn't entirely sure he worked for the campsite?!
Navigating a forbidding tangle of trees to find my pitch I'm sure it was the tiredness causing some wild imaginings, but newspaper headlines flashed through my mind involving a missing cyclist last seen heading alone into the woods and I'm suddenly very aware that no one in the world knows where I am right now.
Soon after and safely (as much as you can be) tucked up in my tent I set about some ninja-organising before tomorrow. My plan was a very early start, assuming I survived the night with Norman Bates on the prowl, to ride the 100 or more km to Regina to meet up with my next Warm Showers host there.
Bags all pre-packed, clothes laid out I merely had to pack up my tent, eat a banana and hit the road come morning.
Now, could I sleep? Hello bear-spray, goodnight Norman.

Day 35:   Broadfell to Regina: 64 miles

Thirty minutes to pack up. How can it take 30 minutes when I only have to pack my tent?!
I'd had some sleep, but not enough and I'm awake at 4.30am and getting ready to roll. Panniers secured and banana eaten I'm heading out with the light, pedalling faster than strictly necessary past Norman's house.

For the first half an hour I relax and enjoy the peace of the quiet roads and emerging dawn, the fields and single strip of road stretching endlessly away in every direction, the view to the horizon unimpeded for miles.
The chirpy headwind greeted me shortly after and we began our daily directionally-opposed pass de deux. Two hours later and I roll up to Indian Head, Tom's intended camping spot. It's still stupidly early so the only place open is a gas station in which I gratefully take a shelter and eat breakfast.

Heading outside I notice that it appears to be getting dark again. Funny, I haven't been stopped for that long. As I cycle away however I see why. It's not sunset but a storm, a big one. Because of the clear horizon I watch it approach with a mix of fascination and alarm. Huge dark thunder clouds chaperoned by a now ferocious wind followed by a horrifying show of the biggest lightning bolts I've ever seen. I'm transfixed but also mildly terrified watching all that loosed electricity, especially thinking about the large metal object on which I'm sat. I ask myself the question, "the tyres will earth it right....?"

Of course, now there's nowhere to stop and shelter. I've left Indian Head behind and there's a distinct lack of trees on the wind swept prairies. With no protection my only option is to cycle blindly onwards into the storm, watching it close the miles between us until it hits.
By the time we meet, the wind is fierce, driving rain into my face so I can't see the road. Almost all light seems to have been smothered from

the sky. I briefly wish my bike had lights but it's not a time for such regrets, fortunately there are few cars about or at least if there are I don't hear them above the crashing thunder on top of me or the crazily flashing electricity splitting the sky.

Instead I opt for complete denial, head down ploughing on, looking only at the road and blocking out the typhoon and my fear.

Drenched, cold, buffeted and scared, I'm wondering if it will ever end when I finally lift my gaze to the sky and there, pushing through the clouds is a small piece of the most brilliant rainbow.

Almost immediately the wind begins to calm and the rain lessens and I feel the most overwhelming sense of peace, my spirit stretches and smiles. It's going to be ok.

Claud rolls on. Enjoying the relative calm we take it a town at a time, counting them off every ten miles or so, progress/survival markers as we damply inch across the map.

At last nearing Regina I spot the cyclists' haven, a roadside diner advertising home-made pie and OAP specials. And who should I see in the window right under that sign but Tom.

Heading through the door I waltz in and plonk myself down opposite grinning. He's already tucking into to a big piece of pie and, as I order another, we exchange news. As it turned out his camping experience was worse than mine. With no campsites in Indian Head he'd been forced to pitch up on a piece of scrub land between two seedy looking blocks of flats. In fear for his safety he'd not slept either, breaking camp early to head out.

Refuelled, we agree to head into the city together, a companionable last few miles to Regina. Arriving earlier than expected and knowing my Warm Showers host was tied up for a few hours we subsequently decide a cheeky celebration drink is in order, especially when rolling past an Irish pub. As of one mind we pull to a stop, propping up the bikes outside and ordering a few pints.

Several drinks and some great Irish stew later I was feeling distinctly mellow as I gathered up Claud and attempted to navigate through this hazy cheer to find my host for the night.

Gordon

Gordon turned out to be a Warm Showers veteran and an incredibly welcoming host.
Arriving to a dry, fully equipped bike workshop for Claud and warm homemade bread for me I was in heaven. It got even better after that ubiquitous warm shower and a dinner of roast chicken and vegetables and when Gordon extended the guest invitation for further night so I could rest up and see the city I profusely thanked the universal gods who were on my side that day it seemed.
That night, tucked up in a clean, soft bed I drifted off musing again on what a difference a day makes. From Norman to Gordon via a biblical thunderstorm. Whatever next?

Day 36:   Regina: 0 miles

Next, it turned out, was a welcome day of housekeeping and home comforts. It was also spent getting to know better both my host and the city I'd rolled up in.
Washing done and emails caught up on Gordon and I embarked upon a walking tour of the neighbourhood, strolling through a string of rolling parks, Lake View and Kiwanis and around the beautiful Wascana Lake.

Gordon made a great guide, full of interesting facts and local knowledge, I also found out he himself was a veteran of many cycle tours, having most recently cycled the road south from Alaska to Vancouver. In a calm, unassuming way he described the desolation, days without fresh water, cars or humans and the frequent companionship of bears. I on the other hand am tremendously

relieved that my only bear encounter to date has been with road kill.
It would be fair to say that Gordon was definitely the 'outdoorsy type' an impression confirmed as he went on to describe his love of skiing, snow-shoeing, marathon running….. Navigating my way around his garage-cum-workshop later in the day this was backed up by stacks of more sports equipment than you could shake a snow-shoe at.

It was lovely though to spend time with someone who was so interested in the world around them. His prolific Warm Showers hosting meant he'd met a huge variety of people from many different places across the globe. It even turned out he'd hosted Arthur, the young French cyclist I'd met back in Marathon. During the day we talked about many things, including route planning and that afternoon Gordon got out his superb collection of maps to help me plan my next steps.

I'd been intending to head due west on the usual cycle route to Swift Current but, after poring over the various maps, the promise of a river crossing by boat trumped that and I revised my route more to the north west.
Finally, ably assisted by Gordon, bike mechanic being amongst his talents, I gave an ever-needed bit of care and attention to Claud fixing and tightening mounts and cleaning and oiling the chain-set.

Later on that afternoon, a quick run into the city centre gave the perfect opportunity to test out Claud's tune up and to meet Tom back in the Irish bar for a cheeky drink, which of course being Tom, turned into 2 or 3. Somehow, during the course of afternoon we agreed to meet the next day to cycle out of the city together. May as well I suppose as we were both going that way.
I debated hotly with myself about going it alone, but, as Tom was only cycling as far as Moosejaw, a day's ride at most before heading off on the Swift Current route, it seemed churlish not to.

A glass or 2 later and it was back to Gordon's for a companionable evening with my lovely host, cooking, chatting and swapping travel tales. An impromptu harmony even filled the kitchen as we chopped vegetables and sang along to familiar tunes, singing being another of his many talents and interests.

Again I found myself wanting to stay longer. The offer was certainly there, and the thought of spending more time with my wonderful host was more than appealing. But the devil was back on my shoulder and the urge to be on the road again was stronger. Despite the ever present fatigue my body was like an addict craving a fix, I needed to be moving. Stay in one place for more than a night or two and I became antsy, restless. Was it just momentum or was there some other, deeper driver? Who knows, but tomorrow Claud and I will roll on.

I have to say I'm dreading facing the wild wind again. That familiar pattern of it building throughout each morning to reach what feels like gale force by the afternoon has accompanied most days since week one, but especially since reaching Manitoba. Those last few days riding into Regina have been some of the hardest, physically and psychologically of the journey so far.

Although it feels personal at times, Gordon assures me it isn't. Looking back as we compare notes I realise both from our anecdotes and my conversations with other cyclists that everyone seems to have experienced seemingly incessant headwinds at some time or another. I've even talked with people riding on the same day as me but in the opposite direction and we've both been hit by headwinds which is downright bizarre.

However, two full days of fighting for headway, pedalling in the lowest gears and even being blown backwards wears at the best of spirits.

Add in as well the odd thunderstorm, driving hail, blast furnace temperatures and the weather really has dominated this stage of the trip. I realise too that my average daily distances have slowed, in part following a more relaxed pace, but also mostly due to wind, thunderstorms and scorching heat and humidity with temperatures up to 44 degrees centigrade. Despite all this, in the last seven days alone

Claud and I have covered over 400 miles (or 650 km), every inch of which has been fought for.

Sister mail:

From: Emma **To:** Cyclinginaskirt
Subject: Bean and her future squeeze
Hey,
Good work on the lad - he is officially fine! Thinking of you in the prairies (no idea on spelling!) hopefully not as boring as you thought - or is this why you have resorted to the toy boy :)

Thought I'd send you a pic of Bean and her friend playing with her toys, although shortly after this she cried her eyes out - I don't think she likes to share her things!

Things are ok here – M seems really stressed over last few days, really short fuse and resorting to child-like temper tantrums! :(am hoping now the weekend is here he can de-stress a bit - Mum and Dad are hopefully babysitting Bean for a bit on Sunday so M and I can go to out. BBQ went well last weekend - bit too well, flippin' loadsa people turned up and all at once! But Bean was so good and let everyone have a cuddle (I even forgot I had a baby at one point!).
Saw health visitor today and Bean now weighs in at 12lbs 14 - so slowed down a bit but still a 'healthy' baby.

Anyway keep the gossip coming! Will you ride with him the rest of the way now? :)
Lots of love, Xxxxx

From: Cyclinginaskirt **To:** Emma
Subject: Bean and her future squeeze
Bean really is starting early with the boys! Sounds like things have been pretty tough with M though, hang in there and if you can, tell him how you feel. It can't be easy for either of you, especially with so little sleep and figuring out how the baby works, hopefully he

can see the need to pull together rather than away from each other to get through this. You both will.

Not planning on keeping the cycle companion, it's been nice but want to get back to being on my own sooner rather than later I think.

Hang in there and lots of love xx

From: Emma **To:** Cyclinginaskirt
Subject: Peek-a-boo
Hey,
Glad you're getting thru the prairies ok, though I hope somewhere along the line it gets at least a little easier for you as your last blog sounded pretty brutal – can't imagine winds like that!

I had a talk with M in the end and I think he got what I was trying to say. If things get stressed again me and Bean can always take a strategic walk and let the dust settle for both of us!
Despite that rocky start we ended up having a lovely weekend, had really nice time going out and stayed up till 12.00 woohoo, crazy :)
Well, got another busy week ahead of me - start booby peer support training tomorrow (not sure what it involves but my brain goes to the idea of a group of ladies sat around supporting each other's' breasts!).
Lots of love and hugs, Xxxxx

From: Emma **To:** Cyclinginaskirt
Subject: Peek-a-boo
Hey u,
How goes it - u still riding with the lad? Had such a busy week but really good - started booby training on Tues, really good course, it's an accredited course so on a selfish note I thought it might look good in the cv if I do look for other work, but also something I think I'm really gonna enjoy doing :) oh something to think about on your

long rides - we need a new name for the 'breast feeding support service' so have a think! So far we've got: 'Knockers at the door' or 'Baps around the corner'? :)

Missing out on B's hen do this weekend which is a little sad but overall I knew I wouldn't make it, to be fair I just don't think I could leave Bean for that long just yet (never thought I'd be saying that!) but on the plus side I found a wicked dress for me for the wedding - one I can feed her in too!
Anyways hope all is good with you and apologies again for missing your Skype calls - whoever thought having a baby would keep you so busy!
Lots of love and hugs, Xxxx

From: Cyclinginaskirt **To:** Emma
Subject: Peek-a-boo
Really glad you talked and sounds like it cleared the air a bit, way to go!

Booby support training sounds like you're going to be handing out bras. I'd hire anyone with that on their CV!
Sorry about the short message, more soon.
Love you xx

Thunder Bay to Regina in pictures

The lovely Sara

Travelling through time

Lake view

Chasing trains

Sunflowers

My first poutine

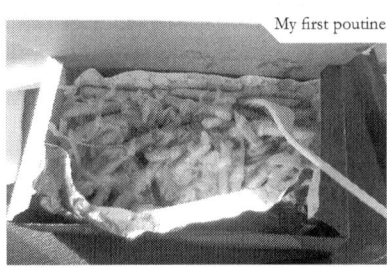

Province number 3

Thunder Bay to Regina in pictures

The first 1000 miles

A bright place

River moon

Camping and clothes drying

One of many "refilled" bottles

Still on the Trans-Canada

Always the left shoes

Sunset on the "longest" day

Regina to Calgary

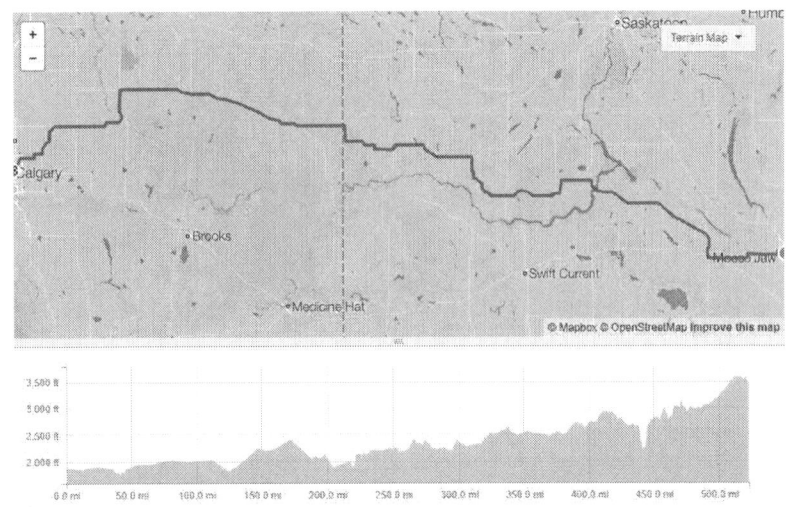

Courtesy of Strava mapping.

Day 37:   Regina to Moosejaw: 45 miles

The insomnia from earlier in the trip has returned with a vengeance. My mind, it seems, is unable to switch off my body and a grand total of 3 hours sleep has left me decidedly groggy and irritable.

Though unwilling to admit it I'm so tired. Not just from the previous night but that kind of deep-bone tired from both the miles and the grind of travel. From having to deal with the unknown day after day; from not knowing what the route will be like, to where I will sleep, to just everything.

The 2 hours between leaving Gordon's and finally getting on the road did nothing to dissipate this charming mood.
Meeting Tom at Tim Hortons at the allotted time, I sit impatiently waiting for him to start, let alone finish breakfast which became a frustratingly protracted affair. After which I had to grudgingly admit that Tom's suggestion of shopping seemed to make sense, taking advantage of the large out of town supermarkets to stock up on supplies. I could of course have just left on my own and I chastised myself for not doing so whilst wandering the supermarket aisles.

If I'm honest, I feel like I've failed somehow for no longer riding alone all of the time.

Up until now, guaranteed, the first three things that people will ask me at any time are:
- *"Where are you heading?....Vancouver –   wow you've got a long way to go"*
- *"Where did you start?....Toronto – no way, gee that's mad"*
- *"Who are you cycling with....? YOU'RE ON YOUR OWN?!!"*

And I'm not exaggerating the capitals.

When asked why I'm travelling solo, my usual quip was that no one was stupid enough to come with me, but in reality, it was totally my choice. I like travelling alone and have done it often, but the amount of horror/fear that is injected in to that last response is surprising and somewhat disconcerting.

A quick, very unscientific straw poll conducted amongst the other cyclists I meet seems to indicate that the general reaction to men travelling alone is one of adventurousness whereas the idea of a woman going solo is a dangerous one.
It has caused me to reflect on the potential riskiness of what I'm doing. After all, there have been (occasional) times in the past when common sense has not been my companion in various escapades.
Examining the main threats to me as a cyclist, these seem to come mainly from traffic and from wildlife, followed by dehydration and exposure, all equally applicable to the male traveller.
Robbery I suppose is a possibility, but I would have to pity the thief who stole my panniers full of sweaty, smelly laundry and half eaten bread rolls.
My conclusion, such that it is, is that the fear stems from a personal perception of risk, rather than any tangible danger, undoubtedly also influenced by the usual sensationalist media reporting as well as someone's own, personal outlook.

If I thought hard about all the things that could potentially go wrong, I probably wouldn't set foot outside the front door. All risk is relative to our own internal parameters and fear can often be a good thing, it keeps us alert and doesn't necessarily have to be a barrier to exploration.

I can also say that throughout the trip I have rarely felt truly alone. I have no problem with spending hours in my own company, a usual day will consist of 8-10 hours on the road, during which time I watch the world go by. I don't listen to music as I ride, and I honestly couldn't begin to tell you what I think about.
Small distractions such as recalling the words to Christmas carols, making up anagrams and designing the world's ultimate roller-coaster have certainly all featured, usually interspersed with deep, profound

thoughts such as, *"oh crap, that's a big hill"* or *"do I want chocolate or strawberry milk for lunch"*.

On the flip side however I would have found the prairies a much tougher place without someone with which to share the pain…..and of course there are many good bits to having another person with whom to talk and laugh with and play silly games.
It's also someone to ride with, to dissect the day with, to experience the highs and lows, to make decisions with on where to camp, when to stop. I'm angry with myself too that there's a bit of me that enjoys that.
What happened to the strong, fearless, intrepid woman…? Well, maybe she never existed but this was meant to be my trip, solo, not tandem.

Solo, you certainly have the full freedom of decision making, no one to hear your tantrums when you are tired and grumpy, to set your own pace and not worry it's too fast/too slow. But you also lack things such as a second voice of reason, someone to say it's time to stop now, take a break, eat something.

Maybe it just boils down to the simple fact that there are always going to be both advantages and disadvantages to riding solo or in company? Having done both it seems neither is definitively better or worse, the experience is just a different one.
My small hope is that by being out there on my bicycle, alone, I can quietly dispel the myth that travelling solo is a more dangerous (and therefore unacceptable) pursuit for women. That feeling of somehow letting myself (and others) down by riding occasionally with someone else, well I'll just have to work on that.

Faffing and musings combined, it was midday before we finally rolled out of Regina with me in a less than sparkly mood. The roads are busy and built up, but not overly so given the size of the city, and especially when compared to the UK. Despite the grumpiness I couldn't help but notice that, amazingly, a tailwind had gotten behind Claud and for once it had become a joy to pedal. I was drunk on speed and the scenery fairly sped by as the road quickly became quieter and more rural. It was then that in the distance, I spotted the gleam of 2 road bikes, shimmying like thoroughbreds up ahead, Lycra-clad riders hunched over the bars. Even more bizarrely, we were gaining on them.

I can never resist a challenge, or a race, and whilst acutely aware of the stupidity of pitting my 42kg bike against these carbon beauties, still I crouch over the bars, legs pumping, lungs screaming and start chasing them down.

It nearly kills me but the gap closes satisfyingly quickly until, pushing 17+mph uphill, skirt fluttering in the breeze (asthmatic lungs wheezing like an 80 year old smoker) I draw alongside. The bikers are amazed (and a little embarrassed) when, with a perky wave and mustering all of my last oxygen to give a cheery hello, Claud and I, panniers bouncing, shoot off up the hill in front.

Needless to say that little episode had consequences and the Karma fairy finally catches me up a few hills later when an asthma attack necessitated a breathing pit stop on a roadside verge.
Lunchtime follows but with the accompanying heat and tight lungs I have no appetite for food; tired and sore and spent, the 'I told you so' noises emitting from my companion did nothing to add to my black mood.

Pushing on after lunch everything seemed achingly slow compared to the morning's high, especially as predictably, even the wind turned against me. Fortunately, Moosejaw itself was not a long day's ride and after a very welcome 45 miles I rolled in to the driveway of my next Warm Showers stay, having said goodbye to Tom who was staying elsewhere. Three days running of not having to camp – this was indeed a high point and probably the longest run of clean sheets since leaving Toronto. I could get used to this.

Glenda and Larry

Glenda and Larry had been hosting prolifically for a number of years and as with all my stays so far, were interesting, articulate, community minded people who were fascinated by the wider world. Hosting, it seemed was a natural extension of their warm, welcoming personalities.

It transpired that the couple also shared their large family home with 9 cats as well as the odd cycle tourist. My bedroom was in the basement where Larry, who reportedly was not a fan (of cats, possibly cyclists) had designated an adjoining space as the 'cat corral'. It was here that most of the menagerie congregated, with only the odd brave one daring to pad through to the upstairs danger zone! Having a human guest in their territory however they were overjoyed at the free warmth and stroking, waiting patiently in knots around my room to be fussed over and curling up on me whenever I sat down for a nanosecond.

In kinship with my other hosts Glenda and Larry were incredibly generous and determined to feed me the gross domestic food product of Canada. Hungry at last, not having eaten since breakfast, I wolfed down an amazing dinner that evening of steak and roast vegetables followed by the most heavenly hot Saskatoon berry crumble (tart round fruits similar to blueberries) swimming in melted vanilla ice cream.

Afterwards, fit to burst and curled up in a chair, my digestive system contemplated this input with wonder and the odd, appreciative noise, whilst Glenda and I talked long into the evening about work, travel and the philosophies of life, with a joyful discovering of much common ground.

Saying goodnight to my hosts that evening the awaiting double bed was the most welcome sight that day, even if I did have to share with a furry interloper or two.

Day 38:   Moosejaw: 0 miles

Another day off – and why not!! My body was definitely in need of it, and with the lovely company of Glenda and the furry family, it was a chance to relax and explore the delights of Moosejaw.

Tom, as it transpired, was also staying, settled into a campsite and in no hurry to move on. We again agreed to meet up in town where, over a morning coffee, we put the final touches to the day's tourist agenda.

Firstly, the 'Tunnels'. Carved out of the earth and rock beneath the town these old passageways had undergone many uses from housing the dispossessed to aiding black-marketeering.

Immigrants fleeing China's harsh regime in the early part of the 20th century had found a dubious shelter there with whole extended families living and hiding in these underground passageways. Their only source of survival was to work illegally, often as free labour for business owners in return for being able to remain hidden from the authorities.

Generations later the Chinese culture is a significant part of not just Moosejaw but many areas of Saskatchewan and other provinces. It also went some way to explaining the baffling proliferation of Chinese takeaways in a swathe of the country where the ethnic diversity of the towns had been nearly non-existent.

The other, rather thrilling use of the tunnels was by old-time bootleggers, the most infamous of which being Al Capone himself; gangs of hoods smuggling liquor through the city to subvert the American prohibition laws.

This bizarre network of underground passages was available to be viewed by the paying public through the medium of a splendidly and wildly over-acted immersive tour.

As participants we were press-ganged into becoming part of a very kitsch 1920s bootlegging gang where a group of enthusiastic actors delivered a performance so hammy it could have provided for a whole hog roast. Guided through in a flurry of feather boas and splurge guns we made dodgy deals and ran rum barrels Al Capone style. It was a bizarre experience but no less fun for it.

And after the surreal hilarity of the tunnels it was time for tourist activity number 2 and something I had been looking forward to for what felt like forever, a soak in the town's famous geothermal pools.
There is nothing comparable with the feel of hot water on tired muscles. Soaking and steaming for hours, the last few weeks and few thousand miles started to wash away. I really believe I could have stayed all night but sadly the staff had other plans.

Floating back to Glenda's in a relaxed daze it was hard not to notice how much of Moosejaw's main street looked like the set of an old Western film. Airbrush away the cars and replace them with horses and women in hooped skirts and a hundred years could easily fall away, give or take the odd mobile phone shop.

The evening was again full of great food and even better conversation, punctuated by some piano playing from Larry.
Again I marvelled at how much the world can change day by day and how amazing these strangers are who take unknown, bedraggled cyclists into their homes and make them feel like family. Have I just been incredibly lucky or is this Canada?

No more home comforts from tomorrow though, back to the tent at least until Calgary. Another city in another province where a tentative arrangement has been made to stay with the cousin of someone I met briefly at some traffic lights in Toronto....I don't know what's funnier, the tenuous connection or the fact that I am considering it?
Whatever the outcome, tomorrow I am definitely back to riding solo, Tom and I wanting to take different routes west from here, we'll be going separate ways.

Day 39: Moosejaw to Central Butte: 62 miles

Today made for a bizarre start. An email from Tom who's apparently decided to head in my direction after all. Seems every time we say goodbye and I've reached a point where I'm ready to go it alone again, plans change. Having spent a bit of time together now though, it's an easy habit to slip back in to. I could decline but I'm not that decisive.

And it's that indecisiveness that sees me waiting an hour later in a cold supermarket car park for Tom, who is as ever, late.

We're finally getting ready to leave when something catches our attention simultaneously. We stop short, both just staring.

Enter 'The Lightrider'.

Pulling into the parking lot is the strangest contraption I've seen so far. A bicycle pulling a trailer covered in metal panels and graffiti, emblazoned with ribbons, carrier bags and the hand-painted moniker – 'THE LIGHTRIDER. Riding atop this is a guy with tattered trousers, a dirty anorak and a serene grin.

Instantly this shabby figure clocks the presence of fellow bike travellers and makes a bee-line towards us.

Tom, in his aversion to anything perceived as 'odd' (hobos, vegetarians, flowers) attempts a quick getaway but I'm intrigued. Plus that annoying politeness-gene would no-more allow me to run away than if faced a whole herd of such curious natives.

"*Howdy*" the Lightrider reaches us, beaming from under his scrubby beard. Dismounting in a flurry of dirty anorak he proudly shows off his steed.

After some discussion it transpires that the metal squares covering the tank sized trailer are solar panels, an integral part of the Lightrider's plan to cross Canada with sun-generated, electric pedal assistance.

A laudable aim, however it turns out that various technical issues have prevented the panels from actually working thus far meaning that the Lightrider had been laboriously pedalling his very heavy, non-power assisted trailer from town to town.

His enthusiasm was undented though as he hit his conversational stride, starting with a lengthy description of his personal belief system regarding travel and the various government conspiracies affecting it, at which point Tom makes a break for it.

He's already on his bike and heading for the highway at speed as I'm still trying to extricate myself delicately from this conversational black hole.

Seizing an opportunity I politely decline an inspection of the overstuffed trailer whilst strategically mounting Claud and pushing off.

I leave the Lightrider grappling with some errant carrier bags which are threatening to escape from the machine's depths.

Waving farewell to each other I manoeuvre out onto the highway, and straight into a tail wind.

Joy of joys, the first 35 miles of the day speed by in a heady 18mph average, the towns hurtling past.

One of my favourite things about all the prairie towns, apart from their kooky names, is their welcome signage; every individual place proudly displaying beneath their moniker the range of amenities available, depicted by small, sometimes baffling hieroglyphic boxes.

A disembodied eye for example, I finally learned, heralded a 'Point of interest', or a 'Point of no-interest' as dubbed by Tom, usually marking the scene of some long ago battle or prairie crossing which had occurred…. but left no discernible evidence on the landscape.

One place for example enthusiastically pointed readers towards a rut in the dirt, purportedly left by carts from the early settlers. More recently however it seemed to have been over-ridden by large farm machinery unless that is, the early settlers had boasted caterpillar tracks.

Lunch was in the very pretty and very tiny town of Eyebrow; sign-icons including a picnic table, a computer, food and ice skating. How could I resist.

After failing to find either a restaurant, internet or any ice in the 30 degree heat I gave it up as a bad job. At least the town's beautifully secluded community picnic area was easy to locate and I gratefully perched on the end of a shady bench making today's bizarre sandwich concoction with peanut butter and coffee crème cookies.

My vague plan today had been to push on to the Riverhurst ferry crossing another 50km away, but a combination of the extreme heat and a lunchtime nap made this seem less than appealing.
Therefore the town of Central Butte, half that distance away, was the lucky host of two cycle tourists for the night.

Central Butte had two distinct advantages that I could see. A liquor shop and a large, empty community campground with a beautifully appointed shady wooden pergola perfect for cooking and lounging in.... sold!
Even better, the campground warden graciously waived the minimal charge for the night, either taking pity on us or not wanting to get too near the overripe smell of sweaty cyclist.

For some reason in our little camp there was a definite holiday feel. Maybe it was the recent rest days or the relatively easy day's cycling? Quite possibly it was also the stash of beer and wine that accompanied dinner.
Lying outside that evening under the stars, for some reason we began discussing our recent tent antics in Whitewood. I'm not sure quite how, but conversation led to action and the encounter I'd viewed as a one-off somehow turned into an unintended encore. Just going with the adventure I suppose.

Day 40:   Central Butte to Beechy: 53 miles

My line in the sand (or grass) remained however, on no account would I share my tent. Sleeping is hard enough as it is without giving over half of a tiny canvass shoe box to another fidgety human being. And let's face it, boys are not known for their rose-scented smell.

Tucked up in my tent, at least I'd been anticipating sleep after the evening's antics but was again disappointed. A strong wind blew up soon after midnight, one which rifled through everything like a nosey neighbour and had the added annoyance of sounding just like a bike thief. Several times I leapt banshee like from my tent, bear spray in hand, convinced someone was making away with Claud, only to be confronted with an empty, windswept pergola, devoid of all but blowing leaves.

Consequently I'm starting the day, sleep deprived, bleary-eyed and maybe a little hungover. That will teach me! Added to this was a cruel scorching headwind which took hold early on in the morning, drying out my lungs to the consistency of old leather. I was not in love with the day and it had only just started.

Sweating and wheezing into Riverhurst a few hours later it was just in time to see the tail of the departing ferry. Pah. My declining mood wasn't helped any by that or the ensuing 40 minute wait for the next boat on a broiling, shade-less highway.

Despite all this, the river had started to work its soothing magic. A broad expanse of blue-grey, shimmering in the heat and breaking up the dry flatness of the prairies, it was almost mirage like in its appearance. There's something exciting too about a ferry crossing by bike, even a little one. Thinking back, the last crossing was all that time ago in Ontario over to Manatoulin Island, it seems like a lifetime away.

The river itself is actually a narrowing of Lake Diefenbaker and is how

Highway 42 manages to continue and cross this large expanse of water. The short 15 minute journey to the far bank was beautiful and worked miracles towards restoring spirits. Rolling off the ferry on the far bank I couldn't pass up the chance for a swim.

Hiding Claud in the shrubs at the side of the road I scrambled down the steep, muddy bank and, without much pause for thought, stripped off.

Tom, slightly aghast opted for shorts but there is something entirely seductive about the feel of water on bare skin. The heat and grumpiness of the day washed completely away as I swam and floated in the wide, warm shallows. Silty mud underfoot and the wide open prairie sky above.

Unfortunately that same heat dried me nearly instantly post swim also evaporating away the new freshness from my body and getting back on Claud suddenly seemed very effortful.

After only a few short miles of pedalling any final benefit from the swim was sucked dry by the boiling sun and harsh wind. Another stop in the town of Lucky Lake and the last vestiges of motivation deserted me, along it seemed with my ability to breathe. Lungs wheezing in the parched air I abandoned any thoughts of a longer ride on to Dinsmore, diverting instead to the nearer town of Beechy.

Rolling up to one of the only buildings, a handy pub, I sank gratefully into a booth and ordered a cold beer. It went down like nectar. I knew then I wasn't moving from that spot.

The rather dubious directions from various locals appeared to indicate that there may be a community campground on top of a large hill outside town, although there was much disagreement over whether the town even had a campground anymore? That question mark settled it and Tom and I agreed to share one of the pub's suspiciously cheap bedrooms for the night.

In hindsight, open-air may have been a better option and the accommodation did much to support that old adage – 'you get what you pay for'. In this case a tiny, airless furnace. The beds were unaired and unmade and looked like they may have had their heyday some 40 or more years before.

I genuinely considered sleeping on the floor as the more savoury option, it was only the state of the carpet however which persuaded against this.

At least the shower worked! Afterwards, a small kitchenette provided a microwave and a toaster, which in turn produced beans on toast, whilst a few more beers added some much needed anaesthesia.
My no bed sharing rule had been ejected in favour of economy with predictable results, including grumpiness at my lack of judgement and lack of solitude.

More predictably, another hot, stuffy, sleepless night followed.

Day 41: Beechy to Eston: 84 miles

A very early 7am start was helped along slightly by strong tea and more microwaved beans (doing my bit for emissions).

The day was distinctly greyer but mercifully cooler than yesterday, much of the light seeming to have been leached from the sky, dampening the sun's previous enthusiasm.
As the gradually more undulating hills flowed under Claud's tyres I was thankful my lungs seemed to have recovered from yesterday, I was enjoying the ride again.
The landscape had also become less arid as marshier, large puddles of standing water formed pop-up lakes bizarrely sporting flocks of ducks. It was beginning to remind me quite surreally of Lake Superior, perhaps I was still stuck in Ontario and the prairies had just been a bizarre dream?!

Lunch, after 60km, was decided by a giant white polar bear which loomed up suddenly at the roadside, the obvious thing to find in the middle of such a green landscape! The aptly named White Bear, again like so many settlements before it, at first appeared to be a ghost town although on closer inspection the local pub was not only open, it was also serving up a very decent lunch, even if there were no other customers.

It was slightly strange being the only occupant there (Tom having ridden on ahead) but I was getting used to it and it certainly didn't stop me polishing off my burger, despite the dower gaze from an array of stuffed and mounted animal heads. A particularly suspicious deer seemed to have eyes which followed my every move.

Heading out again after lunch the wind was there waiting like a malevolent shadow. All too frustratingly the map in my bar bag confirmed what I could already feel, I was heading due west now, straight in to the full force of a headwind.
My eyes didn't leave the map as I crawled millimetre by millimetre across the page, all focus on the few turns in the road which would hopefully provide at least a little respite.
After an hour or so of slow grind I took a small break in the town of Tyner where I met Tara, who, as it turns out, was the town's sole occupant. Apparently the population occasionally doubled when her son came to visit but apart from that she had the place all to herself so was quite glad of the company, however brief.
Break over, after devouring the rest of my burger from lunch, it was off again, this time to be faced down by the most monster-sized hill.

I could actually see it looming on the horizon a good few miles off but had stubbornly refused to believe it to be anything but a mirage.
I was wrong.
Faced with this behemoth and the still roaring winds I felt like crying, I truly thought I'd finally reached my limit. Always waiting in the wings of my consciousness, the ever present doubts now gleefully leapt in. How could I reach the top of something that was near vertical? And if I couldn't do that, how could I even consider climbing mountains in

the Rockies if I can't ride up a hill on the prairies? My confidence and energy were haemorrhaging fast.

What I needed was an incentive, a motivator powerful enough to help reach the top. Bribing myself with food or beer wasn't going to cut this one, it needed the big guns and then it struck me, it wasn't a what, it was a whom?
People, specifically the ones in the world I would most dearly like to see right now.
I began imagining. I imagined my beautiful sister, family, friends, loved ones all waiting patiently for me at the crest of the hill. When I made it up to the top we'd have the biggest reunion ever, the chance to talk, laugh, to hug all those whom I miss so much on a daily basis.
It's hard to fully describe the power of this thought I could visualise these people all so strongly, so much so that I fairly flew up that hill with anticipation, only to be unbearably heart-sore when, on getting to the summit, I don't actually find them there.
But they got me through and I learned then that thinking of them was a most powerful gift to possess.

The final 20km stretch to the town of Easton was covered by sheer bloody-mindedness and the fact that I'd agreed to meet Tom there having separated much earlier in the day.
Finally rolling into the town with barely enough strength to turn the pedals I spotted him sat on a bench outside a gas station. Practically falling off the bike I collapsed on the seat to gain back some strength, only slightly heartened to hear that he'd struggled just as much as me.

Half-heartedly pulling up at the local grocery store we were approached by a guy on a Harley motorbike. All leather jerkin, tattoos and attitude, his swaggering approach looked ominously like the precursor to running us out of town. Like I had the energy to move another step!
Planting his large, leather booted feet directly in front of us, legs apart he stood like a hairy colossus sizing up the two puny cyclists. Opening

his mouth to speak, I waited tiredly for the command to move on, however it never came.

"You look like you really want the camp ground, it's close by but tricky to find, let me show you where it is."

Gosh, wasn't expecting that. Too tired and stunned to speak we meekly followed Ron, our new guide, who chatted away as he led us the slightly convoluted route to the site. Leaving us pitching the tents he returned barely 10 minutes later, his young daughter in tow, with a huge bag of fresh produce for us from his garden.

Yet again, such unsolicited kindness was almost overwhelming. Waving away our thanks he roared off up the road leaving us to take full advantage of this unexpected windfall. The greens especially made a welcome addition that night to palettes jaded by too much convenient junk food.

Crawling into the tent after dinner I reflected on the day, a tough one and a testing one for sure but a good cycle and a not so shabby 83 miles.

The countryside is also getting more interesting again as the prairies are roughening up. I hadn't quite realised how much I missed the variations in scenery from other provinces.

Now, sleep would be nice.

Day 42:   Eston to Alsask: 70 miles

Hallelujah, an amazing night's sleep, I'd almost forgotten what it was like. Heading out on my own I celebrated accordingly with breakfast on the road in a little diner and then splashing out on lunch at a café in Estonia. Even the very grumpy waitress who charged me $10 for hot chips and gravy still couldn't put a dent in my spirits and by the end of the day I rolled in to the provincial border town of Alsask feeling really damn good.

The sky didn't see fit to match my sunny spirits however and was now a dark, foreboding grey as I hurried to pitch my tent ahead of what felt suspiciously like a massive storm. The eerie grey light prompted me to set up camp in record time.

Just as I was heading towards my 3rd diner of the day a couple of cycle tourists rolled up, two young college girls on bikes who were touring the province on their summer break, they also looked really, really tired. We exchanged the usual pleasantries and route information before I headed off to the warmth of the diner which turned out to have a really friendly waitress and some excellent Chinese food.

Stuffed, dry and warm I lingered in this little oasis as long as I could before heading out into the car park, saying good night to the waitress who was getting out of her car. She look confused, even more so when I complemented her on the delicious food.
Now I know I may not have the most memorable of faces, but as one of the only customers that night I was really surprised when she looked at me blankly. One of us must be going mad surely?
The situation resolved itself just a few moments later as the woman's doppelgänger emerged from the diner, still in waitress uniform. Turns out this identical twin was there to pick up her sister from work. As you can imagine, not the first case of mistaken identity for these ladies but it made me giggle all the way back to the tent.
Also turns out that was the last laugh of the night.

Day 43   Alsask to Cactus Corner Services: 83 miles

The storm hit somewhere around midnight, lashing rain and winds which made the trees under which I'd pitched seem like a less than great decision. Sleep, with the cracking of branches and flashing of lightning all around, was an elusive thing.

My usual start to the day followed just as predictably as, tired and grumpy, I packed up my soggy belongings preparing to hit the road.
Sticking my 4th Provincial flag on to Claud's mudguard did lift my spirits slightly as we rolled past the boundary sign into Alberta,

however it was a damp and subdued cavalcade which headed out that morning, consisting of myself, Tom and the 2 college-girl cyclists from the campsite.

Soon, Tom and the one of the girls were pulling away in front. My body was stuck in slow mode after so little sleep but unfortunately that competitive streak just wouldn't keep quiet.

I began pushing myself, riding harder than faster than I knew was wise. Predictably my lungs began to complain, an asthma attack lurking in every pedal stroke, then, to top it off I heard that tell-tale hisssss-ing sound that makes the heart of every cyclist sink into the road.

A front puncture. Tom hovered around but my pride wouldn't let him near so I imperiously ordered them all on, I didn't need them anyway. Sitting by the side of the road watching them go I struggled to hide annoying tears of tired frustration and to get my wheezing breathing under control. For me, tears always herald the start of an asthma bout, with the wheezing soon turning to being winded. If you've ever had the breath knocked from your body by a fall you'll recognise that feeling of desperately trying to re-inflate your lungs and replace the air whilst feeling like you're suffocating. The inhaler means I'm fine but my chest always feels like it's been in a fight afterwards.

Breathing under control and puncture changed, the road ahead is clear and I begin to settle, the emotional tempest subsiding for now. This was how I liked it, no pressure of keeping up with the pack, no one to interrupt my flow.

Head down, lungs like a vice I plough on. But the crying jags which accompanied the asthma continue, not helped by the rotten night's sleep and I feel like an emotionally exhausted wreck.

As is the way of the world when feeling like that I also started analysing my time with Tom.

Going off on one……:

There is always a delight for me in getting to know someone, finding out about their lives, loves and likes, why they're on the journey they're on. With Tom it had also been an exaggeratedly accelerated experience, a friendship developing in the super-compressed, supercharged environment of cycling and camping, mushrooming under the huge expenditure of energy and heightened emotions.

I remembered Thunder Bay Dan talking about that extreme connection forged under trauma. Of course cycling is no bear attack but, sharing such big highs and lows has certainly forged a relationship quicker than a few nights down the pub. I wonder, not for the first time, if, under any other circumstances we would ever have been friends?

Tom was/is a city boy from London, working in the capital and embracing all that the lifestyle entailed from partying to promiscuity, a life of money, fashion, possessions, having the right labels, friends, a life of easy loss and easy gain.

In so many ways it completely the opposite of how I live, what I value. My career, for instance has always centred around those areas of society that people would rather ignore, addiction, mental illness, homelessness, working with people for whom life is a daily struggle. No bling, no labels and definitely no money at the sharp end of social care.

Whilst my dress sense also appalled Tom, his made me laugh. At home I loved nothing more than charity shop apparel, Tom anything that was labelled, on trend and as far from a thrift store as it was possible to get, I called him the fashion victim, he called me a hippy.

Our opinions too differed as much as our clothing. My views can probably be summed up as to the left of liberal, in my work you can see the best and the worst of humanity, sometimes in the same day. Those strong, starchy, entrenched views I held in my teens and twenties have long since softened and flexed into the general mantra of 'who am I to judge?'

Tom on the other hand, still wore that arrogance of youth and comfort on his well labelled sleeve. Life thus far had provided him little exposure to anything away from middle class suburbia and city excess. There were noticeably increasing incidences where I found his black and white judgements on issues both naïve and infuriating.

Maybe only time and experience can soften those edges, I certainly couldn't, and we'd begun to butt heads more and more as his harder views met my more liberal ones.

Despite increasing tensions and on a lighter note, there was one place where our differences were more comically apparent and that was in our gear for the trip.

Me: bike, tent and most equipment bought for a song from thrift stores or online second hand sites, picked up on route or donated by friends, a montage of colour, brand and style.

Tom: Matching top range panniers, high end clothing, tent, camping equipment and technology.

But the funniest thing – when equipment broke, tore or ceased to work, guess whose it was, certainly not mine. There's a lot to be said for thrift.

All of this churns in my head as I surge along. I'm angry as I chew over the above. Why am I still riding with someone with whom I have so little in common, especially as we both seem to annoy the hell out of each other.

The benefit of all this navel gazing is that I don't notice the miles pass by. Suddenly it's nearly 3pm and more than time for lunch. I'm passing Youngstown so I decide to pull in and who do I see lounging at a picnic table outside the convenience store. Tom. And annoyingly, I'm surprisingly pleased to see him. He's actually been concerned at what kept me and I explain about the lengthy puncture repair and rubbish breathing, omitting the internal monologue.

Chatting away, the fug of the day lifts somewhat and we head off together after a break, cycling at a relaxed pace, banter flying. It's suddenly ok again.

Noticing the world around me for the first time that day I see that the highway has gotten busier and worryingly, the shoulder has gotten smaller. And smaller. And smaller, until it's mere inches wide. Cars and lorries are thundering past now and there's seemingly no escape.

It takes a great deal of concentration to stay upright and safe, balanced on a knife edge between roaring trucks and a precipitous drop verge until the final shreds of my energy trickle away. It's been a long, emotionally and physically tough day.

This morning I'd been hoping to reach the small town of Hanna but just a few miles short a rest area and truck stop with attached services loom and I pull in with gratitude.

Enough.

With a tidy, free camping area alongside the services I pitch my tent in record time and head into the truckers' lounge for warmth and food.

Taking advantage of the comfy dining chairs, electricity and free Wi-Fi I treat myself to the largest slice of sponge cake on the planet and a glass of red wine. As the day blurs around the edges so too do the doubts and the discomfort. A good end it seems to a rather shit day.

Day 44: Cactus Corner Services to Drumheller: 60 miles

Despite yesterday's 80 miles and utter exhaustion, sleep did not want to be my friend. I wake up at 2.30am and that's it. By 3.30am I give up, crawl out the tent to go back into the (thankfully 24 hour) services. The highlight of this is an unexpected and much needed Skype chat with Emma helping to put into perspective a little the previous 24 hours. Two hours later I finally head back to my sleeping bag to wring out a couple more minutes of shut-eye before the encroaching dawn.

Seven a.m. and my body is poleaxed with sleep, or rather from the lack of it. That's it though, there's no more to be had so I lever my protesting body out of bed and start packing, getting a vicious stab of pleasure from Tom scrambling bleary eyed out of his tent in a panic as he hears the sound of my deflating air bed being packed. He doesn't want to be left behind it seems!

19 km of road later we pull into the small town of Hanna for breakfast.

Maybe it was the name, reminding me of a friend, but the feelings of home-sickness were stirring in my gut, especially after that long conversation with Emma last night. Still feeling the physical and emotional effects of yesterday I needed a pick me up.
It arrived in the form of Harry's cafe, primarily chosen after cycling loops of the town looking for somewhere, anywhere that was open.

The eponymous Harry, owner and name giver was a sardonic man, initially of few words, his gruff no nonsense approach to ordering appeared to brook no discussion and no menu.
Sit down, tell me what you want, nothing fancy.
Ooooh-kay!
It turned out though that Harry enjoyed a bit of banter, especially with two cycle tourists of the world (who were very gullible). As we warmed to each other Harry was especially pleased to learn where we were headed that day, the famous Drumheller, land of dinosaur remains and somewhere I've been really excited about seeing (I know there won't be real dinosaurs).
Harry really got in to his stride showing us photos of a family trip, although with each picture little fantasy-busting warning bells started to ring, the place looked more 'tacky theme park' than Jurassic-park. Surely this was just the kid's part, not the real dinosaur bit? Burying my head in sand (honestly, I know there won't be real dinosaurs) I listened, looked, thanked Harry and prepared to leave. As we were heading out Harry caught us up and thrust a bag of home-made muffins into my hand. For the journey he said gruffly. I was incredibly touched.

Heading off, Tom was grumpy, stemming from my making conversation with strangers and delaying things it seemed. I reminded him he was free to go without me.
I take an interest in people and I can't help it but, as ever, that politeness means I also find it very hard to cut off a conversation and

walk away if someone is mid flow. This can be both difficult and wonderful. When you feel someone is truly listening to you it can be the most fundamental of human experiences and connections. Everyone has a few stories, at the very least, to share and I'm genuinely fascinated. In so many ways that is what this trip constantly unearths like hidden gem stones, people; amazing, friendly people who give you both kindness and a small window into their lives.

Oddly this sociability was born from an acute shyness. As a teenager I was terrified when faced with a group of people or even one-on-one and used to clam up in all but the closest company. To tackle this I developed the habit of encouraging the person/people I was with to talk about themselves.
Find the things they were interested in, passionate about, and people will talk for hours leaving me free to listen and not lead. Instant conversation, shyness solved.
It's a trait that's served me well both in work and socially but can sometimes backfire if I get stuck with a conversationalist who doesn't draw breath, or, as I've found on occasions, if someone reads more in to the attention than friendly interest.

Over the years though I've met some truly amazing people, I'm astounded as rich seams of personal history have been shared and friendships formed. It's been a huge part of my work for many years too, this listening, understanding, the teasing out of information. In many ways I do it well as it suits who I am. Too well according to Tom.

But, back to the dinosaurs, like small children we had both been childishly excited about visiting the dinosaur isle. The photos had put a bit of a crimp in that, seemingly revealing Drumheller's dinosaurs as a more brazen bunch, a plastic T-Rex behind every diner, pterodactyls lurking in trees.
Enthusiasm for the dinosaur quest remained mostly undiminished however and heading down Highway 9 on a beautiful sunny day, food

in my belly and the world was again a glorious place, or at least it would be without the usual cow of a headwind.

At Delia a sign from the highway for a tea shop quickly persuaded us to turn off in the dual hope of cake and a bit of (head) wind relief. A few miles later however and no tea shop was apparent, anywhere.
I finally found someone to ask at the only place that wasn't shut up tight, a local store in a hamlet of a dozen houses. As it turns out the tea shop was most definitely shut.
Mourning the lack of tea and cake we debated the possible routes. Backtrack to the windy number 9 or... A friendly customer tuned into our conversation and sure enough asked the usual, "where were we headed", Drumheller, "well why not just carry on on this road" he said, "not only was it prettier, but a shorter route and nearly flat with just one small hill".
Why oh why didn't alarm bells ring?! A quick map consultation seemed to show it as longer but what did the cartographers know, surely local knowledge trumped a piece of paper? Fortified with chocolate bars and faith in this local sage we headed back out.

The road was indeed pretty and dramatic, wide open vistas punctuated by sheep, bushes and fields of corn rippling wave-like to merge with the horizon like a golden ocean. A shepherds' hut leaned in to the wind at a crazy angle, like us, braced against the gale, beaten but not subdued. The road was also most definitely going steeply uphill.

In the blazing midday sun we sweated upwards, stopping every now and then to breathe and take pictures whilst we seemed to be winding up the side of a mountainous rocky peak. It was well over an hour later when sweating and scorched, we gratefully reached the summit, walked into a field of corn and collapsed under its tall stems.
I was tired but elated. Hill done I lay back and looked at the blue, cloudless sky framed by a tunnel of corn stalks towering above me and filtering the golden light. It was one of those unreal time-out moments, like sitting on that highway in to Winnipeg. Those, 'My god

this is me, now, having an adventure' moments when my life in England seems a thousand years past.

Leaving the vague shelter of the corn stalks and back into the furnace of sun, I was at least now anticipating a downhill run into Drumheller. The guy back at the store had said just the one hill right…?
As the hours wore on I realised how wrong he was. That one hill turned into 3 which then turned into several more, all the time the road shimmering like liquid in the heat. Even better, we were heading back into the wind.
It eventually transpired that an extra 15km had been added by taking the detour from Delia and goodness knows how many more feet of climbing. The thought that kept me going though, it would be worth it for the dinosaurs.

As Claud slouched along I also noticed an odd feeling in my back wheel. To be fair it had been present for the last few days but I'd been managing to ignore it or put it down to the unkempt highway. There was no denying now though, it was definitely worsening and there was a distinct lurch which produced a swaying movement when I rode.
The spokes were also beginning to work themselves loose, so much so that I needed to stop every few hours to tighten them. My lack of mechanical experience meant there was no finesse when doing this, I just tightened loose bits. Unbeknownst to me, all this tightening in fact was making things worse, pulling the wheel more and more out of shape and exaggerating the buckle.
I cycled on obliviously.

After what felt like forever the road finally started to descend, leaving the grass plains and plunging down through sheer, craggy rock faces of long abandoned quarries. All very atmospheric, the stark colours and raw vista just oozed prehistoric. Racing downhill finally I burst from the last descent through a steep, jagged valley into the flat and very modern-looking town of Drumheller.
Parched beyond reason I stopped at the nearest shop to drink them

dry of slushies. Never a good choice when thirsty as severe brain freeze set in almost immediately precluding drinking. The slushie-fest went something like gulp, ouch, gulp, yowl.

Next task was to find a campsite. It seemed the only one in town was a tired affair although we both got the shock of our lives at the price, $33 per person!!
The instinct to say 'stuff that' was overwhelming, I was dog tired and hungry but really, that was a crazy price. We cycled on, seeking out the tourist information centre for further inspiration only to find it closed until late afternoon.
So, for the next hours or so we explored Drumheller. I don't know what I'd expected in the way of dinosaurs, obviously not the real thing but….. I couldn't help nursing a severe sense of disappointment. The main square itself held a few garish fibreglass replicas (congruent with Harry's photos) which reminded me of the sad, weather beaten models from run down seaside resorts back home.
The largest, most impressive, a tyrannosaurus, at least boasted the chance to climb up inside – usually- but today a sign blocked the staircase saying 'Closed for repairs'. Also closed was the dinosaur museum. Spot the theme.
After finally getting into the tourist office we were regretfully informed that there was indeed just the one camping option in town and with the town squeezed into the only flat plateau in the valley, spare land seemed non-existent, putting paid to wild camping. Tired and pissed off we retreated to the campsite and paid fees.
To add insult to injury there was even an extra charge for the showers. I didn't like Drumheller.

It was in an extremely bad mood that evening that I cycled back into town for dinner. Parking Claud behind a local pub I got chatting to one of the staff, Les, who taking his break there.
Les, in true Canadian style was really friendly and really interested to hear about the trip and we chatted for a good while before I gave up on the idea of walking any further and just headed inside after him.

It turned out to be a good call. After a great dinner in the pub, a few games of pool and some very agreeable orange citrus beer I dragged my tired body and bike back to the tent.

By this time I was recognising the need for a long rest and a few days off but was also conscious of the fact I had a place to stay lined up in Calgary and, due to a family wedding, they could only host me if I got there the day after tomorrow. This meant a 140km ride (at least) in 2 days and, given the current terrain, goodness knows what the hills were going to be like over that.

Oh well, that was tomorrow's problem.

Day 45: Drumheller to Beiseker: 42 miles

Hurrah, finally I slept well, bizarrely lulled to sleep by a weird rocking sensation caused, not by beer, but by the dodgy bike wheel. You know that feeling you get when you step off a long boat trip on to dry land and your body still sways? It seems that buckled wheels can have the same disconcerting effect.

After a long lazy start and a lot of time with the bike upside down trying to fix the wheel it was nearly midday when we pulled out of the campsite. Claud continued his lurching progress as I bid farewell to the plastic monsters and shut up shops. Cycling past Les's pub I couldn't resist popping in to say goodbye....and maybe for some more of that citrus beer and, whilst I was at it, it seemed sensible to have a bit of lunch too.

Les was pleased to see Tom and I and enthusiastically introduced us to all the other staff. After a great lunch we were approached by the owner of the pub whom Les had told all about the trip, much to our astonishment he told us that lunch was on the house, a gesture I was really moved by.

An hour or so later and a few more glasses of beer, I now absolutely didn't want to cycle, but Calgary beckoned and if I didn't leave now it would mean covering 140km in one day the thought of which was not a happy one.

Bidding farewell to Les I reluctantly headed out into the blazing afternoon sun, finally questioning the wisdom of such a late start, especially when immediately on leaving town I was faced with a huge hill. My heart sank as I faced the prospect of that long, long climb out of the valley which I'd so happily whizzed down into yesterday, all in temperatures that would melt steel.

Sweating and swearing, less than half an hour later Tom was already pulling ahead when I heard that familiar hissing sound.
The buckled back wheel had punctured. Wearily I pulled into the side of the road and begun unloading my stuff. Tom, unaware I had stopped and with no way for me to tell him, disappeared over the brow of the next hill and was gone.
Inner tube changed with relative ease I then hit a snag, I just couldn't get the back wheel back on. No matter how I manoeuvred it nothing worked. Because it was so bent out of shape it now wouldn't sit in the forks without pushing up hard against the brakes. With nothing in my tool bag to help I was just contemplating the long walk back to Drumheller when, from over the crest of the hill came a Landrover, one of the first cars I'd seen in a while. And miracle of miracles it seemed to be pulling over.

Enter Kees and Marcia, two Dutch travellers who, even more miraculously, also had a substantial tool kit and an even better knowledge of bike maintenance. Whilst I chatted to Marcia, Kees took charge, levering the tyre in to place, adjusting the gears and the brakes. He also pointed out the now very obvious wheel buckle which had impeded my putting it back on without tools.
Oh dear! It was however with huge gratitude that I waved my roadside-guardian angels goodbye, with equal promises to email them that I'd arrived safely in Calgary.

Thank you Universe.

Now however I find myself just a few measly miles into my journey and with the afternoon shadows drawing in I needed to pedal and fast. With no bike lights I didn't want to be on the road after nightfall and there were a good 30+ miles still to cover.

As the afternoon dragged on the hills kept rolling up at me. I half expected/hoped to find Tom on one of them as my motivation was flagging, but no, each solitary crest came and went with barely a car, let alone a cyclist in sight.

The setting sun bathed the rocky landscape and fields in a russet-golden glow, but the spectacular sunset was tempered by the number of miles still left to cover.

As the light faded I was alone in the dusky gloom on what appeared to be a particularly deserted route, especially when a damp, chilly mist began to descend, the heat of the day suddenly giving way to a surprisingly cold night.

In the fields either side of me I could hear, and occasionally see huge farm machinery rear up out of the murk. The odd car that did pass did so suddenly, leaping upon me out of a fog that was now so thick I couldn't see more than a few yards. Of course I should have had bike lights but I didn't (or rather I did, but no batteries). I hadn't expected to be night riding.

The cold affected my breathing too, as well as the growing sense of fear the familiar wheeze and ache in my chest reappeared.

It was at this point, for some reason, I really wanted to talk to my mum. This may not seem especially strange but for me that maternal relationship has never been a close or a comfortable one, we're both too similar (stubborn) and too different to ever be great friends.

On occasion I've thought wistfully about it but it's not how things are. Here though, now, that childish instinct was bizarrely strong, I wanted her with me and I began making promises to the sky gods, that when (and if) I was safe I would make more of an effort to build that relationship. Bargaining with the universe of sorts.

It was a very cold, scared cyclist who finally pulled into to the Beiseker campground that night, breath coming in gasps and wheezes.

The campsite attendant pointed out the tent area and lo and behold, who was pitched there under the light, Tom. Was I glad to see a friendly face!

It also turned out he'd been really worried. Having realised I'd dropped back he pulled over at a lay-by a few miles further on, however when I didn't show up he started to get concerned. Finally, in desperation he'd leapt into the road to flag down a passing car. It transpired that yes, they had seen the cyclist in a skirt being assisted roadside by two motorists. Reassured, he'd cycled on but hadn't realised how long the repairs would take and how far behind I'd got.

After catching up on our journeys Tom gallantly went to organise some food for dinner which we cooked and ate huddled in his tent against the cold. We then said our final goodbyes before heading for bed. Tomorrow I would be leaving early for Calgary which Tom would bypass; his plan was to skirt the city and go straight towards the Rocky Mountains. With my city stop I wouldn't reach the Rockies for a good few days yet so my journey would finally diverge from his.

I couldn't avoid the city either, today had shown me that Claud was in need of some serious attention and the best place for that was a large town.

Falling asleep that night it was the old, familiar mix of sadness at saying goodbye to a friend, fear at being on my own again and exhilaration at the same time. All accompanied by the gentle rocking of that buckled wheel.

Day 46:   Beiseker to Calgary: 49 miles

I'm on the road by 8am hoping to make Calgary and more importantly the bike shop by early afternoon.

The sun is out and warming the overnight chill from the fields and my bones as Claud's bent wheel bobs along transcribing a funny little shimmy with every rotation
I find myself enjoying the solitude again and that feeling of freedom and possibility. Alberta is rapidly becoming more built up as I head towards its capital city, the sparse hamlets leading into neat, prosperous farms and clusters of new-looking houses.
The influence of the oil industry and its money is everywhere from the drills silhouetted against the skyline to the wealthy-looking horse ranches and advertisements for shopping malls that I pass.

My plan had been to cycle into the city on smaller roads, avoiding the heavy traffic of previous towns. Taking a break at a quirky 50's diner/caboose around mid-morning I decided to sound out the locals for advice on how to reach the city.
After much discussion and disagreement they settled upon a route called the Stoney Trail, quiet and bike friendly apparently, it sounded perfect. In my head this trail was a delightful, shady, tree-lined cycleway on which I would arrive with ease away from exhaust fumes and large vehicles. Lost in my idyll I pedalled onwards.
Now, either I took a wrong turn somewhere or the serene version of Stoney Trail had only existed around the time of the pioneers, after which, some bright spark had whimsically decided to name a FUCK-OFF-GREAT-BIG-SUPER-HIGHWAY after it.

Going west into the city, following this ring road was an experience that knocked all the others into a different galaxy.
A full six lanes of speeding traffic thundered past me as I wobbled my way down what appeared to be the hard shoulder of a giant motorway. Worse still was the life endangering task of negotiating the exit and

entrance ramps down which huge articulated trucks hurtled to join or leave this speeding mass of traffic.

In desperation I began to throw Claud kamikaze style across the end of each slip-way, teeth gritted and praying to any and all gods that I'd make the 'relative' safety of the next bit of shoulder. Claud's back wheel now wobbled uncontrollably, my nerves shattered, body jangling like bag of broken glass. Stretched to breaking point I finally reached my 16th Avenue turn off and headed west into a whole different set of problems.

The avenue was only slightly quieter and dominated almost exclusively by huge, impatient 4x4s. This time though there was no shoulder, just an uneven strip where road met sidewalk, punctuated by potholes and manhole covers.
Fending off wing mirrors as trucks determinedly squeezed me against the kerb I cycled on blindly through huge intersections, up and down steep, seething streets until, when I was beginning to give up all hope, I at last spotted my turn off.
I was shaking when I finally began to leave the main city behind, winding my way through the mercifully quieter residential streets. Somehow I'd managed to cycle right across town, through the heart. It may have been the most direct route but it nearly gave me heart failure and a few too many close calls.

I literally wobbled right into the bike shop and deposited Claud on the floor where the staff looked less than thrilled at the sweaty, grimy cyclist and bike in their midst.
A long chat with the mechanic and he began to thaw a little as he was briefed on Claud's long list of ailments and, in deference to my ailing finances he agreed to repair/rebuild where possible. With Claud now in good hands I begged use of the shop phone to call my host for that evening to let him know I'd arrived.

David

I could write reams and still fail miserably to describe my next host. Funnily enough, how I ended up staying at all was a combination of the most bizarre set of circumstances.

David was the cousin of John. John was a random stranger I had met briefly in Toronto a few weeks earlier whilst waiting at some traffic lights on Claud.
John and I had got chatting, he too was cycling, and he wound up offering to take me on a tour of the city. A pleasant afternoon and neighbourhood tour followed after which we met up the following evening for dinner at a beautiful sushi restaurant to swap stories. During the meal we'd talked about my planned trip and John's previous tours, organised forays in France with luggage transfers and 3 course lunches. His was a definite world of comfort over adventure and I think he was both genuinely horrified and taken with my intentions.

On parting that night we had vaguely agreed to keep in touch in the way that you do when passing through a place and as the weeks progressed we'd swapped the odd email. I was especially heartened to learn some of that spirit of adventure must have rubbed off on him at dinner as, not long afterwards, he'd made a foray both out of his comfort zone and out of the city for the first time ever, retracing my first day to East Caledon to visit friends. Good for him.
As it turned out John also had a cousin in Calgary whom he'd agreed to contact on my behalf if I ever needed a place to stay. I did and here I was.

As I waited outside the bike shop I knew nothing about John's cousin David except that he was retired civil servant living with his wife in the outskirts of the city and that they were willing to house a complete stranger for a night or two!

I was often asked if I was ever worried about staying with strangers but so many good experiences had given me a sense of security. Ironically John had been full of doom and gloom about the world and its many evils but so far Canada had proved him wrong. David as it would turn out was no exception.

David pulled into the parking lot in a huge truck-type minivan and a squeal of tyres. On the phone he'd instructed me to meet him at the car, matter-of-factly stating it was easier not to faff around getting out due to the wheelchair. Had no one told me he was tetraplegic? Stunned is probably an understatement.
On the drive home David was highly amused that John had neglected to mention this and proceeded to tell me briefly, and equally matter-of-factly how, in his late teens he'd been life-changingly injured in a sporting accident.
This constant stream of narrative was also interspersed between dinner plans and exclamations of delight at my adventures so far. He was an unstoppable force and I felt instantly at ease.

Home was a large, modern house beautifully furnished and entirely accessible. David wasted no time instructing me how to help retrieve his wheelchair from the back of the car before using a system of lifts and ramps to access the main house. Heading inside we were enthusiastically greeted by Garbo a boisterous, poodle type mop of dog who joined in with gusto whilst David took me on a quick tour of the house before showing me to my room.
A huge comfy looking bed beckoned but I resisted. Prioritizing a shower and laundry and feeling my human-ness return, I took my tent and sleeping bag outside to dry off. I am always acutely aware of how sweaty and smelly I must seem to others; on the bike I don't notice but, in polite company and lovely surroundings, I sometimes find myself trying to hold my own breath and stand downwind.

Cleaned and scrubbed, David was waiting for me in the garden and I soon succumbed to a comfy sun-lounger and glass of wine. Chatting away I found I was enjoying myself immensely.

David's wife Sarah joined us soon after and we all trooped off to a sushi restaurant – booked after David had consulted John on my food preferences. A family friend came too to make an enjoyable little party. However, as hard as I tried to make intelligent/coherent conversation the day's adrenalin had caught up with me and my tired brain could add little to the evening.

The big comfy bed beckoned but before falling asleep I marvelled again at how my surroundings and my comfort changed from hour to hour. From last night's dark, dank battle from Drumheller, through today's awful, crazy highway and run into the city today to the womb-like comfort, peace and luxury of kind strangers.

Day 47   Calgary: 0 miles

The joy of a long lie in and a great breakfast was tempered somewhat by a phone call from the bike shop. Claud, it seemed, was not a happy bicycle. In fact he was going to need quite a bit of work before he was back on the road again including a new back wheel, 2 new tyres, both being filled with glass shards (that explains the punctures) and new front bearings, somewhere in the region of $260.

Considering what I'd asked a $100 (£60) bike from eBay to do so far – just over 2500 miles to be precise- this wasn't entirely unexpected or unreasonable, but I still had a little knot of dread at the cost and my rapidly diminishing finances.

Sadly, there was no question that it needed doing so, whilst the bike shop started work on the job, David took the opportunity to introduce me to downtown Calgary, in particular to visit a charity which helps those with spinal cord injuries and with which he was actively involved. The charity has its headquarters in Calgary and David was keen to visit their newly funded rehab gym. The staff there are hugely friendly and welcoming and I found myself fending off questions about the trip in favour of learning more about their work there.

Over the next hour I was treated to a whistle-stop tour of all the centre had on offer and how it supported those who'd experienced life changing spinal injuries.

Listening to explanations of the slow, painful rehabilitation of limbs it struck me, not for the first time since meeting David, at how incredibly lucky I was, to have the ability to travel. At least my legs could feel that ache from over work, I took the fact that I could move so much for granted. I guess that we all do, but it's situations like this that bring that fortune home; a reminder of how life can change on the flip of a coin. It's difficult to write about it without sounding trite but a large part of this trip has been about meeting different people and glimpsing, just a fraction, those lives they live.

I was reminded too of James my previous host all the way back in Manatoulin, Ontario. Two individuals, four provinces apart for whom life had dealt that specific all-changing moment. Two individuals who had picked themselves up from these seemingly knock-out blows and, rather than throwing in the towel, had gotten back in the ring for another round, throwing themselves into their lives and their communities, fearsome and fearless fighters.

After the rehab centre the next stop was to buy new tyres – not for Claud but for the wheelchair. As I compared tread and tyre pressures with the sales staff I'd realised I'd never thought about wheelchairs getting punctures before, but wheels, are wheels however they are ridden or driven, it was yet another eye opener. David even insisted I try out his spare chair that had just been fixed – a road test. It's a very surreal feeling sitting in a wheelchair when you don't need to and it felt very disquieting in a way I can't quite put my finger on, almost like a nose-thumbing to fate whom I didn't want to antagonise, especially at present.

But boy, just those few short minutes in the chair served to give just a tiny insight into all the many challenges a permanent residence could throw up, innocuous things such as doorways, conversations and of course punctures all took on a new degree of challenge.

I was ashamedly relieved to get out of the chair and with no small sense of luck that I could just stand up and walk away. It was a thought-provoking experience however and one that will remain with me for a long time.

Released from the frigid air conditioning of the shop back out to the blazing sunshine, one more chore remained, to drive to the bike shop to collect Claud.

The mechanics had done an outstanding job. Riding round the car park it was wonderful not to wobble around all over the place – 2 round wheels made for a very smooth ride, as did the new, ultra-sexy and tough Schwalbe Marathon Plus tyres with, I was informed, kevlar puncture resistant technology. We shall see!

Returning from my test ride I went to pay the bill only to find there wasn't one. My hosts, it seemed, had taken it upon themselves to make my trip as easy (and as memorable) as possible. I was speechless as this most generous act.

I tried, unsuccessfully over the next hour or so to gently refuse this too generous a gift however my hosts were equally as stubborn as I.

All I could do is promise myself that one day I would pay-forward their kindness.

A lovely dinner with Sarah and David that evening was followed by an earlyish night in preparation for heading off the next day.

Again, as with so many hosts, it would have been lovely to linger, to talk more and share stories about life in all its forms but they had guests arriving for a family wedding the next day and me, I had some mountains to get to. I'd glimpsed the tantalising foothills of the Rockies on my way in to Calgary and I was eager to reach them.

The pull of those mountains was upon me and my feet were twitching after a day of rest. Time to roll away on those puncture resistant wheels.

Regina to Calgary in pictures

Province number 4

Dinosaurs in Drumheller

Strong winds hereabouts

Not much to cycle on

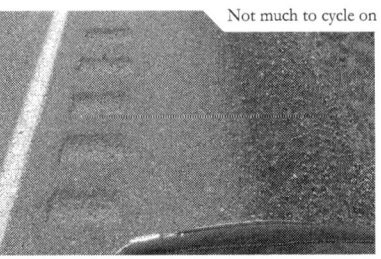

Too much to cycle on

Going into the canyon

Regina to Calgary in pictures

Rear view

Shadow cycle

More creative sandwiching

Waiting for the Riverhurst ferry

Graffiti train

Just the one eyebrow

Polar bear territory

Descent to Drumheller

Calgary to Vancouver

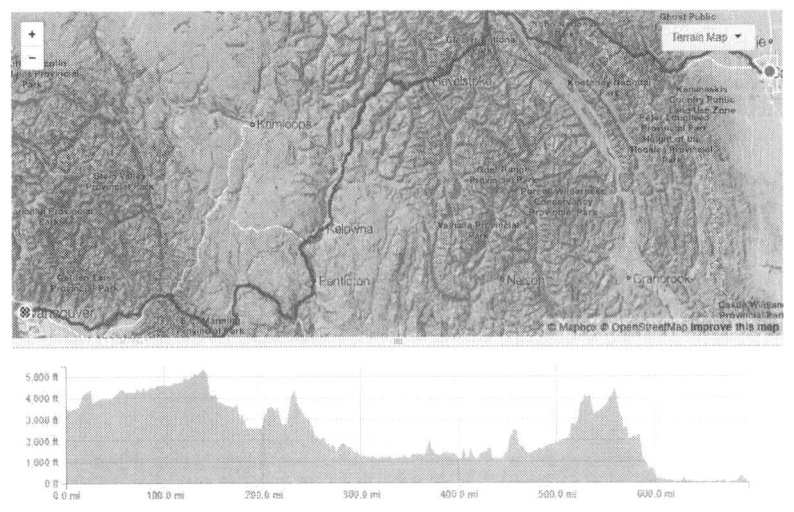

Courtesy of Strava mapping.

Day 48:   Calgary to Canmore: 60 miles

I'd hoped to make an early start before the heat of the day but David it seemed was in no hurry to get rid of me the next morning and chatting away, the time galumphed by. He was also worryingly keen to drive me to the outskirts of Alberta to save a climb over some big hills. I was horrified however and firmly assured him I had set myself the task of riding every inch of the way. After coming this far there was no way I could do otherwise. The skirmish of two stubborn people ensued and eventually we settled on the compromise of instead of riding from the house in the city's suburbs, David would take me back to the bike shop so I could begin again where I left off.

After a few more detours and errands on route we finally made it back to the shop where I'd wobbled in less than 48 hours earlier. It was also a lot later than planned and nearing midday as I said a sad farewell to my surprising, funny, amazing host and, underway again, pedalled off to join the highway.

Slogging uphill 10 minutes later, the midday sun broiling down, I was truly cursing my late start. Head down, teeth gritted I couldn't understand why a car kept honking at me, head filling with foul retorts I looked up to see it was David, parked at the top of the hill, camera and a wave at the ready.

How could I not smile?

Calgary behind me I turned firmly towards the beauty and majesty of the Rocky mountains, or at least the lower slopes. I knew there would be far bigger peaks to come but I was excited. The inaugural province of Ontario, which seemed to have taken forever to cross, was now far behind me, as were Manitoba, Saskatchewan and much of Alberta. I'd ridden across pages and pages of my road atlas and the miles were slipping away faster and faster. The Rockies had been a significant marker, in my mind at least, and now here were the very things I had been focusing on for all those miles, the gateway to British Columbia and the final part of my trip. Maybe I was going to make it after all?

That thought began to lose its shine however as the climbing and the sun grew more intense in seemingly direct proportion. Two hours of heat, headwind and hills and I had begun to feel distinctly faint and light-headed. I was also having bizarre fantasies about ice cold, diet cola. This obsession has come to completely dominate my thoughts as I reached the top of yet another steep climb and wobbled, woozily into a remote rest area.

I was desperate to cool off but there was just no shade to be had at all apart from a small patch of shadow cast by a lone camper van. As I crouched miserably in its wake, draining the dregs from a tepid water bottle I marvelled at the latest mood swing from high to low.

Suddenly, the camper's door swung open and I steeled myself to be berated by its owner for squatting too close. Not at all, the universe had more surprises it seems.

Ron and Louise had seen me pull in and were curious as to what a be-skirted cyclist was doing in the middle of nowhere in the middle of such a blazing hot day.

Even better, as I gave my usual summary of the trip they invited me into their van, straight away pulling out a big bottle of ice cold diet cola.

I was floored. My obsession had just become a reality, in a lonely rest stop in the middle of nowhere, two people had just produced the very thing I wanted most in the world. I guzzled happily, not believing my luck as the pair described their camper travels and delivered copious warnings about the dangers of bears and weird strangers!

Leaving the van some 30 minutes later I felt like a different person in a different world. The wind had dropped significantly and even the hills levelled out. I practically flew the rest of the way down into Canmore and the hostel I'd picked for the night. Truly in mountain country now surrounded by soaring, snow covered peaks I felt a sense of calm permeate my skin.

The Bear hostel was a great find. Looking out on the mountains on all sides, it boasted spacious communal areas resplendent with large squashy chairs as well as well-designed, small dorms where even the little bunk beds had privacy curtains. A restorative dinner of a microwaved lasagne and a gin and tonic commenced before I gratefully took advantage of one of the large, comfy sofas. Sat reflecting on an amazing few days, at the generosity of strangers and how the universe had provided exactly what I needed, bike fixing benefactors and diet cola. It was then I suddenly heard an unmistakable English voice. It could only be one person - Tom!

Day 49: Canmore: 0 miles

Turns out that Tom had encountered some of those 'weird strangers' that Ron and Louise warned me about. Since parting after Drumheller a string of bizarre camping experiences had unsettled him somewhat, hence the hostel that night. It also seemed his route around Calgary was actually quite a long one so he'd only arrived here earlier in the day. The strange thing was that it wasn't even strange seeing him, I just accepted what came along.

Tiredness had set in again though, especially after the craziness of the last few days. My body really wanted more time off and for once I was happy to give in. Canmore was gorgeous. It wasn't a chore to spend a few more hours in this chocolate-boxy beautiful town with its mountains and wooden chalets.

I had a great time visiting the upmarket supermarket, all 3 bike shops and – joy of joys, a second hand sports shop selling just about every piece of equipment imaginable from tents to ski goggles.

I grazed good food, ate ice cream in the main square and just soaked up the fresh air. It was also a chance to send my previous hosts a small thank you gift seeing as they would accept nothing in return for their hospitality.

Back at the hostel I chatted to a pair of delightful elderly ladies from Britain who were excited to be exploring the area on their first ever bus tour and to be staying in such exotic surroundings (of a hostel). I also greedily took advantage of the excellent Wi-Fi to catch up with friends and family by email.

From: Emma **To:** Cyclinginaskirt
Subject: Thinking of you….
Hey you,
Just read your latest blog and I have to say it brought a tear to my eye, find it hard to think of you struggling like that and wish I was there to help you thru it! But I have to remind myself that this is your adventure and as well as the downs I can also see the ups! :)

Had a hard couple of days myself, it transpires that Bean is just the worst for falling asleep, have never seen someone fight it like she does! This results in her getting overtired and then she just screams and boy do I mean scream, uncontrollably and inconsolably! Been reading lots and it appears that the more tired babies get the more alert they appear so you continue to play with them when in reality you have just 10 swift minutes to get them down before they're overtired and so impossible to put down they cry themselves to exhaustion!
Had my second major meltdown a couple of days ago too after she had screamed relentlessly at me for 2 hours! Fortunately I've now started to pick up on a few of her sleepy cues and last night I got her in bed by 6, sat with her for an hour but then she put herself to sleep no crying so I know it can be done!
I even managed a bath with a glass of wine - amazing!!!! Brings back quite fond memories of my labour and you sitting with me whilst I was in the bath at 3am, including playing with that wind-up frog you got for the birthing pool!!! Really brings back to me how I couldn't have done that without you!!!!
Right, I've waffled enough and must dash - got another baby group to go to! Hope you're enjoying the Rockies, it is truly stunning,

All my love and a Bean hug, xxxxxx

From: Cyclinginaskirt **To:** Emma
Subject: Thinking of you....
You do help me through it, every single day. You and Bean are the most important things to me in the world. The thought of you gives me strength when I need it the most.
Sorry to hear things have been difficult, you sounded more positive when we spoke the other day. Hang in there, I know it doesn't feel like it but she will settle, and this won't last forever. Not surprised you lost the plot, lack of sleep is often used to torture people, you are coping the best you can, and very, very well considering.
Funny, I was thinking about your pre-labour in the bath and talking to another mum about it yesterday. I wouldn't have missed spending that time with you for the world, I just wished then, as I do now, that I could/can take all the hurt, pain and difficulty away for you. But you know what, you coped and more than that you rocked delivering a kid, just as you will rock being a mum :-)
Hang tough.
The biggest hugs I can possibly send.
Love you X

From: Emma **To:** Cyclinginaskirt
Subject: Thinking of you....
Morning Sis, Oh my, Bean's got a bit of a cold - the result - it took 3 hours of jiggling, 2 bottles and a lot of boob, 1 dose of Calpol and a desperate car trip to get her to sleep - that said she's now been asleep for 14 hours and counting, poor kid!
Hopefully speak to you later – can't wait.
Love and hugs, xxx

All of this was followed by a long, emotional Skype call.

Physically and emotionally replenished with good things I retire to the kitchen for a nightcap gin and tonic, served in a coffee mug, where I run in to Tom and we catch up on our respective days and, out of habit, make a plan to leave together the next morning. Heading off to bed, somehow I end up in Tom's dorm which smells overwhelmingly of male locker-room. With his odorous room-mates out on the town and with breath-taking nerve looking back on it, we discover the many advantages to having fully a curtained bunk-bed.

Laughing at just the whole surreal-ness of the last few days I sneak back to my bed and fall in to the deepest ever sleep.

Day 51: Canmore to Banff: 17 miles

Another late, lazy start, I'm definitely reluctant to leave the relative comfort of the hostel, especially the big squishy sofas. Finally out cycling though, it's hard not to be dazzled once again by the amazing views.
Claud and I are in serious mountain country now. No more foot hills as the peaks climb steeply all around us. Far off, snow-capped summits pointing the way ahead, every pedal rotation bearing us inexorably deeper and higher into the heart of the Rockies.

That must be why it's such flipping hard work! I'd assumed the general lack of breathing ability and aching limbs was caused by the usual combination of asthma and tiredness however, I was somewhat relieved to find out that Tom struggling too. It gradually began to dawn on me that, after all that steady climbing, it was the effects of the altitude that were beginning to kick in.
Looking back with the benefit of hindsight, it was more than obvious that there had been a gradual climb all the way from Calgary. Now, well into the mountain ranges, the air became thinner still as I huffed my way along a relatively tiny, but beautiful 17 miles, past clear lakes and headily scented forests to the beautiful town of Banff in all its kitschy glory.

Coasting down the sun-drenched main street it didn't take much imagination to airbrush in liberal coatings of snow and skiers enjoying the wooden clad bars and restaurants, picking out designer on-piste gear along with their après-ski. Although off season, Banff itself was still surprisingly crowded, with coach loads of tourists browsing both the high end stores and the novelty sweet shops.

On the way into town, large notices adorning the side of the road consistently warned of the dire penalties for non-permit camping, scaring us into a long wait at the tourist information centre to find out what our options might be. Not much as it transpired. When I mentioned about the bicycle, the harried, slightly anxious assistant informed me that the nearest and only campsite was a long, long, long way out of town up an appallingly steep hill. Would I not prefer to stay in town? Sure, how much?
One glance at the accommodation prices swiftly ruled out that option so, with a sense of dread, I accepted a map and directions and we headed out of town wondering what on earth I was going to face.

Practically nothing as it turned out. After quickly leaving the main drag a relatively short, not too steep hill led to a very pleasant campsite, just a stone's throw from town. Perched amongst the pine trees I discovered a handful of other hardy campers and bike tourers, happily pitching up in a quiet, woody, pine-scented glade which offered beautiful views over Banff and the surrounding snow-topped peaks.

With the tent pitched relatively early that day Tom and I set off back down the road, this time on foot to the handy bus stop. We were heading towards a source of much anticipation, a visit to the thermal baths, one of the town's most famous attractions.
What better way to get rid of the aches and pains of all those miles than a long soak in hot, steamy water.
I was beside myself with excitement (obviously it didn't take much) as the bus chugged through the town and wound its way down narrow lanes to the middle of nowhere disgorging us and 20 or so other eager

people clutching towels by the side of the road.

The pools weren't immediately obvious however and it was a slightly confused group who began to wander up and down the deserted stretch of tarmac. Just as I was beginning to wonder if this was some elaborate tourist joke some bright spark amongst us finally spotted a signpost leading through a parking lot to a foot path.
A few minutes later and we were all trooping through the lobby of a large stone building and paying our entrance fee in the steamy underground reception. Given the number of companions on the bus I should have guessed that the pools would be less than exclusive although not even that had prepared me for just how popular they were. Emerging from the gloomy changing rooms, blinking in the bright mountain sunlight, I took in the sight before me.... A smallish rectangular pool of muddy brackish looking water, filled almost to bursting with semi-naked bodies. Not quite the stuff of my fantasies for the last few days.

The first challenge was actually just finding somewhere to enter, it was that busy. Squeezing politely but determinedly through the bobbing masses I finally slipped my cycle-weary body beneath the warm brown waters. It was blissful, especially if you closed your eyes (and ears) to the shouting, laughing, jostling throng surrounding you.
Ignoring the press of bodies I managed to stake a claim to my own little spot at the side of the pool and, turning my back on my fellow wallowers, I gazed out on the imposing silhouette of Mount Rundle letting the warm water caress away the aches and tensions.
Suddenly my head is engulfed in a wave of soupy warm water as Tom pops up out of nowhere causing a mini tsunami. I'm mellow enough now though and we lounge and chat away.
As often happens, the conversation turns to sex and relationships and to differences from the 'norm'. In what's becoming an increasing pattern Tom's take on things is radically different from mine and my good humour of the afternoon deserts me. A belligerent discussion ensues and one in which we can only finally agree to differ, after

growing bone-weary chasing the debate round in circles. I'm irked nonetheless and, as I have more often lately, I wonder why two so dissimilar people don't now part company and go our own ways.

The familiarity of habit is becoming ingrained it seems. It's funny, it was so nice to see a friendly face just a couple of days ago back in Canmore but already the tensions and irritations have returned. Cycling so many miles takes its toll physically, mentally and emotionally and spending so much time with someone on a daily basis when you're tired and depleted is enough to test the strongest of relationships, let alone that of near strangers. The company has been lovely, but both welcome and frustrating. It somehow feels like the time for saying goodbye is nipping at our heels.

With this washing machine of a debate going on in my head it's a thoughtful journey back to the campground that evening.

Before going to sleep that night I open the side of the tent and stare through the trees at a nearly full moon, rising against the backdrop of snow covered peaks and a smorgasbord of stars. It's a surreal sight, I almost can't believe I'm there. I experience again that sensation of being somewhat removed from my own body; as if I'm watching this scene at the cinema and my senses and feelings are just out of reach on the other side of the screen, along with the incredible view.

Maybe it's the fatigue or the overload of new experiences and beauty, but more and more I find my senses and emotions either numbed or unbearably heightened, like today in the pool. Too much or nothing. I wonder if this will right itself when I finally finish? Some days too I do really want to stop; days when I'm tired beyond sanity but then again the thought of stopping terrifies me because I have no idea what I'll do next. It's all too much to contemplate right now, especially when gazing out on an infinite universe of stars. So I push the thoughts back down inside, close the tent flap on my spectacular view and miraculously, fall instantly asleep.

Day 51: Banff to Lake Louise: 40 miles

Another morning of faffing commences including a long stop for coffee, food buying and window shopping (the only affordable kind).

Not usually one to bear a grudge I find that I'm still pissed off from yesterday and I nurse this feeling, along with an increasing inability to breathe, as the morning progresses.
The wheezing and sullen contemplation sits alongside me on the road too, festering nicely mile after tough mile, developing with the altitude until, a few hours in, it all disgorges itself in an ugly mess and I have a meltdown in a layby. Under the gaze of a stunningly beautiful mountain lake, I heave Claud to the ground and sit sucking greedily on my inhaler, muttering like a semi-crazy thing.
A hug from Tom and the chance to vent did much to fix the situation, as did the restoration of oxygen to my sore lungs, but the day continued to be a slog.

Whilst the cycling dragged, some sensational mirror lakes and forested slopes drew the eye and made the time pass more quickly. The air temperature too was noticeably colder now, with more mountains showing their snow covered slopes. By early afternoon the day had begun to take on a heart-sinkingly grey hue and sure enough, just shy of Lake Louise, the first drops of sleety rain begin to fall.
An icy mist quickly followed suit and, huddled under my rain hood, visibility is reduced to near zero. It's definitely time to stop now so, after a slow 40 miles, I steer Claud into the tourist information centre in Lake Louise and call it a day.

The lake area is famous for its ski resorts and deep, turquoise waters as well as being known as the gateway to the frozen north, to Jasper, Whistler and beyond. It's also an area I'd been hankering to see. A big part of me had hoped to continue cycling north to Jasper on the famously beautiful Icefields Parkway, heading on via Princes' George and Rupert islands to the Glacier Bay National Park, flirting with the shadows of the Alaskan wilderness before dropping back down into Vancouver. Sadly however it was not to be.

It seemed that the weather and the ski season were both closing in rapidly, evidenced by the mountain chill and plummeting temperatures. Although it didn't look that far on my map (nope, still haven't learnt my lesson), to visit Jasper by bike turned out to be an extra 250km, just too long a detour for the time of year and the summer equipment I had.

So keen was I to go, I briefly considered the idea of stabling Claud for a few days and hiring a car for the visit but both availability and cost proved prohibitive, as did the lack of buses or other transport. The universe was obviously trying to get a message across, maybe something to leave for another time. It did help however to cement the route I would be taking from here. Departing Lake Louise I would again be reunited with the ubiquitous Trans-Canadian Highway 1, all the way over the mountains to Revelstoke by way of Rogers Pass.

Decision sorted, I made a bee-line for the shop next door to the Tourist Centre to buy myself a woolly hat as it was flipping freezing. Shivering through the sleety mist, I finally stumbled across the campsite after 20 minutes of circular riding. Pitching the tent took another 30 very cold minutes, sacrificing more than a couple of tent pegs to the rock hard ground.

Although I'm very cold and dirty, the idea of crossing the wide expanse of icy forest trails only to turn blue in a sub-zero shower block also didn't appeal. After pathetic attempts to light a fire fell flat however, a shower won out over a long evening shivering in my tent.

Happily, the showers turn out to be a great move, steamed and lobster red I emerged to find a little cooking hut still open. Even better, I also locate the last of the gin and tonic and a bottle of whiskey. A bit later, warmed by shower, food and copious amounts of alcohol, the world once again begun to look rosier. I would though, still be wearing every item of clothing I possessed tonight.

Day 52:   Lake Louise to Donald: 68 miles

Leaving early the next morning I designated only a brief and chilly stop to admire Lake Louise. Ooh, look, a blue lake.
The town still had a hold though and, passing the shopping centre, a quick map-check somehow segued into a long breakfast at the local bakery. Stuffed full of spicy pasty, coffee and cookies I browsed the internet map sites and tried not to think about the literal mountains to be climbed in the days to come.

Looking at the maps and plotting distances I knew that the road had been gradually climbing from Lake Superior to Canmore. What I hadn't realised is that this translated to a gain of over 1000 metres above sea level.
For the first time since starting in Toronto this actually meant the east to west route was possibly a little more advantageous. Despite the winds the route appeared to give a longer (in distance) but more gradual climb to the Rockies over the whole trip, whereas the (smug tail-wind) west to east folks were having to do much more climbing at the start of their trip. With fresh, but unseasoned legs, they were tackling bigger gradients. Conversely I suppose it meant they could practically coast along after the mountains of course…. Hmm, maybe not quite the advantage I first thought then.
Pulling away from the town my body actually felt good and relaxed. The sun was even trying to throw a few rays through the gloomy mist to brighten the day and the road ahead.
Forgotten already was the freezing gloom and laboured breathing of yesterday as Claud and I barrelled along more stunning mountain roads. The soaring peaks matched my spirits as we tackled some huge climbs up and through Kicking Horse Pass at 1,627 metres (the Kicking Horse area incidentally produces some rather nice coffee of the same name).
The climbs were more than rewarded too by plenty of adrenalin fuelled downhills, swooping down through gorges bursting with ice melt. Eagles soaring alongside on invisible thermals in the vast, open

sky, plummeting out of sight after unseen prey, all the time cocooned by mountains so vast they were unending.

A leisurely lunch break in the town of Golden set the tone before the final stretch of the afternoon, Claud and I climbing and swooping our way into the small alpine hamlet of Donald.
Situated off Log Dump Road and Big bend Highway (I kid you not) but still nestled amongst the mountain tops, Donald was mercifully perched at a lower altitude than Lake Louise and the temperature felt positively balmy as I pitched my little tent in the lush orchard of a tiny and all but deserted campsite.
The sun shone on my endeavours as, joy of joys, I discovered a small, well heated ladies toilet and shower block which became mine for the evening. Treating it as my own private office I was able to cook and hang up my damp clothes from the previous day. It even had a Wi-Fi signal and plug points so, whilst my food simmered and my soggy socks aired, I charged up my tablet, wrote another blog post and caught up on emails.
How amazingly civilized and warm.

Tom knocked on the door from time to time, the gents I think, being somewhat less salubrious than the ladies' facilities, but I was in the mood for solitude and after a while he retired to the joys of the laundry room, leaving me to my little haven of peace.
Today I had cycled over a mountain pass and I felt great. Were the Rockies and I developing at least a mutual respect, if not an outright friendship?

Day 53:   Donald to Canyon Hot Springs: 55 miles

The answer, as it turns out, was no.

There's nothing that makes the heart sink faster than waking up to the steady drumming of rain on canvas. Ignoring it for as long as possible I dragged out breakfast in the laundry room hoping that the weather would ease somewhat. When it became clear that it had other plans I grudgingly accepted the inevitable and packed up my gear in the rain; always in the back of my mind the sinking feeling that, cold and tired at the end of a long day's cycling I'll be unpacking the same soggy tent this evening. Oh well, nothing to be done but to don my rapidly disintegrating waterproof coat and pedal on.

The rain continued to pour as the road set off steeply uphill. Forty five minutes of climbing later and not a downhill in sight, I'm wet through and freezing. The road has also produced the craziest optical illusion, it looks like I'm riding downhill even though I'm still heading upwards.

The road itself runs in a rough spiral and staring at the concrete barrier marking the edge I would swear blind it is sloping downwards but, my legs are very, very definitely pushing uphill. For once it's not even the wind pressing against me, it's not even that windy, I'm just cycling upwards on a road that looks like it's going down.

I begin to think I'm losing the plot and my fevered imagination has finally flipped into crazy land but, when Tom experiences it as well, at least I know I'm not cracking up (or that we both are).

This weird down-up hill continues, as does the rain, relentlessly. My waterproof coat, which has been much patched with sticky tape, is now sporting some seriously large holes through which moisture pours with impunity in icy rivulets.

I'm wet through anyway as the less-than-breathable material produces a 'boil in the bag' effect, trapping sweat inside and turning it into cold clamminess. To complete the loveliness, my gloves, trousers, socks and shoes are also sodden.

Drenched and freezing cold, I begin to shiver uncontrollably, big, juddering shakes.

If it weren't so uncomfortable it would almost be funny as shivering spasms take over my body so that the whole bicycle is wobbling down to my toes which are clipped tight to the pedals, huge shudders starting at my rattling teeth but stopping dead at my immovable feet.

It's not even as if there's any view to distract from the grind. The wet duvet of mist is obscuring everything except the Escher-esque up/down impossible road. No houses, people or cars for the last 2 hours either, just 2 stupid cyclists.

Grinding miserably along I genuinely consider the possibility that a) I've entered some weird mountain twilight zone and b) I may seriously be developing hypothermia, when, rounding another mind-bending bend, I finally spot a large hunting-style lodge looming amongst the trees. Salvation! I wonder if they have a kettle?

Crunching up the deserted gravel driveway I'm well aware that if this were a film the swirling mist would be accompanied by a Hitchcock-inspired sound track, screech owls and me shouting at the TV screen to 'get the hell out of there and run'.
But hypothermia can help overcome the most sensible of reasoning so, up the front steps I marched and rang the bell.
It sounds deeply within the house but there's no answer. I try again. Still silence.

I'm frighteningly cold now and shaking uncontrollably. Decisive action is needed so I shiver myself down the front steps and hunt out a back entrance. Stepping cautiously through a side door I find a wood lined corridor. A few steps in and I can pick out the faint sounds of voices coming from somewhere ahead. It seems like someone is at home after all, but who?
Rounding a corner I find myself at the entrance to a large, open wood-panelled hall. A soaring ceiling and plentiful glazing give the huge space a lightness, even on this dullest of days. It's also a hive of activity. Boxes, chairs and dust covers are strewn everywhere as though the whole place was being packed away. Incongruously though, set to one side of the chaos is table fully laid for dinner for 20 people or more, gleaming plates and glassware all looking mightily out of place amongst the chaos.

I stand there watching, equally mesmerized and unsure what to do next, however my shivering does the job for me, making my metal shoe cleats clatter on the floor like a small army of tap dancing mice and alerting people to our presence.

The room, as one body becomes silent. Heart in mouth, there's nothing for it but to stammer out a greeting and an explanation in between uncontrollable teeth chattering.

Would they mind, whoever they were, if Tom and I just sat in a corner for a little while and dried off/got warm and ate our sandwiches? Please…..?

Silence, for what seemed like an age, then an explosion of warmth and welcome. It turned out we'd stumbled into a hotel which was closing up for the season. This was the staff packing down on their final day, hence the chaos. Despite this chairs were pulled up to a less crowded part of the main room, a towel found for me as well a generous offer to help ourselves to some of the hot food being prepared in the kitchen.

Once again, I'm overwhelmed. The staff apologise that they need to keep packing, they're on a deadline to close but usher us into the steamy warmth of the canteen where there is a joyful abundance of hot soup, vegetables, bread and chocolate brownies. One kind soul even lit the oven for me so I could bask in its heat for a while.

Making sure our plates are filled up the staff then melt away leaving us in a quiet corner to thaw out.

Minutes later I'm cradling a bowl of broth in one hand and tea in the other trying not to shake them out of their containers. I watch with happy detachment the bustle of activity around me, the blue tinge finally beginning to fade from my cold lips.

I can't describe how tempting it was to stay here all day, even being locked in for the winter didn't seem so bad. The idea of heading back out into that freezing misty rain and crazy up/down road was exactly the last thing I wanted to do. This feeling was only heightened when, getting ready to leave, I had to force my protesting body back in to a cold soggy rain coat and wet shoes.

Saying a heartfelt farewell to our impromptu hosts I sloshed and squelched my way back out to an equally wet Claud. Leg muscles and fingers cold and stiff, today was definitely not up in my top 10 of favourites, but, pedalling keeps you warm and there was still plenty to do.

At least the mist had finally lifted somewhat, taking with it the worst of the rain and leaving just a dull greyness. It was a bonus.
Soon after, I pass a sign informing us we're entering Glacier National Park. I'm strangely excited by this as it means we're nearing the second of the big mountain crossings which will take us into the heart of the Rockies.
At 1,330 metres Rogers Pass is lower in altitude than Kicking Horse but I've also started the day at a lower elevation. The climbing therefore promises to be full on.

It's a challenge Tom has been building up to in anticipation and fear for some days now – riding up this mountain. Having previously gained a small amount of experience riding in the Pyrenees I feel somewhat worldly in mountain cycling, I'm actually looking forward to these peaks. Unlike the incessant headwinds which have never left me, mountains at least have a finite end point. Once you reach the summit then, relatively, it's all downhill.

How do you tackle a mountain? One pedal stroke at a time.
Full of adrenalin and bravado I set off, onwards and upwards until one hundred yards later I'm brought to a stop by a lengthy set of road works.

Waiting for the human signallers to give me the green light I stare up at the mountains ahead and at the Columbia river disappearing through the same pass I'll be climbing, but far below rushing headlong through the gorge. Above it, the mist has all but gone, replaced with a glimmer of sun and a brilliant rainbow.
My heart swells. It's another of those many moments when I have to pinch myself to see if I'm really here. And I am, completely in the

215

moment, face upturned to the light, eyes closed, car horns hooting.... The signals have changed and it seems that I'm holding up the queue of traffic.

The construction worker, his board now turned to 'Go' sends me on my way with a cheery, *"Get going girl"*, so I do, waving on my way past, the line of cars squeezing by me and roaring on ahead up the slope.

For the next hour I am completely focussed on nothing but the next few metres of road ahead as it winds steeply upwards through a series of narrow tunnels carved or boxed into the mountainside. Between the tunnels the noise of the river drops away as it disappears into its lush greenery far below, replaced by the sounds of birds, dripping water and a cyclist breathing very heavily.

There's a fair amount of traffic too, frighteningly so in the long dark road tunnels in which there's no comforting shoulder to cycle on. The road is barely wide enough even for two lanes and the approaching cars sound monstrous as their straining engines echo and roar in the dark. Most terrifying are the huge trucks that also monopolise this route. I'm shaking again but this time in fear as relentlessly I'm squeezed against the dripping rock walls by these metal behemoths, passing with just inches to spare. I shoot from the exit of each tunnel like a small, sweaty cannonball, heart in my mouth, pedalling like a fury.

Some of the dozen or so tunnels at least have little slit windows cut out of the rock which illuminate small patches in the cave like darkness, others don't. A few are short enough to have a welcoming arch of daylight visible on entry but most seem to wind into the rock for miles (probably only few hundred feet) until it feels like I'm being swallowed by the mountain itself.

My nerve is beginning to fail as I enter yet another gaping black tunnel mouth. The road behind had seemed empty and I was hoping to pedal like a dervish to clear the tunnel before encountering any more traffic. More than ever I'm also aware of my huge oversight in not having any lights. As the blackness envelopes me however my heart sinks to hear the roar of a powerful, grinding engine behind me. Please no, not another truck, not in here. The blood is thundering in my ears so I almost don't hear the shouting. Stupefied and afraid I realise someone from the approaching vehicle is yelling at me with full throated vigour. My frayed nerves finally start to give way and I want to cry.

As the truck pulls alongside the driver slows and leans right out of his window. I brace myself for abuse or worse, objects being thrown. He opens his mouths wide before yelling deafeningly at me. "GREAT JOB, BRILLIANT, YOU'RE DOING AMAZINGLY, KEEP GOING, CARRY ON" And with a thumbs up and a wave he's gone.

I'm stunned and my lip is trembling but this time with emotion. Scared and tired, near the end of my resources, those few words are like a shot in the arm. My courage returns and my determination. Suffused with a warm glow from a few simple words of praise I rocket out of the tunnel mouth, the last one as it turns out, and shortly afterwards I'm pulling into the visitor centre which marks the Rogers Pass Col, standing proudly at 1,330 metres above sea-level and over 540 metres of which I'd just climbed.

The Centre was the second oasis of the day, warm and welcoming the kind staff let me use their kettle to make a hot drink and then didn't bat an eyelid as I stripped off (almost) all my wet clothes and hung them around their large log fire to dry. Shoes and socks steaming away on the hearth I appropriate a comfortable arm chair and sink gratefully into its warmth.
I'd made it, I'd climbed a mountain. What I hadn't realised too was that this mountain was now in my 5th and final province of British Columbia. At some point yesterday between Lake Louise and Donald, whilst crossing Kicking Horse pass I'd slipped out of Alberta and over the provincial boundary.
I reflected how exciting it had been on that day barely a month ago, after 4 weeks of travelling, that I'd finally left Ontario but still with 4

more provinces to go. Now, just over 30 days later and I'm entering the final stage. It's almost too much to take in in my cold, tired, emotional state so I sit back in my fireside chair and let my mind drift to a delightful tourist information film playing on a looped TV.....
Stunning Canadian scenery plays out in front of me with healthy, adventurous families enjoying the delights of the great outdoors until…. Enter the bears. For the next 10 minutes the film lectured in alarmingly graphic detail on the difference between brown and grizzly bears and what to do in case of an attack by each.

Having successfully thus far avoided thinking too much about bears, this wasn't helping. Especially now. These TV bears all looked the same to me, huge teeth and claws, I just hoped I'd never have to be close enough to identify one let alone remember how to deal with it.
The film succeeded in scaring me from the comfort of my chair and back onto the road. Tiredly gathering up warm damp socks and Tom who'd also rolled in. We pointed the bikes towards the final straight for today.

There was now a fission of excitement, partly because the place I was aiming for tonight was a well-known hot springs resort and partly because the route promised a pretty much uninterrupted 20 miles of pure downhill.

Still not quite believing this could be real, I picked up the pace until soon, I was no longer pedalling. Oh. My. God. It was true.
Claud was flying, twisty hairpin bends, the opposite of this morning's counterparts, shot by in a blur. Rocky walls and evergreen clad slopes flashed by alternately as the road circled steeply downwards, the freezing mountain air rushed past as I let go the brakes and shrieked and whooped with all the emotions of the last few days.

For a whole 30 minutes I didn't push the pedals once. Claud just streaked and bounced down the mountainside, two eagles soaring next to us for part of the way, we were descending from the sky like Gods, literally coming down through the clouds.

At one point an unseen large pothole shot me perilously close to a catastrophic plunge from the edge but I was going too fast to do anything other than sit tight and hope. Nothing could stop our progress it seemed until, breathless and frozen, with a permanent grin carved on my face, we rolled into the Canyon Hot Springs Resort.

After such a day, heaven couldn't come any closer than an hour long soak in thermic water naturally heated to 40 degree Celsius, all whilst gazing out at the snow topped mountains from a steaming and deserted outdoor pool.

Two days, two mountain passes, two Canadian provinces. Well over a thousand metres of climbing and the same descending. Hypothermia, hot pools, random log fires and strangers sharing hot food. Wind, rain, sleet, mist, sunshine and rainbows.
This journey continues to amaze every single day.

Day 54: Canyon Hot Springs to Revelstoke: 23 miles

Duh-duh, duh-duh, duh-duh….4.30 am and I'm woken by the ground shaking and a thunderous rolling growl.
Exhausted, sleepy and disorientated I lie there briefly wondering if it's an earthquake and if so, if it really matters if I just stay in my tent and go back to sleep.

It's freezing too, and as the cold air drags me into consciousness I realise that it's less likely to be an earthquake and more probably the goods train line, helpfully situated behind the campground at the hot springs.

Something I have learned, Canadian trains last forever. Having grown up in the UK, where trains are mostly short affairs, Canadian rolling stock is a force to behold. I'd gotten used to it watching the Soo-line trucks roll across the prairies, line upon line of carriages for Canadian Tire, or carrying grain and other goods. I'd always abandoned in the end trying to count of the number of carriages attached to these monsters, but in general it would be a good half an hour or more as the beast slowly rumbled its way past.

Fine, when watching on a warm day whilst travelling along a highway. Not so fine when you're sleeping next to it (or trying to) in the early hours of the morning. I'd increasingly noticed that for some reason train lines and campsites seem to be situated in parallel, this wasn't the first goods train alarm call I'd received. It was however the coldest.

Levering myself out of the depths of my cosy sleeping cocoon, the thermometer by the poolside bathrooms showed as a disturbing -2 degrees Celsius, officially freezing, supported by the frost dusting both the ground and Claud. Winter was definitely on its way. Despite it being only mid-September the mountain seasons arrived early it seemed. Maybe only a week or two more and snow could well have made yesterday's crossing impossible. Shivering at the thought I returned to the relative warmth of the tent but sleep had fled.

Loading up Claud was a thoughtful slow-going process, the highs and lows of the last few days having given way to a tired calm.

My legs were also less than enthusiastic at having to pedal again too, feeling they deserved a better rest.

Out on the road and after 23 miles the beautiful little town of Revelstoke came into view. A pretty high street lined with not one but 2 bakeries made an easy no-brainer for the morning's coffee and cake stop.

Tired though I was, I'd gotten so used to just pushing on even when I didn't necessarily want to I never questioned that I'd get back on the bike today, constantly fuelled by that strange mix of guilt about stopping and the need for motion. So, it was a physical sense of relief when Tom, obviously feeling the same, suggested we simply stay put. Relief and guilt then commenced a heated, but short battle. "Stopping after only 23 miles" my inner voice chided, but deep in the recesses of my tiny brain I knew it made sense. My body was running on fumes again, especially after dealing with the cold and climbs of the mountains, this was a beautiful little town, what better place to rest. Deal done, conscience nearly squared, we rode through the pretty, quiet streets, away from the main square and out across a rickety iron river bridge to find a lovely, sunny campground.

Laying myself and my frozen tent in the sun to thaw, I dozed for an hour or more before taking pleasure from life's little necessities such as laundry and cooking. It was also with great pride that I stuck my final provincial flag to Claud's mudguard.

The mountains smiled benevolently as I made use of the crème de la crème of campsite accessories, the enclosed camping kitchen, where free utensils, sinks and work tops as well as little gingham covered tables giving the small-tented camper somewhere comfy to cook, eat and write.

A quick trip back to the well-stocked supermarket in town fixed my food needs, as did another sneaky visit to the bakery.

Looking back over the journey I find I'm thinking increasingly about one of the biggest parts of life on the road – food.

After all, it's the stuff that has helped me cover over 2,500 miles (4,000 km), get through five provinces and two mountain passes. To date though I've had a bit of a love/hate relationship with the stuff and the sheer amount I am having to consume.

To put it into context, I'd received an email from my Pa a while back in which he'd put his considerable engineering skills to the test and; after a string of complex calculations based on weight, speed, the alignment of the planets, he worked out that I needed to consume approximately 770 calories an hour whilst cycling (with another 1200+ a day for general functioning).

Put in simple terms that's 1.7 donuts an hour (Tim Horton's maple frosted being my current favourite).

It has surprised me how much fuel I actually need. I'm a grazer by nature, preferring to eat little and often and at home I have a pretty healthy diet, low in fats, little or no meat, bread or dairy products or alcohol.

Well, not anymore!

With a typical day now equalling 7-9 hours on the road that's a staggering 6,590-8,230 calories at the very least. Whilst the general healthy-living guidelines recommend that the average adult female needs approximately 2,000 calories per day to get by, my output, however, means that I should literally be eating for four. It's not as simple as it sounds either.

Donuts and cakes quickly lose their appeal in any quantity, plus the energy contained within them is minimal as it's coming primarily from sugar. As runners, cyclists and most sporty folks will know sugar gives you a great initial energy rush, which quickly peaks and dies leaving you feeling slow and lethargic. Food at roadside diners and service stations also leaves a lot to be desired on the healthy eating front with fried food and snacks being the predominant, easy-grab fare. Convenience is definitely king when it comes to eating and I swear I have consumed my body weight in cake and chips since the start of the trip just because they're the easiest thing to hand.

The weather also plays a part in diet. Hot days sap the appetite as well as energy, meaning all you want to do is drink fluids. My saviour at these times has been chocolate milk, cartons of the stuff, energy, protein and down in a few gulps. And to compound all this, at the end of a long day's cycling, the last thing you feel like doing after finding a camping spot and putting up the tent is cooking a meal.

With this in mind my staple diet and highly technical fuelling strategy can be divided roughly into 3 parts:

    1) Drinks: coffee (for the wonderful caffeine hit), water and

chocolate milk by the gallon. The discovery of Canadian brand beer and whiskey have also contributed to happy camping (purely medicinal of course).

2) Sandwiches: anything that can be conceivably captured between 2 slices of bread makes an excellent snack/lunch. My current favourites include biscuit, banana and peanut butter or marmalade and granola sandwiches…..don't judge until you've tried it; it's delicious.

3) Evening meals: same principle as above but with super noodles. Ready in 2 minutes, combine noodles with any random item loitering in the food pannier including nuts, more granola, avocado, tinned tuna and sachets of tomato sauce/mustard. These can be freely obtained at most roadside restaurants and I'll guiltily admit to leaving most service stations with pockets full of random condiments.

Back in my new favourite campground I indulge myself in my food and wine spoils whilst taking full advantage of the rare opportunity to speak with friends and family via Skype.
Never the most reliable medium, especially given mountain reception, time difference and (for some) a young baby, my typical Skype attempts ran thus:

Emma to Cyclinginaskirt: 07:00 GMT. Skypey skype skype
Sounds like a good call on the cake stop in Revelstoke! Good for Skype if you can make it that'd be great. Hopefully speak soon x.
Cyclinginaskirt to Emma: 07:15 GMT. Skypey skype skype
You awake now? X

Emma to Cyclinginaskirt: 08:20. Skypey skype skype
Sorry I was, managed to get madam back to sleep then dropped off myself an extra hour! You about now?
Cyclinginaskirt to Emma: 08:45. Skypey skype skype

Online for half hour now if you're about? X
Emma to Cyclinginaskirt: 09:32. Skypey skype skype
Damn think I might have missed you? Email me when you log on X

Cyclinginaskirt to Emma: 10:37. Skypey skype skype
Are you around in 5 mins? X

Cyclinginaskirt to Emma: 11:01. Skypey skype skype
Hello...anyone there? Email me if you're awake and I'll turn Skype on.

Emma to Cyclinginaskirt: 14:15. Skypey skype skype
Hey,
Don't know what happened today, I was online but couldn't see that you had logged in - think it might be me not understanding my new phone! :(Really sorry we didn't get to speak. Glad to see you're enjoying the Rockies, brings back lovely honeymoon memories! Looks like you're thinking only another week or so before you hit Vancouver!
Lots of love and warm hugs, Xxxx

Oh well, it's the thought that counts I guess!

Day 55: Revelstoke to Mara: 60 miles

It was always going to be very hard to leave a town that has not one, but two amazing bakeries, not helped of course by legs that feel like lead. A weariness seems also to have set in, not just in my body but a heaviness of spirit. Way back at the beginning of the journey I'd expected to be ecstatic by the time I got to this point, barely a week from Vancouver, but instead it's the reverse. The closer I get the more troubled I feel.
I'm pondering this conundrum from the warmth of Bakery number 2

whilst waiting for Tom to get his act together. Following on from my food-related blog "Eating for four" there had been a barrage of messages, including some expressing relief having misinterpreted the title, people having thought me in the family way! All however offer much needed words of encouragement and excitement at the impending end to the trip.

Gina, David's housekeeper has also sent me a message. It seemed that after having talked to her briefly about the trip she had been really taken by the idea and the adventure and wanted to contribute in some way. Thanking her profusely, I suggest that people have already been so kind to me but maybe she'd like to make a donation instead to a cause that's close to her heart, so she's chosen a local food bank she tells me and my heart swells for her generosity and that of the people I've met in general.

Emotions in turmoil I leave the warmth and happiness of the bakery to join Tom who is loading up his bike. The need to be moving is upon me however tired I am, so, readying myself once more I turn Claud towards the Monashee mountains.

In Revelstoke I'd been reading about a local tourist attraction, a Ghost Town and château situated at Three-Valley Gap, nestling on the shores of a lake with the same name. It sounds intriguing, exciting even....
As I draw alongside the lake and look down on the 'Château' - a hotel perched on the shore, I'm reminded fondly of something akin to the Kellerman's Holiday camp from the film Dirty Dancing'.
Billed as a heritage site, with historic buildings from the days of the first pioneer settlers I'd been expecting ghostly and gloomy fortresses, all dripping stone and hushed awe. This was all, to be frank, very modern looking and brightly painted wood.
Wandering round the near deserted complex (ghost town was right) it finally dawned on me that actually, the historic ancient buildings in Canada are most likely to be less than 200 years old, modern in European terms. Growing up in a country with more castles and

cathedrals than a bored teenager ever wants to be dragged around it was actually quite refreshing to get a different perspective on historic. The creepy 'ghost town' feeling was present though, ironically from being the only two humans on the complex.

Walking across a small bridge by the lake, I eventually discovered a very modern side to the place, a helicopter tour company tucked away behind the hotel. I was sorely tempted to take a flight over the glacier and the lake, partly to rest my aching legs and mostly to sight-see without the effort of pedalling, but the $200 price tag was beyond my limited budget, especially not knowing what the next weeks would hold for Claud and I. Reluctantly I trailed back to the highway and got moving again, pedal power it was.

Lunch was a rest stop outside of Sicamous which boasted its own trash museum before more rolling road and another cheeky stop at a Tim Hortons for coffee, and cake – got to boost that calorie intake after all. At some point during lunch the companionable headwind joined me and gallantly accompanied the rest of the ride.

Sicamous also marked a departure from the Trans-Canada Highway 1 after deciding to take a more Southern route into Vancouver through the Fraser valley rather than heading due west to Kamloops.

Huffing away against the wind I couldn't help but be drawn by the beautiful Lake Mara marking the way on my right-hand side. As the road bent around the lake I threw admiring glances at the sleek, expensive boats bobbing haughtily against their moorings, like the local society-set keeping a wary eye out as a sweaty interloper or two pass on by. Worn down by the headwind by now I was immeasurably glad to spot a campsite ahead of me on the lake, however, pulling in to the driveway a few moments later my heart sank at the big notice informing all that it was now 'Closed for the Season'. Winter it seemed was now chasing me, not only for the weather but the accommodation too.

Looking around, stealth camping options were not seeming good, with the lake butted up against one side and wall to wall houses lining the opposite shore. It reminded me a little of the Tobermory situation. Considering Canada has so much land, there seems to be an awful lot of it covered in houses when you don't want it to be.

Nothing for it but to cycle on, keeping an eye out for any opportune patches of wasteland or friendly looking front gardens.
Luck however was on my side as barely 2km down the road was a sign for another campsite. To be fair, it didn't look very open at all. In fact it looked like someone's wooded driveway but hey, it was worth a go.
The luck held as the owners, an elderly and slightly bemused couple agreed to let us camp. They had all but closed (apart from their roadside sign) not expecting any trade that time of year but were more than happy to let us pitch in the woods. Even turning a wheezing old tap back on for us and unlocking the wooden outhouse which served as a toilet. It was basic but it was a place to stay for the night.

A local deli provided pasties and wine and Tom and I set up our usual camp in his more spacious tent for dinner. Talking through the last few weeks the same feelings of this morning, successfully repressed by cycling, returned to plague me. Tom's plan had always been to continue on after Vancouver, cycling South down through the U.S towards Mexico.
My 'what next' however was looming blankly. I think I'd hoped to have some epiphany on the road by now, some thunderbolt of realisation as to where my life was taking me, what I should do next, my raison d'être….? Leaving Toronto, it seemed I'd have forever ahead of me to reach that decision (seriously doubting I'd ever get this far).
Now, the urgency was nipping at my heels. With just a few days remaining I hadn't a clue.
Help.
Actually, whiskey helped, at least to postpone the inevitable a bit longer. Tomorrow would bring the answers. Maybe?

Day 56:   Mara to Oyama: 48 miles

OK, it might not have brought the answers but it did bring rain. Coffee and bread from the local store were consumed back in Tom's tent, neither of us in any hurry, we began watching a film on his iPad, Ground Hog Day, very apt. Still raining, it seemed like a good way to pass the time until, miraculously the sun finally made an appearance.

Cruising round the lake I began to enjoy the empty deserted feel of autumn. I could imagine how, in the height of summer, the area would be heaving with assembled tourists and seasonal dwellers. Now in the damp morning air, just the few true locals remained, repairing boats, mending cabins, chatting on porches and waving at us on occasion.

Finally rounding the end of the lake I was sad to see it leave my side, I was missing the dramatic mountain views too. After days punctuated with superlatives and just plain awe-struck 'Oh wow's' at the unfolding panorama, the valley in which we now were felt quite tame by comparison and I mourned the lack of drama.

The road forged on through the town of Armstrong which made a surprisingly great lunch stop. Not exactly picturesque, the Cheese Shop and café more than made up for that with its warm, fuggy welcome, hot spicy soup and cheese scones. A mecca for cheese lovers everywhere and with a superb deli I was tempted to do a Revelstoke and stop again. Sanity and the lack of camping spaces prevailed however so it was reluctantly onwards through Vernon and a hilly cycle trail around Kalamalka and Wood Lakes.

After the morning's late departure and stopping to help Tom with a flat tyre outside of Vernon it meant that the day was drawing rapidly to a close by the time we reached the small town of Oyama. Twilight had definitely taken hold as too had the cold air.
Another sign of the turning of the seasons, we no longer had the luxury of long summer evenings or the corresponding warmth. Lungs

tight and breathing laboured in the chill evening air, it was definitely time to shiver to a stop and make camp for the night.

A wonderfully ethereal woman at the campsite (instant hippie diagnosis by Tom which meant I would be doing the talking whilst Tom huffed and rolled his eyes in the background at such new-age-ness) showed us to a lovely clear pitch with a view of Wood Lake, tempered somewhat by the fast falling darkness but, looking up beyond the lake, a vast canopy of stars was already appearing.

I wasn't in the most social of moods either, lungs hurting, body jaded. I felt tired, mentally and physically. The same tired internal discussions going in the same weary circles. What was I doing and why didn't I go it alone?
Definitely time to be on my own again.

Day 57: Oyama to Kaleden: 66 Miles

Again, rather than lifting overnight, the bad mood slept with me and I woke with the same grey blanket of irritation under which I'd gone to sleep. This wasn't helped by trying and failing to talk with my sister on the ever idiosyncratic Skype.

Cycling along, mind elsewhere nursing the grumpiness, I was brought back to the present with a jolt by a loud car horn, blasting aggressively behind me. Not the nice 'cheery hello' peeping of previous drivers but a 'get out of my way won't-ya' from some arsey motorist in too big a hurry. It didn't end there though and it seemed the closer I rode to the city of Kelowna, the worse it became.
Stopping thankfully in the teeming city centre Tim Hortons, Tom and I faced each other and made plans.

Mine were to continue on the same road, through Penticton and crossing out of the Rockies through the Alison Pass between Princeton and Hope, re-joining the Trans-Canada Highway 1.

Tom had different ideas however, it seemed that Roger's pass hadn't been quite the daunting challenge he'd imagined it would be. Wanting to tackle something else he determined to turn off on the outskirts of town to take the higher Okanagan Connector road to Kamloops and Highway 1. A quicker route but reaching a higher altitude over that shortened distance.

Once again it was time to say goodbye it seemed. Twenty five km after Kelowna the road forked and Tom and I, with a brief wave, went our separate ways, quite possibly for the final time.
Or maybe not, who knew?
Depending on how fast we rode there was the potential to meet, in a few days, in the beautifully named town of Hope the other side of the mountains before the final run into Vancouver. But no plans, no promises, just a wait and see.
As I cycled away I let out a huge breath, releasing it seemed to dispel a good deal of the pent up frustration and angst from the last few days. On my own I had only to concentrate on what I was doing, far less time for maudlin reflection and less people to argue with, just Claud and I, the highway and the headwind stretching on ahead.

As if joyful to have me all to itself again the wind increased, gleefully buffeting and toying with the bike. Lunch was a stop in the quaint town of Peachland and its very welcome autumnal weekend market.
It was here I discovered the joys of pierogis, little crescent shaped dumplings filled with egg and bacon, beautifully warm and spiced they hit the spot like nothing else could have. The woman running the stall was delighted by my virginal pierogi eating state and kept plying me with extras to ask my opinion. Stuffing myself with both sweet and savoury I listened whilst she described how, fed up with living the corporate dream, working all hours to the exclusion of everything else, she had turned her back on a city career to open up this stall.
Like so many of the people I'd met she'd opted out of the 9-5 in order to chase that little spark of a dream. Warmed inside and out I cycled on.

The afternoon can only be described as windy to the point of insanity, battling along in my near lowest gear the skies around me darkened ominously until, as I reached the aptly named Summerland, the heavens finally opened unleashing an almighty deluge. Soaked and squinting at the final bit of grey splodge that was Lake Okanagan, faintly visible through the downpour, I headed onwards.

I now had the choice to camp for the night at Penticton but, stubbornly refusing to stop short of my target some 8 miles hence, I put my head down to the handlebars and grimly, soggily pedalled on. Only another 8 miles….

At least the rain had mercifully abated somewhat but an icy wind and near black skies accompanied a long climb out of the town (which I had stupidly not stopped in). It was now just a grim struggle, mile by mile to get to Kaleden.

As ever, I'd forgotten to factor in gradient along with distance. After Peachland the terrain around Lake Okanagan had levelled off quite a bit. Past Penticton however the hills returned with a vengeance. You'd think after so many thousands of miles I would have learned to read the gradient of the map as well as the distance part. It seems not.

The first campsite sign appeared on the outskirts of Kaleden where I gratefully peeled off the highway and down an incredibly long steep hill ending at a near deserted lake site with a forbidding air.

It was blowing a gale still and there seemed to be little shelter as I huddled miserably against the wall of the site office waiting for sign of the occupants. After nearly half an hour waiting around in the cold someone finally appeared to give me an eye watering price for the showers, let alone a pitch for the night.

An internal tug of war now commenced. Do I stay and suck up the cost, the sensible option or do I drag a cold, wet, tired body back up that huge steep hill on the off chance of finding another place to stay somewhere that felt more welcoming?

The less than warm reception, cost and cold outlook grudgingly made my mind up. Claud was turned around and we headed back up to the road. Having all but run out of strength I pushed him back up that long hill, cleats skidding on the slippery, mossy road, losing my footing and falling in the mud more than once. At the top I cursed both my pride and stupidity before forlornly remounting and pedalling away, having already made up my mind to camp in the next available space be it campsite, field, fire trail or hedge. Enough was enough.

Thank the universe. A mere quarter of a mile along the road was another site and, despite the massively steep uphill drive it was bright, welcoming and more importantly, affordable.
Nearly closed for the season the damp campground was all but barren, however the delightful Korean owners, on seeing my drowned rat appearance somehow produced a cup of hot tea. I also managed to purchase a can of lentils for dinner so things were looking up.

Tent pitched in record time I set about the crucial practice of finding a base for the evening.
Over the weeks I have definitely developed a few campsite survival techniques which, when available, centre around taking possession of the laundry room. These invaluable places offer a wealth of possibilities to the weary camper and I have learnt to unashamedly turn these little nooks into a makeshift office/kitchen.

Laundry room luxury
The best ones are equipped with a plastic chair and accessible electrical sockets into which electronic items can be plugged for charging.
A camping stove can be set up on top of a washer and food cooked in relative comfort and, if the campsite has the holy grail of Wi-Fi, one can also spend a happy evening sending emails huddled by the warmth and fabric scented fragrance of the tumble drier.
I've also got to chat to some lovely, if slightly bemused, people who've come in to use the laundry facilities and found me squatting on top of the machines eating instant noodles and doing my emails feeling right at home.

This evening I had a very nice chat with Bonnie and Jerry a lovely couple who'd come in to do their washing and found my dinner bubbling away on a stove on top of the drier surrounded by electrical devices plugged into any available socket.

Two hours later, warm, fed, tired but satisfied that I could still survive alone, I quit my laundry room lounge and snuggled up soundly in the tent. Adventure resumed.

Day 58:   Kaleden to Princeton: 63 miles

Such a civilised start to the day, waving good morning to Bonnie and Jerry I headed to my laundry office for a quick Skype call with Emma. It's amazing how much a few crackly pixels can make your heart happier and the world seem a better place. I miss her though and seeing her both lessened and heightened this.

A cup of tea with the Korean couple and a conversation about their decision to immigrate to Canada. Just like the pierogi lady and so many other's I've met, it's another person, another family making a life-changing move in the hope of something more, something different, something better.

For this couple it was about their son, their obvious pride and joy. Despite the numerous difficulties in getting here, Canada clearly offered the family better life chances and a better future for their children and grandchildren. Not so dissimilar really to those early pioneers who, not so many decades before walked this same route for much the same reasons.

Journeys that shared both purpose and hope but spanning generations.

Time to cycle what turned out to be a very hilly 10km of road leading out of Kaleden. It seemed to take aeons to cover a relatively short distance, however after that first grinding climb the route became kinder, long flat and downhill stretches helping somewhat to offset the ever present wind.

Passing through the tiny settlement of Olalla gave rise to a pleasing verbal tattoo which ran through my head, turning over in synch with Claud's wheels, Olalla, Olalla, Olalla. This earworm remained whilst the road rolled along before finally dipping down into the town of Keremeos where I was both to have lunch and to pick up the wonderfully named Crowsnest Highway.

An early noshing opportunity presented itself in the form of one of the many tiny diners dotted around the area. I'd come to love these places, warm and fuggy with good home-made food and friendly people. Local customers amongst whom you often stand out, but are always welcome for that difference.

So much nicer than the chain owned, homogenised offerings which front the main travel routes back in the UK where, such is the proliferation of standard branding, coffee, fast food, snacks, you could step through their doors and be anywhere from Devon to Newcastle and have the same layout and choice presented.

Tracy, the diner's sole waitress, kept me company as I ploughed through a chicken burger and fries, keeping up a patter about the local area and asking questions which I tried to politely answer through mouthfuls of gorgeous, greasy carbs.

Sated and happy, Claud and I left Keremeos to continue at a more leisurely pace (being full of fries) through the core of the Okanagan Valley.

The town and valley were apparently named after the native Similkameen word "Keremeyeus" meaning 'creek which runs through the land'. This fertile plain lying in the heart of the Rocky mountains is famed for its abundant fruit and vegetable output. Even on a grey day like today the roadside is alive with colour, fruit and vegetables stacked and gleaming lining the route as far as you can see.

Wooden stands, some tiny and some the size of several houses all displayed boxes and tables of glistening autumnal produce, buckling under the weight of what seemed a hundred varieties of apples, peaches and cherries, squash, garlic, tomatoes, onions, potatoes and too many more things to name. This display was then duplicated, large and small for mile upon mile upon mile.

It was like cycling through the produce aisle of the world's largest supermarket whilst all the while under the stern gaze of the Rockies' mountainous slopes, not the snow covered peaks of a few days previously but large jagged masses which formed the valley walls.

Stopping for a break and a look around one of the beautiful, inviting stalls, I was also told by one of the customers that the Valley was famed for its winds. It seemed that locals joked that the only time you didn't feel the wind was when it was blowing from all four directions at once! I could empathise with that.

It was truly a joy riding through the festooned streets and I was sad when, on the outskirts of town, I finally saw see the last outpost of stalls slip past Claud's wheels.
After that, the valley and the Crowsnest highway, continued pretty much interrupted by town or people for the next 40 miles.

A short break in the only intervening town of Hedley furnished me with some fresh baked rolls and an abundance of chocolate before the last few miles to Princeton which lay at the foot of my final mountain and the Allison Pass which would take me out of the Rockies and eventually down into Vancouver.

I'd originally hoped to continue past Princeton for another 10 or 15 miles that day and get stuck into some of the climbing but the lack of handy food stops and towns had perturbed me, as did the weather which was again damp, grey and cold. With the temperature dropping I checked in at the Princeton Tourist Information centre for the latest forecast and some guidance about the road ahead.
I really wish I hadn't! The two ladies at the Tourist Information were perennially cheerful and also told me that, as far as they knew there was absolutely nowhere to even pitch a tent for the next 20-30 miles ahead.
They also very helpfully (and with gleeful smiles) gave me a little piece

of paper which explained exactly, including pictures, how arduous that route would be.

The hill profile for the Princeton to Hope section looked like the ECG trace of someone having a major coronary. Jagged peaks and troughs spanning approximately 80+ miles, all of which I would potentially need to cover in one day, even better, some 55 miles of that would be climbing. Big, big hills.

More than anything, I was scared.

Gloomily I trundled Claud away from the happy Tourist Information staff and back into the town of Princeton. In true form most of the camping facilities were now shut for the winter, however a soggy park on the outskirts of town had a few pitches left.

With a freezing cold shower block and no warm laundry to sit in I couldn't face cycling into town through the downpour so dinner was cooked early and a big no-no, in the porch of my tent.

Sod the bears, they're probably tucked up in bed by now I thought defiantly, forcing down the usual instant noodle/tuna concoction. In a fit of organisation I also boiled some eggs I'd bought in the valley earlier to make sandwiches for tomorrow's trek. I love eggs and they are great fuel but make terrible pannier fodder given their propensity to smash and leak everywhere no matter how carefully packed. I'd be looking forward to these.

With nothing else to do and nowhere to go I huddled in my sleeping bag for warmth and, after a few aborted attempts to read, made a try for sleep.

12.30am still awake. Seems I've pitched my tent on a slope and no matter how I lie I keep sliding stealthily towards the bottom.

03.15am sleeping bag in heap at foot of tent again. Awake, listening to someone snoring.

04.45am Really, really need to sleep but cold and scared. Keep thinking about the day ahead. Also really need to pee but far too chilly to move.

05.10. Aarrggghhhh, bollocks to it.

Day 59:   Princeton to Hope: 84 miles

Having been awake for most of the night the day dawns feeling like it's old already. Old and grey, with the pernicious wet mist shrouding the world like a damp blanket. There's a crick in my right side from having tried to wedge myself in position all night and I'm grumpier that the meanest grizzly as, with dawn breaking, I pack up my soaking wet tent and push Claud out onto the deserted highway in search of breakfast.
I'm not sure why I'm so concerned about today. If worst comes to it, there's got to be somewhere to camp overnight, but in my head it's all about targets and by the end of today I'd told myself I'd be in Hope. Even if it kills me.

Too antsy to eat much I grab a shockingly bad breakfast from the only place open, a gas station staffed by a sleepy, spotty youth who looked like he thought he might be hallucinating as I clopped around the meagre shelves in my skirt and cycling cleats, muttering and grabbing chocolate bars off of the shelf.
Leaving the attendant rubbing his eyes and blinking at me through the window I force myself to eat breakfast, a nutritionally balanced meal of chocolate, cookie and chocolate milk. Surprisingly fortified and with a new resolve, I hit the highway. Hope, here I come.

The first two hours made me glad of 3 things:

1) That I hadn't attempted to try free camping last night. With one side of the road a sheer drop and the other a solid rock wall it would have been near impossible.
2) That, being tired, I'd stopped cycling at Princeton. This route would not have added to the experience on the back of a long day.
3) That I was only ever going to cycle this route once!

The gradient made it excruciatingly tough going, climbing and climbing up sheer roads which wound continuously into the thick grey mist. It felt like cycling into the sky. Disorientated and dizzy I circled upwards.

At least mitigating the relentless climbing was the odd downhill section and whilst it was depressing to lose some of the hard won altitude, descending 9% gradients was a thrill, albeit a freezing cold one.

The road, for the most part however, continued upwards, although after those first leg-tearing hours the gradient was far less steep. Looking at my map from Princeton, the bit I'd been dreading, a 20 mile uphill section stretching through the Provincial Park, turned out to be a comparative doddle. As the road entered the Manning Park's east gate I found myself accelerating away, actually changing up front gears to the middle cog for the first time that day.

Surrounded now by tall forest and bird song, hardly a car had passed me for hours let alone any other human life. The climb was gentle and satisfying and in no time I reached the Park's main rest stop somewhat elated by this discovery.

On a bit of a high, especially at over 1000 metres I was itching to keep going, but a sliver of common sense prevailed. Contemplating food, I was annoyingly unable to stomach the idea of the egg sandwiches I'd so carefully prepared yesterday, instead resorting to more cookies and a cup of hot tea to thaw my cold extremities. As I sipped my tea I also checked my emails, a few messages from family and one from Tom.

He'd made it to Hope the previous day after a long, wet ride up the Coquihalla Pass. The lucky bugger was now resting in a tent in the town's campsite and drinking beer, wondering what was keeping me. My reply was brief and to the point. "Save me a bottle, I'm on my way down".

Topped up on sugar I surged out of the rest area, determined to reach the summit of Allison Pass which I knew wasn't far away and sure enough, just a few miles later there was the sign indicating I'd reached the col. Posing and trying to take a selfie whilst shivering uncontrollably in a sudden hailstorm, I recorded my topping of the pass at the post marking its 1,342 metres, squinting against the icy pellets thundering from the sky.

Desperate to get warm, we were quickly away again, Claud and I pelting along as my legs tried to pump heat around cold muscles, 48 miles of climbing done, 32ish miles still to go.

Optimistically (and looking at the hand drawn map) I'd expected the majority of those miles to be downhill given the morning's efforts. Life and roads aren't so straightforward it seems and there were an unaccountable number of hills still to climb, however the descents, when they came were both steep and spectacular.

For once, I thanked my lucky gods that I wasn't doing the usual east-west crossing. I would not have fancied cycling up some of those precipitous slopes if travelling the other way. The odd brave road cyclist who passed me from the opposite direction could be seen, face a rictus of concentration, veins popping from arms and forehead as they focussed everything on those killer climbs. I would like to say I empathised with their struggle, felt solidarity, but that would be a lie. Mostly it was a 50/50 mix of smug and relief that, for once, I was going the easier way!

I couldn't entirely gloat however as a tough, rolling 15 mile section of road brought on more climbs of its own. Relatively I was still descending overall but, swooping down the mountainside, the road offered high percentage plunges into a valley which would all too often be followed by the requirement to climb out again the other side. Really not fair.

Excitingly though I could feel the air warming as the altitude fell away. The foliage too became more green, lush and plentiful and I could feel a sense of hope burgeoning in me at the thought that today's journey at least was coming to an end.

A handful of miles and some more winding descents later the roads grew suddenly busier, traffic thicker.

Hope is definitely something of a destination hub. It's also a geographical meeting place, for both the Coquihalla and Fraser rivers and four main highways which converge on the town from all points of the compass.

The eastern terminus of Highway 7 arrives in town along with the western terminus of my route, the Crowsnest (Hope-Princeton) Highway and the Southern Terminus of the Coquihalla road (Tom's route). All of these routes then converge to join the main artery and my companion since Ontario, the good old Trans-Canada Highway 1.

Navigating around some of these busy intersections I cross a spectacular iron bridge over a river gorge and, in no time at all, the mountains are behind us and I'm entering the promised land – also known as the town of Hope.

Skirting the spaghetti junction of converging roads the overwhelming thought, obliterating anything else, is that I've made it! After being so worried at the start of the day I've now covered 84 miles, 5,000 feet of climbing and nearly 7000 feet of descent.

I also desperately need food!

Having survived all day on biscuits and adrenalin I'm now half crazed with fatigue and hunger in equal amounts. Pulling into the nearest parking lot of a handy McDonalds the world is momentarily reduced to the size of a chicken burger meal and extra-large thick-shake.

In the seconds it took to consume them my whole body heaved that contented exhalation that comes with both complete exhaustion and complete satisfaction. I sit back in my plastic moulded seat just staring, stoned on food, looking benignly at my fellow man and not wanting to move from this spot for a very, very, very long time.

As welcoming as the staff were however, I wasn't sure they'd let me stay the night. Reluctantly I heaved my body away from the rest and the warmth and gathered up Claud for the short ride to the campsite.

Circling the camping area I spotted a familiar tent pitched behind an even more familiar bike. Tom, strolling across the campsite a moment later, looking annoyingly bloody fresh and rested, "*So, what kept you?*"

I growl at him and point at an unopened bottle of beer, which was pretty much all I could manage after the day in hand.

Very gallantly, and un-Tom-like, he pitched my tent for me (I must have looked knackered) whilst we filled in the gaps of the missing few days. Had it only been a few? It felt like a life time.
It seemed that Tom's route through the Coquihalla Pass was as steep as he'd anticipated and then some. Not helped by that ferocious storm I'd gotten caught in around Penticton, it had drenched him too, resulting in a night spent huddled in some underground toilets, bizarrely with a couple of Swiss touring cyclists.
After that though, the route was considerably shorter, so much so that he'd arrived the day before and hence why he looked so sprightly whilst I could hardly formulate a coherent word.

A few hours later, a warm shower and the food were taking effect, helped along by a visit to a wonderful local diner (much better that my fast food blow out) for some hot soup, followed by some wine and whiskey back in the tent.
Curling up in my sleeping bag I found myself nestled against something squishy.... Dubiously I fish around and finally extract my packet of egg sandwiches, carefully prepared back in Princeton and now flattened to a pulp by a day's hard labour in the panniers.
Too exhausted to move from the tent and risking the curiosity of a hungry bear, I put them aside as a potential breakfast. It's 9.30pm and time for lights out.

02.30 am and my brain switches back on with a vengeance. Try as I might after that, sleep just wouldn't come. Thinking back, I was definitely lacking in food; sadly however, the egg sandwiches just weren't appealing, so after much tossing and turning and cursing and grumbling I finally waited out the remainder of the night in the warm toilet block catching up on emails, writing and waiting for dawn.

From: Emma **To**: Cyclinginaskirt

Subject: Thoughts for Vancouver….

Hey,

Sorry Skype was a bit rubbish the other day but it was lovely to hear your voice! Things are going a lot better - to be fair we had a really good night last night and she slept till 8 which was fab! Maybe I'd be writing something different if she had been a mare about going to bed! One thing that makes me feel better is that whenever we have a crappy night I know at some point we will be having a good one - 'hope' I guess :)

Couldn't really talk much about M as he was home when you called, so far things have been a lot better since I had my last melt down, he's been a lot more supportive and little things like offering to look after her whilst I pop out for an hour or make the breakfast whilst I'm feeding her in bed, don't get me wrong it's not perfect but I think he's now beginning to appreciate how hard work being a full time mum is and see the need to help out more even with just the smallest of gestures!

Anyways hope the last bit of your trip finds you well and that you manage the last bit of the ride with or without Tom :)

Enjoy Vancouver, I liked the park there! Whatever you decide to do next on your trip I just think it's fantastic what you've done so far, what you've seen, experienced, amazing that only a few people can say they've done that, very inspiring. Go with your gut instinct for the next step - it'll tell you what's the right thing to do.

Love and squishy hugs xx

Day 60:   Hope to Mission: 55 miles

If my body had an independent voice right now it would be screaming this. I DON'T WANT TO CYCLE, I DON'T WANT TO CYCLE, I DON'T, I DON'T, I DON'T!

Lucky then it didn't have a say and by 8am, with relatively few hours of sleep, I was back in the fabulous diner ordering a large helping of fruit pie and ice cream. The waitress looked at me slightly askance then obviously thought better of commenting.
It's amazing how cheerful a slice of pie and ice cream can make the day however, even the sun had come out and I at least enjoyed an hour or so of wandering around Hope. It really was a pretty little town. Nestled at the bottom of the Fraser valley, surrounded by the mountain's lower slopes and bubbling, dancing rivers it had a distinctly alpine feel about it, a little similar to Canmore.
As I wandered around in the sunshine running errands and visiting bakeries I felt relaxed and happy. I DON'T WANT TO CYCLE yelled my body just in case it made a difference.

Arriving back at Claud I found a red rose tucked under the bungee cords of my panniers. 'Happy world friendship day' was printed on a neat red label around the stem. Wow, this town even gave me flowers, how could I leave?
But, that weird itch was back as strongly as ever, despite a protesting body and a burgeoning anxiety about what I will do when I finish, I still needed to push on. This dynamic tension continued to push and pull. I don't want to get to the end but I do want to finish, to stop, to rest to....... (insert ideas here)?

I push on. Leaving behind the beautiful sunny town of Hope, the burbling river and the red rose giving locals. Back to the highway and, after the town of Assizes, a headwind accompanied by the most enormous hill.
I should have known and it was almost fitting, when the kindly woman

at the Assizes Tourist Information told me that the road was pretty much flat now all the way to Vancouver! At 11% average gradient the hill towered above me almost vertically. Clunk, click, clunk, click went the gears as I dropped down through them. With nothing left to shift to it was up out of the saddle and pumping for all I was worth until, rounding the steepest, vertical cliff of a right-hand bend I just couldn't propel the bike forward another inch. Claud stopped dead. As did I, still clipped into the pedals. There were those few, achingly long fractions of a second when the world stood completely still, balanced on a knife edge, breath held, on pause. Then the world, and gravity crashed back in and I was sliding backwards, downhill, with my feet stuck in the clips. Seconds of wrenching, which felt like aeons and I wrestled my feet free just in time to half topple, half leap sideways until Claud was lying on one pannier in the road, wheels spinning gamely.

I don't know if you've ever tried to remount on a hill, a steep hill, with cycling cleats. Trying to get a purchase on the tarmac, let alone enough momentum to push off is nearly impossible. Luckily a handy gateway gave a metre or two of flat ground, enough to re-launch Claud at the last part of the hill and triumphantly, heart hammering, over the crest.

After the monster hill, the rest of the day dragged by in a grind of achy legs and nondescript scenery. On leaving Hope, I was heart-sore to notice how quickly the mountains had receded into memory. I already desperately missed the dramatic, majestic landscape, swapped instead for a steadily more urban one. No more snow-capped peaks pricking the sky in the distance, only chimneys and houses, farms and stores.

As the city grew around me I felt hemmed in once more, the shock of the traffic too was immense. Changing course to some slightly quieter back roads I at least felt I could catch my breath, look around me, until SMACK.
I was nearly jolted from the saddle, the bike swung wildly across the

road and I was suddenly wrestling desperately with the bars to stay upright and in one piece.

Riding along in a dream, staring gormlessly in to space, it seemed I hadn't noticed a large boulder squatting evilly in the middle of my path and had ridden right into it. Adrenalin coursing through my whole body like an electric shock I checked Claud over, feeling the tyres and frame tenderly like that of an injured animal. Incredibly we both seemed to be intact so, wobbly-legged, I cautiously cycled on.

The adrenalin was probably the only thing which helped to fuel those last few miles to a tiny and deserted campsite on a fishing lake outside of Mission.

Setting up my tent under a fishing shelter next to the lake and beside Tom, it dawned on us both that this was to be the very last night before we reached Vancouver.

I couldn't take it in! We did however need to celebrate and so we would, in style with a Chinese takeaway.

Ordering from the phone in the camp office the wonderful owners, on learning of the journey so far couldn't have been kinder. As I showered, they opened up their clubhouse, closed now for the season, put on the heaters and decorated the place with candles. When the takeaway arrived they even brought us china plates and cutlery. So, along with a bottle of wine I'd bought earlier we sat down, at a proper table, for our last meal together.

The evening was a blur of food and wine, of remembering places and people. The ranch and quad bike riding in Manitoba, the hot pools in Moosejaw, trying to find our ways (separately) out of Toronto and a little bit of forgetting too, of the arguments and petty annoyances.

The club house even boasted a very old VHS player and collection of similarly dated films which we coaxed back into life. Curled on the sofa, watching the 1980s unfold on a static-blurred screen, full of rice, noodles, wine and warmth it felt entirely surreal. From the start of the adventure in Toronto two months ago to right now and the thousands of miles in between it had been the most incredible journey and, in less than 24 hours, for me and Claud, it would all come to an end.

Day 61: Mission to Vancouver: 49.24 miles

The morning of the last day dawned chill and misty. As I lay, encased up to the nostrils in my warm sleeping bag, I let the many emotions and feelings ebb and flow through me like a troubled tide.

My introvert musings were interrupted however by a low muttering, groaning sound just outside the tent.
Surely Tom wasn't that hung over, it's not as if we'd drunk that much? Curious, and looking forward to the opportunity of laughing at a friend's discomfort I braved the chill air and went to investigate.
Behind the pitch Tom had his bike upended on the soaking grass having woken up to a puncture on the last day. I'd like to say I was helpful or even sympathetic but that would be a lie. My appreciation of schadenfreude was just too strong to pass up the opportunity to laugh at him.

Oh, that will teach me.
Leaning over, on a whim, to inspect Claud I found my own front tyre as flat as the proverbial pancake.

I was actually quite shocked as it had been weeks now since any such occurrence and not since my brand new tyres back in Calgary.
What I was looking at though was a pinch-flat from that rock I crashed in to yesterday which had kindly left me a little end-of-journey present.

Role reversal now and Tom's turn to laugh like a drain as I muttered and cursed Claud's impenetrable kevlar tyres which proved to be just that. Trying to wrestle off rubber which had welded itself to the rims

with hands numb from cold I spent a full 20 minutes trying to part them from each other but only succeeding in parting skin from my knuckles. In a complete, emotional hissy fit 1 threw the wheel on the floor and tyre levers and spanner at the lake.
Luckily, I can't throw for toffee and they plunked harmlessly on the grass whilst Tom, not even bothering to hide his smirking, took up the cause.

Between us, we finally managed to get the tyre off and puncture sorted, during which time the sun grudgingly started to make an appearance, lightening the day and the mood to one of resigned amusement at the final day flats.
After a dawdled-over breakfast of leftover Chinese food we at last hit the road somewhere nearing midday and, as ever, later than planned.

True to form I possessed no detailed bike map for the run into Vancouver. My trusty road atlas which had served so well since leaving Toronto had now entered its final page and, as my orange highlighter wobbled to a standstill, I had no real idea of how far the city centre was or which roads, other than the main freeways, would take me there. Neither as it turns out did Tom.

Consequently, and perhaps fittingly, there now began many hours of wandering around in ever decreasing circles, hopefully following bike route signs and disappointedly losing them again. I have no idea where I cycled. At one point the tarmacked road gave out on to a gravel driveway that said 'Private: Psychiatric Unit'. Soon after which it dead-ended in a vegetable patch.
Nonplussed. I retraced my steps.

The only other apparent turn off led to a railway line, whose level crossing gates were currently firmly closed.
In consultation with the only other human being in existence, a man in tattered overalls, hopping constantly between feet whilst clasping and unclasping his hands, I determined that a) he was on a day pass from

the neighbouring hospital and b) the train would be through in about an hour.

After a few futile attempts to source a better alternative, i.e. jumping over the tracks (not with a full bike) I settled down glumly to wait. Over the next hour more people joined the crossing queue and it became quite a social occasion. I briefly got excited when, after just 25 minutes a train appeared but, how could I have forgotten so easily, this was a Canadian train. Canadian Tire carriages rattled by non-stop for the next 30 minutes whilst I got to know my fellow waitees, many of whom gave me earnest, but conflicting directions for the next leg.

When the train had finally cleared I set off at full pelt, or as much pelt as I could muster. My brain felt like it was processing things through treacle.
Various cycle paths appeared but, like all the others, they too seemed to terminate in the middle of nowhere, or this time a timber yard.
I was very aware that my next and final Warmshowers host would be going out for the evening at 5pm and the last thing I wanted to do was loiter in some cold front porch waiting for their return hours later. The day however was ticking away.

With any thoughts of peaceful mountains now long gone, I find myself fully enveloped by the urban sprawl of roads and housing on Vancouver's outskirts. The main road I eventually ended up taking into the city reminded me of my Calgary arrival, traffic heavy and very hilly. It was fortuitous that Tom had now found a GPS system on his iPad so, for the last hour we grimly followed the little blinking cursor as it almost imperceptibly crept forward across the screen.

Heading towards Vancouver's east side, the very British, geographically diverse place names were bizarrely familiar. Cycling past (New) Westminster and Richmond, signs for Guildford and Hastings, it was a strange experience indeed, but then it was a strange day.
Finally, at some time a little after 4pm I pulled up to the curb in the

middle of Main Street alongside Tom. As he was staying elsewhere in the city this is where we would finally say goodbye.

It had been the intention to stop for a drink, take finisher's photos, to reminisce and more but, now we were here, the idea felt leaden and flat, just like the mood.

I'd been so focussed on just getting into the city today that I'd barely stopped. My original rosy vision was of a triumphant, leisurely cycle in, stopping for pictures outside of quirky Vancouver landmarks and waving graciously to acknowledge the adulation from the adoring crowds lining the route. I'd even being preparing my speech...I would like to thank my supporters, friends and family..... OK, so it's not the Olympic homecoming parade but, I had expected a definite sense of occasion at least internally if nothing else; a sense of completion, satisfaction, exhilaration.... something. Instead, I just felt hollow. And very tired.

So, no momentous, celebratory arrival and no lingering congratulatory farewells. Just a *"See ya then"* an awkward, bike mounted hug and a parting of ways.

Twenty minutes or so later and I'm slogging up – yes up – the steep street of my final host. It seemed fitting, if not karmic, to finish my journey on a hill. At least a watery sun was poking through the clouds making the day distinctly warmer than it had been for a while.

Finally locating the house, I heaved Claud through the narrow side-gate and rang the doorbell.

3,090.2 miles and 61 days after Claud and I had set out from Toronto, we'd arrived in Vancouver. We'd done it!

Calgary to Vancouver in pictures

Beautiful British Columbia

Beautiful British Columbia

Rainbow's start to Rogers Pass

Rogers Pass climb

Arriving at Canmore

Cloud level

Dry out at the top

And the bottom!

Calgary to Vancouver in pictures

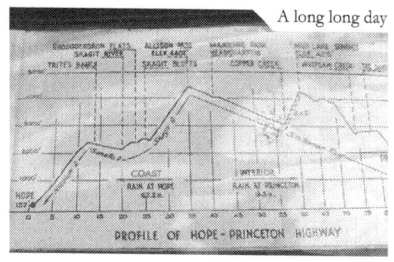

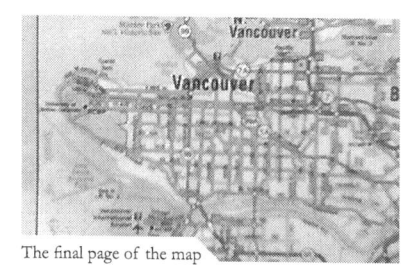

Allison Pass summit

All 5 provincial flags

Thermal pool heaven

Not quite cordon bleu

Okanagan abundance

A long long day

A last feast

The final page of the map

Post-match Analysis

During those 3,000+ miles or 5,000 km, Claud and I have:

- Had 9 days of rest (only 2 consecutive).
- Gone through 5 provinces,
- 4 mountain passes
- 3 time zone changes,
- 4 punctures, 2 tyres, 1 new wheel, chain and set of back cogs

- The highest temperature I took note of was 44 degrees Celsius, the lowest -2 degrees Celsius
- The highest altitude 1,342 metres
- Longest single hill climb, 48 miles/77km (Allison pass, Princeton to Hope)
- Longest day 103 miles/166km from Ignace to Vermilion Lake (Ontario)
- The shortest day 23 miles/37km, Canyon Hot Springs to Revelstoke (BC)
- Number of chocolate bars, peanut butter sandwiches and packets of instant noodles consumed....both innumerable and obscene.
- Number of other touring cyclists encountered 57 (with all but 4 going in the opposite direction).
- Number of new friends made, countless

The statistics are the easy part however, over the last 61 days I've also been through a full spectrum of emotions, often over the course of just a few hours.

Anger, frustration and tantrums at the wind, hills, heat, thunderstorms, hailstorms, oh and did I mention the wind....?

Tears and utter exhaustion after cycling some ridiculously tough days, finishing when there is nothing left in you and your body feels like it has been turned inside out.
Exhilaration, flying down the side of mountains at eye-watering speeds, weaving in and out of city traffic and overtaking buses, tractors and other (non-laden) cyclists....competitive? Just a bit!

Alongside this there's also been so much joy, wonder and open-mouthed awe at some of the spectacular scenery that is everywhere you turn in Canada. Sunrises over Lake Superior, fields of golden sunflowers glowing in Manitoba, oceans of wheat and corn melting into the bluest, clearest horizon in Saskatchewan. The dramatic, dinosaur canyons of Drumheller and oil-fuelled prosperity of Alberta and finally, fittingly dramatic, the Rocky mountains, the wild, arresting, heart-pumping, lung breaking gatekeepers to British Columbia.

Looking back at my original plan, such as it was, I was expecting the trip to take approximately two and a half months, I'm surprised it's been quicker, but I have been on a roll.
There are certainly more than a few places I could have lingered, mostly because of the people and at times I've questioned that I'm not doing enough of the 'touristy' things such as visiting museums and galleries or hiking and exploring the trails. But that's for another trip. Cycling through the landscape has, I feel, given me a unique perspective most tourists, and many Canadians don't get to experience. It's a vast country and I can't begin to see it all whichever way I travel.

One of the single, overwhelming emotions on this trip though is gratitude.
Firstly, for the huge number of emails and messages that people have taken the time to send. Every single one has been gratefully received and keenly hoarded, precious words that have helped at some of the most difficult times.

Secondly, I had no idea what a difference it would make to also receive those kind and encouraging words from strangers whom I've met at rest stops or even traffic lights.

Thirdly, I've been truly humbled by the wonderful people I've met, planned and unexpected, who have scooped up a tired, dishevelled cyclist from the side of the road and shared their homes, their lives (and laundry) and helping me to get me going again.

Contact, in whatever form, with family, friends (both long-standing and new), has been the one thing I couldn't be without. I know now that I can happily live with just a few panniers full of clothes, no problem, but what is most important is that which I can't bring with me, the people I love and care about. I miss them, yet I'm thankful for knowing that they are there for me, always.

Throughout the journey there has also been a growing sense of peace and calmness, when the road stretches out before you, your legs find a rhythm and your mind can freewheel. Cycling is one of the simplest activities, and that's what this trip has really been in essence, just a bit of a long bike ride.

So, what next? The short answer is I'm not sure, but getting on the bike every day has become a way of life, like going to the office to a job I enjoy. There are days I get up and grumble because it's cold, or I'm tired but when the reward is all of the above, why would I want to stop?

I will definitely be taking a break in Vancouver, to recharge rest and repair my ailing skirt. But I can say that I have truly fallen in love with Canada and the temptation to stay longer, to return to the start and to reconnect with friends I've made along the way is a strong one.
I'll spend some time deciding, but the road also continues, from Vancouver, either up to Alaskan wilderness or down on the Pacific Coast Highway to Mexico and beyond.......

The Beginning Of The End

It's a bright, crisp day in Vancouver and, after nearly a week of monsoon weather it has finally stopped raining. I've given up loitering outside in the cold and am now nursing a coffee and scone in a warm café, waiting.

I'm wearing my brand new, fluorescent green raincoat and feeling, if not refreshed, then a least a little more rested following a four day holiday of sorts, my longest time off the bike in over 2 months.

I'm just thinking I could happily sit here all day, any inclination to move slowly draining out of me when I spot someone cycling towards me. With a sigh born of much more than a few late nights I leave my window seat and head out into the chill air. Claud is there, leaning patiently against a nearby pillar, like the faithful friend which he has become, the final provincial flag for British Columbia shining proudly on his front mudguard alongside the other Four. Ontario, Manitoba, Saskatchewan and Alberta.

I pat him fondly as I clip on the bar bag and, checking the waterproof covers on the panniers, I swing myself in to the saddle and coast out on to the road. The cyclist up ahead is dawdling along at a leisurely pace and I catch him easily.
Pulling up alongside Tom turns and grins at me. *"What kept you then?"* he enquires.

And that's all that is said as we ride in companionable silence away from the city, through the lush, traffic free roads of Stanley Park and over the spectacular Lions Gate suspension bridge.
A couple of hours later, after the usual ups and downs of the road we pull in to Horse Shoe Bay, just in time to wave off the departing ferry.... on which we should have been aboard.

Mañana as they say in the more laid back parts of the world. At the harbour side is a fish and chip restaurant and in 2 hours another ferry will come along which will take us to Nanaimo on Vancouver Island. Just one more little bit of Canada to do.

True, the island is the size of England but it would be rude to have come this far and not visit right?

After that – who knows? But I don't have to decide today. For now, all I have to do is stop pedalling and catch a ferry.

And Then....

I can't believe how cold it is. I'm shivering like crazy as I crouch in the passenger foot-well of a friend's car trying not to be seen. I'm wearing a red, flimsy Chinese-style summer dress, brought in those hot, heady few weeks in Toronto before Claud and I left on our adventures. On this occasion however, I feel the shivering owes more to nervous anticipation as much as clothing choice.

My friend returns to whisper frantically through the window. *"Keep down for another minute then run for it. If you keep low no one should see you."*

My leg muscles are seriously protesting by now and I desperately need to pee but I keep my position, counting down until I stealthily slip open the door. Crouching against the side of the car to keep hidden I check the coast is clear before darting across the empty parking lot and in through the front entrance of the large community hall. Standing alone in the lobby, I peer nervously through the small, smeary glass door pane at the party in full swing within.

Tables are laid out café style decorated with lacy cloths, pretty china plates and cups whilst around the room are stacked the offerings of a high tea; sandwiches, delicate cakes, scones and clotted cream, along with tea pots and milk jugs in constant supply. The hall is filled with smiling, happy people dressed up for an afternoon tea party but, as I'm watching the laughter and chattering peter out.

The room becomes silent as every guest, moving as one, turns to stare up at a large projector screen which is filled with a slide-show of baby pictures. Slowly, as the pictures scroll though, the chubby baby becomes a dark haired little girl, then a gap toothed school kid, an awkward teenager, a beautiful young woman, a university graduate, a bride and finally a mother.

The slide-show then segues into a video clip. The person in the clip is shown against a background of sun-kissed trees, t-shirted and brown limbed. I can't hear what they are saying but I don't need to, I know the words by heart. I should do as I spoke them, recorded just a few weeks earlier and thousands of miles away.

I'm telling my little sister how much she means to me, how from the moment I watched her being born she was my best friend, a best friend whom I love more than anyone in the world.
I was also telling this best friend that I was so sorry I wouldn't be able to make it back for her 30th birthday party as I was continuing on my bike trip but that I missed her very much.
The film ends and for a second, before the slide-show resumes, silence.
My sister red-eyed, crying, breaks through the absence of sound to give a lovely speech thanking everyone for organising and attending such a wonderful surprise party. After this, slowly, the room once more resumes its clatter of tea cups and chatter of voices as people return to their food.

Amidst the bustle, quietly, I push open the door, slip through and become a part of this scene that I've just been watching. People pay me no attention at first, some faces I don't recognise, some don't recognise me. It's been a while. Emma's friends glance my way and then lose interest, but slowly a few people notice me and a ripple of murmuring and nudging starts and expands outwards.
Emma is just metres away from me now. As she turns around to see what the disturbance in the air is I see her gaze travel around until it rests on where I'm stood. There are then the longest few seconds of incomprehension as she processes what her eyes are telling her, against what her she knows shouldn't be.

It has, after all, been many months and I've just told her, as pixels on a screen, that I won't make it home for her 30th birthday but…..

The tears really come then and the rest of the room seems to drift away as the two of us cry and laugh and embrace.
The journey home, to be here, was a fantastically long one but it was maybe the best thing I've ever done.

The noise of the room fades back in, like emerging from underwater into a crowded swimming pool. My parents are in shock, as is everyone. A secret well kept. Nobody knew I was coming home, but I have.

In my bag is a return ticket to Canada, but now isn't the time to talk about that. In this moment, I am here with my family, the people who matter the most in the world and right now there's nowhere else I'd rather be.

The end, for now.

The Bicycle And The Baggage

For those who are interested here are a few details about Claud the bike and what I carried with me on my trip.

Bike: Claud Butler Classic Alloy series 7005. Shimano Tourney front and rear mechs and 7 speed shimano shifters. Front triple chainset 48-33-28, rear cassette 11-34. V brakes.
Wheels and tyres: 700cc x 32 with Schwalbe Marathon Plus tyres
Luggage and panniers: Back: Ortlieb city back roller, front: Axiom. Dry-bag, bar bag, seat bag and frame bag all unbranded. Mirror and bell.

Camping:
Tent, Lichfield Treklite 200, 3000mm hh
Inflatable, gel-filled, full length camping mat and inflatable pillow
Sleeping bag: Mountain Hardwear's female specific Lamina 20 (3-4 season) synthetic fill and separate silk liner.

Clothing:
Toiletries (sunscreen, toothbrush, toothpaste, moisturiser, shampoo, comb, lipstick, petroleum jelly, shower gel which doubled as laundry liquid), 1 down-jacket, 1 pair of bib shorts 1 pair of padded shorts, 2 short sleeve cycle tops, 1 pair arm warmers (made from cut-off 50 denier leggings), 1 long sleeve cycle jersey in a very impractical white, 1 thin long sleeve top, 1 pair of neon leg warmers, 3 bras (2 sports and 1 regular) socks and pants, 2 pairs of gloves, long and short fingered, a woolly hat, 1 buff, 1 light shower proof jacket, 1 rain jacket which disintegrated, 1 pair of cycling leggings, 1 pair or cotton leggings, 1 lightweight dress and thin cardigan, 1 merino jumper, 1 vest t-shirt, 1 cotton t-shirt, 1 pair of shorts, 1 bikini, 1 colourful cotton scarf and cotton sarong (both had multiple uses), 1 lightweight towel, shoes x 5 (cycling cleats, lightweight sneakers, camping crocs, flat sandals,

strappy heels) and of course a skirt!

Other essentials:
Camping stove, gas and solid fuel tablets (never used) pans, foldable bowl/cup, travel coffee press, 1 spork (spoon and fork), washing up liquid, sponge, multi-blade penknife, gas lighter, nylon cord, road atlas, pens, phone (used only for photos and Wi-Fi as unable to get call/messaging plan abroad), HP Slate (tablet), chargers and converter, money, paperback, food and 2 x 750ml water bottles (not enough)! Multi-tool, 2 x spare inner tubes, spanner, tyre levers and mini-pump.

Food: Generally, tinned tuna, dried noodles, crisps (chips), whiskey, chocolate, cake.

Total weight of bike: 16kg (approx)
Total weight of luggage: 26kg (approx)
Combined weight: 42kg
Rider weight for comparison: 52kg

Acknowledgements

There are many people without whom this book would have remained a dusty diary of memories on a shelf.
My heartfelt thanks go to Hannah, Kim, Mike, Gaz and Jacqui for helping bring the book to life, for the inspiration, practical support, encouragement and blatant nagging to get it finished.
A huge debt of gratitude also to those wonderful friends and family whose messages of love and support meant so much. To Tom, for all of the adventure and last, but by no means least, to the truly fantastic individuals of Canada who shared their homes, stories, wisdom, humour and beer with a random, dishevelled cyclist.
To all of the above, a sincere and heart-felt thank you.

Thank you for reading my book, I hope you enjoyed it. If you would like to leave a comment or review the author would love to hear from you. Feedback is always appreciated and can be left on Amazon/Good Reads or you can find more information about my travels with Claud and beyond at www.cyclinginaskirt.co.uk
Happy pedalling and happy reading.

About The Author

Lorraine, also known as 'Cyclinginaskirt' is a forty-something female writer, traveller, passionate cyclist, adventurer and consumer of cake. She possesses limited common sense, but still insists on trying to fathom out this life with style and a sense of humour.

She cycles in a skirt to remind herself not to take life (and riding) too seriously.

She likes to think and write about personal development and the taking up of challenges, about travelling solo as a woman, about pursuing passions, ditching the pension plan and choosing the road less travelled (or cycled).

Her philosophy is:

"I will never reach the end of my life wishing I had spent more time in the office"

Printed in Great Britain
by Amazon